Ianto Ware started cycling because he couldn't afford a car and started watching the Tour de France because it was the only thing on Australian television at 2AM. After a youth spent playing in terrible bands and writing fanzines, he now works in cultural and urban policy. He grew up in Adelaide and lives in Sydney.

TWENTY ONE NIGHTS IN JULY

A PERSONAL HISTORY OF THE TOUR DE FRANCE

IANTO WARE

Hunter Publishers
PO Box 81
Flinders Lane
Melbourne 8009
Australia
www.hunterpublishers.com.au

Cover: Design By Committee
Text: Anne-Marie Reeves

National Library of Australia
Cataloguing-in-Publication data:
Ware, Ianto
21 Nights in July: How I learned to stop worrying and love the bike. / Ianto Ware
ISBN: 9780980740509 (pbk.)
1. Tour de France (Bicycle race). 2. Tour de France (Bicycle race)—History.
3. Cyclists—Biography. 4. Bicycle racing—France.

796.620944

Dedicated to my Grandfather, Dean Ware,
on the occasion of his 85th birthday

CONTENTS

TWENTY ONE NIGHTS IN JULY

A PERSONAL HISTORY OF THE TOUR DE FRANCE

July 1st, 2006
Strasbourg

FLOYD LANDIS WINS (AND LOSES)

Muscle does not make the sport: that is the evidence of the Tour de France ... It is not muscle that wins. What wins is a certain idea of man and of the world.
— *Roland Barthes*

In 2006, for the first time in my life, I watched every single stage of the Tour de France. I'd hunker down on the couch in the middle of the night, in the middle of the Australian winter, and stare at the *peloton* as it wove its way through the glittering French countryside. I was a chronic insomniac and the grandeur of the race seemed so much more fantastic than anything I could have dreamt up, even if I had been able to sleep. That was also the year Floyd Landis won and then subsequently turned out not to have won because he was doped to the gills. His testosterone levels were so high even the World Anti-Doping Authority was shocked. Dick Pound, their comically named president, declared, 'You'd think he'd be violating every virgin within one hundred miles. How does he even get on his bicycle?'

That was the start of my passion for the sport of cycling. It is a passion that has grown over the years, much to the bewilderment and alienation of friends and loved ones, who find the sport both dull and confusing. I'm still not sure why it was the Landis Tour that triggered it. It wasn't a good race. Things started badly when nearly all of the favourites were implicated in the Operation Puerto drug scandal. It started badly for Landis too, when a mechanical fault cost him three seconds on the starting ramp for the opening prologue in Strasbourg. He'd crawled into the lead by the alpine stages, taking the yellow jersey on Stage Fifteen, losing it with a spectacular collapse on Stage Sixteen, and then making up for it on Stage Seventeen to Morzine, when he produced a one hundred and thirty kilometre attack over five major mountain passes. At the time it seemed heroic, audacious, and unbelievable. It turned out only the latter was correct. He tested positive a couple of days later.

In hindsight, Landis's ride into Morzine looks cartoonish. But in the moment, home on the couch in front of the television, I thought it was spectacular and I suppose enough other people did too. Evidently, there's a substantial discrepancy between what's believable and what people are willing to believe.

When I discovered the Tour, I was in my mid-twenties, studying for my doctorate and working an extremely mundane office job. I was a chronic insomniac and, being in Australia, it was the only thing on TV after midnight. I'd chanced upon the 2005 Tour and watched Lance Armstrong seize his final victory. I remember him on the podium, announcing, 'I'm sorry for you. I'm sorry that you can't dream big. I'm sorry you don't believe in miracles.' I was sorry for myself too, because it is hard to dream big when you spend your days doing data entry for the minimum wage.

By that point I was already riding a bicycle everywhere because I couldn't afford a car. I'd bump through the morning traffic every day on a battered mountain bike, getting yelled at by the local motorists, before spending eight hours locked in an office that was, quite literally, a glorified stationary cabinet. Then I'd ride home, study for a few hours, and stare at the television until I eventually fell asleep. The ride to work was frequently the only enjoyable part of the day; a sudden burst of adrenalin brought about by near-death encounters with cantankerous bus drivers, operating as a counterweight to the anesthetization of my working life.

When the Landis Tour started, I purchased a copy of the annual *Ride* magazine form guide, so I could better comprehend what was going on. I'd sit up all night, half-frozen and lulled into a state of sleep-deprived hypnosis by Phil Liggett and Paul Sherwin's droning commentary. Watching hour after hour of failed breakaways and alpine attacks that dissolved like the morning mist, the whole affair took on metaphysical dimensions.

Out on the roads of regional France, fundamental truths about the human condition were being played out. At home on the couch, I was a mass of youthful confusion. As I watched the Tour, it told me fables of persistence, of grace in defeat, of effort rewarded or thwarted, of luck both good and bad, and those stories resonated with great profundity. It was like I'd gone on some sort of transcendental peyote retreat, except it lasted three weeks and I didn't have to endure the company of emotive new-age stoners. Life-altering epiphanies rolled in thick and fast.

Oddly, I think the deluge of doping scandals around that

3

time actually helped. There was something appealing about the idea that people like Armstrong and Landis cared so much about the sport that they'd cheat and lie for their big dreams. I couldn't imagine caring that much about my office job.

The Tour fascinated me and I began reading and watching anything I could find on professional cycling. The more I learnt, the more overwhelming the epiphanies became. In 2008 I started writing them down. My approach was methodical; through each stage of the Tour, I would take extensive notes and, the following day, I would write a detailed summary of the race, followed by an examination of the philosophical lessons it revealed. That was the year Carlos Sastre won and, when I gathered together my twenty-one essays, I felt sure they formed a compendium of profound truths about the human condition.

After that, I began to delve further back into the Tour's history, seeking out its most famous stages, and trying to understand the lessons they contained — from Fausto Coppi's victory on Alpe d'Huez to Jacques Anquetil and Raymond Poulidor's battle on the Puy de Dôme; from René Vietto's shameless weeping to Greg LeMond soiling himself in his struggle against Bernard Hinault.

Over the years I have made a yearly ritual of spending the nights of July devoted to this task. In solitude, with nothing more than my television, my laptop, and my reference texts, I have tried to codify the thing that makes cycling so all-consuming. Like great works of art and literature, it is a pursuit that goes beyond the simple sporting schemata of winning and losing. There are no goals, points or runs, no definite ninety-minute time period, and sometimes, as was the case in 2006, there's not even a definite winner. Instead, the collective energy of its protagonists — the riders, the fans, the directors, the sponsors, and the landscape itself —

accumulates to offer a panorama of effort, will, endurance, failure, ambiguity, and chance.

When we study the Tour's finest moments, we see a sport where people celebrate the act, and not the outcome; a great defeat, audacious failure or glorious collapse will be celebrated as much as a win. In this way, cycling is both an examination and a celebration of the full gamut of human experience.

THE DAY I LEARNT TO RIDE AND ALSO LEARNT TO CRASH

My first really solid memory of cycling occurred when I was six and rode without training wheels for the first time. My mother took me down to the car park of the old university campus near our house and explained the theory of using your weight to roll into the corners, rather than turning the handlebars. I can remember quite distinctly the initial thrill of shifting my weight to take tight turns. It felt like I was defying gravity itself, weightless and flying across the bitumen.

Notably, that was also the day I had my first memorable bike crash. I leaned in too far on a tight bend, lost traction and plummeted downwards like a small, screaming Icarus. Looking back, I view this incident as a neat illustration of the paradox inherent to cycling; a dream of skimming across the surface of the earth like a god, underwritten by the knowledge that, when men try to be gods, they can easily find themselves hurtle back to earth with great velocity. At the time, my six-year-old self felt the injustice acutely. I threw a tantrum and blamed the incident on my bike. My mother wasn't overly sympathetic and I still corner really nervously.

I'm sure I had other crashes when I was a kid but it wasn't till twenty years later that I had another really noteworthy one. Oddly, it was only a couple of hundred metres further north, just up the road from where I had that first crash. I was riding home on a bike path that goes through a narrow underpass, below a bridge with a bit of a blind corner. I'd been through it hundreds of times so I guess I didn't check it was clear and went into it too fast just as some guy on a mountain bike lumbered through the other side. I swerved to miss him and we scraped past each other. I remember thinking 'That was close' and then I looked down at my front wheel and it was jack-knifing back and forth. Then I crashed and landed on my face, cracked my helmet, and burst open my chin and lips, but somehow avoided breaking my nose or cracking any teeth.

I've heard it said that you should take a crash like a lesson in physics. Personally I tend to take it as a lesson in metaphysics. Whenever I crash I always feel there's a greater philosophical truth to be taken out of it, like a glimpse into some transcendental realm where you see how futile your claims to self-determination are in contrast to the grim reality of human frailty.

I was having a bad time of it that month. I'd just finished two years on a postdoctoral scholarship. The halcyon days of scholarly life had faded away and I found myself rudely hurled back into the workforce. My last real job involved working in an office, doing virtually nothing for several hours a day, so the return to my 'career' wasn't particularly welcome. To add insult to injury, I was embroiled in a tumultuous relationship with a woman who seemed to actively dislike me. I disliked her as well, so it's a mystery as to why we were seeing each other. A couple of days after I crashed she dumped me for the second time, which didn't improve my mood any.

6

Then I got a job interview for a research administration position, filing papers for academics. The job itself sounded horribly dull but it paid well. Having worked in an office prior to the scholarship, I had no desire to return to another one, but I felt a sense of obligation to engage in some sort of paid employment, plus I needed the money pretty badly. I went to the interview hoping it would go badly, which wasn't an unrealistic expectation given I had still a massive scab all over my face from the bike crash. Unfortunately it went extraordinarily well and they offered me the job, on my birthday no less. It was a grim omen.

It was also the first time I really noticed that my love life, my 'career', and my relationship with cycling have a weirdly symbiotic relationship. When something happens to one of them I usually see a change in the other, like some sort of cosmic ballet danced by whatever petulant Fates control my destiny. I first felt this symbiosis a few years earlier, just before I turned twenty-five, back when I was still doing the mundane office job. I'd recently stopped driving automobiles altogether, mostly because petrol had gone over eighty cents a litre. At the time I considered this a moral outrage and I made a pledge that I wouldn't drive again until it went back to at least seventy-nine. Obviously that never happened and I subsequently gave my car to my grandfather.

Around the same time, my girlfriend moved overseas. This became a bit of a recurrent theme throughout my twenties. Every few years I'd start going out with some nice girl and then a year or so later she'd move to another country. One moved to Japan, another to Germany, and a third one to the UK. The first time this happened, I had a simultaneous burst of good luck, winning a scholarship and quitting my job, whereupon I got a payout for unused annual leave. I used this to buy a Giant CRX-1; a sturdy little hybrid commuter. It turned out this was quite a good compensation for heartbreak.

Without a girlfriend or a job, I started riding every day and quickly came to the conclusion that it was doing me a great deal of good. Compared to the existential angst and protracted whinging my working and romantic life provoked, there was something uniquely grounding about riding a bike for long distances. Perhaps it was the hypnotic rhythm of the pedals as they ran in unison with my heart, lungs, and legs, or the all-encompassing physicality of being at one's limits, or perhaps it was simply the humility that came when I discovered dehydration tended to loosen my bowels. Regardless, cycling provided some counterpoint otherwise lacking in my life up until that point.

Over the course of two years on a university scholarship I wrote my PhD and learnt how to ride centuries. Slowly, cycling's improving influence began to seep into other elements of my life. In 2007 I began an uplifting affair with a woman known affectionately as the Furniture Removalist. She was called this because she helped me move house with great aplomb in the early weeks of our relationship. She used to plod around on a reissued Schwinn cruiser, with a three-speed hub gear, foot brake, and the double, curving crossbars US bike companies used to go nuts for back in the Fifties. She didn't ride much but she looked amazing when she did. The bike was huge and she'd sit perched among the various looping bars, bolt upright and decidedly smug as she glided along at just above jogging speed.

After she moved to Germany, I began working full time and, flushed with cash, forked out $3000 for an Orbea road bike. Unfortunately I didn't have any time to ride it. I'd get home from work after dark, gripe about my long working hours and lament another failed affair of the heart. That year was particularly cold. After work I would ride home to sit in my house at night alone, cold and exhausted. I purchased a heart rate monitor and rollers so I could better focus my energies and retain good form despite the ravages of work and winter. It was in this light that I watched the 2008 Tour de France.

That was also the year I stumbled upon the sports writing of Roland Barthes. He's better remembered as the French philosopher who was killed by a laundry truck in 1980 but he was also a devout cycling fan. I'd read him as an undergraduate studying literature but hadn't really paid attention. But his writing on cycling answered a question I found myself contemplating; why does the Tour matter so much? Buried within the pages of his landmark 1957 book *Mythologies*, amid his rambling essays on steak and chips and wrestling, he offered an answer:

> Every day and everywhere, man is stopped by myths, referred by them to this motionless prototype which lives in his place, stifles him in the manner of a huge internal parasite and assigns to his activity the narrow limits within which he is allowed to suffer without upsetting the world.

Like much French philosophy from the Fifties, *Mythologies* is essentially a diatribe on how mass media, the state, and various other nefarious institutions generate a popular mythology that being happy means being white, middle class, heterosexual, and buying things from shopping malls. It's an old argument and probably contains some merit.

Of course, this isn't a book on the ideological apparatus of capitalism, mass media hegemony, and the mechanisms of oppression. This is a book about cycling. Barthes wrote an entire chapter on the Tour de France in *Mythologies*, arguing that it wasn't just a race, it was a mythological story of what it meant to be human, like Homer's *Odyssey* but played out on bikes every July. A couple of years later, in an essay called

'What Is Sport', he wrote:

> Muscle does not make the sport: that is the evidence of
> the Tour de France. Muscle, however important, is never
> anything more than raw material. It is not muscle that
> wins. What wins is a certain idea of man and of the world.
> This idea is that man is fully defined by his action ...

I can see his point. In each year's Tour, a mass of grown
men in brightly clad lycra will haul themselves over three
thousand kilometres, traversing both the French Alps and the
Pyrenees as part of a race virtually all of them will lose and
around a quarter of them won't even complete. What strikes
me about this situation isn't the victories or the losses, but the
exhibition of a wholehearted, passionate devotion borne out
of a belief that riding a bike means something.

Of course, others may beg to differ. Over the years, many
people have suggested I take cycling too seriously; that it's just
an overblown game played by skinny men in garish uniforms,
a meaningless pursuit instilled with a value far beyond its
worth. That's quite possibly true, but then no one has been
able to offer me a better alternative. In the absence of anything
more profound, I think cycling offers a very solid foundation
for one's world view.

STAGE 1

July 2nd, 2006
Strasbourg to Strasbourg

JIMMY CASPER TAKES A TUMBLE

I'm sorry you don't believe in miracles.
— *Lance Armstrong*

L et us now return briefly to the 2006 Tour. With Armstrong absent for the first time in seven years and Landis nine seconds off the lead, the first official stage win was taken by one of my favourite sprinters, Jimmy Casper. It was a great victory and one that I consider the harbinger of an age.

The *peloton* had chased down a lone breakaway by Walter Bénéteau before coming into the final kilometres for a jittery, high-speed, bunch finish. With no single, clearly dominant sprint train, the run-in to the line was chaotic. Amid the hubbub, World Champion Tom Boonen botched his sprint, the aging Erik Zabel lacked his former kick, and Robbie McEwen was still coming into form. Thor Hushovd, in the yellow jersey after winning the previous day's prologue, crashed after colliding with a huge green novelty cardboard placard — one of the numerous unusual objects given to fans by the Tour's sponsors. From out of this confusion emerged the second-tier sprinter Jimmy Casper, bursting through the pack to cross the line with an expression of unrestrained joy. The commentary barely noticed he was there until he'd actually won, and even then seemed surprised.

To be fair, Jimmy Casper isn't exactly the kind of rider you'd expect to win something as prestigious as the opening stage of the Tour. In theory he's most famous for winning the Grand Prix de Denain (twice), the 2007 edition of the Three Days of West-Flanders, and the GP Le Samyn. In practice he's more famous for being the last place finisher of the 2002 and 2004 Tours and for having the most unimaginably horrendous crashes. His crash in the first stage of the 2003 Tour de France, in which he crumpled in the final metres of a mass sprint and caused a pile up, appears in not one but two films — *Wired To Win* as well as the classic tribute to drudgery and suffering *Hell on Wheels*. It's hard to describe what happened. It looked like his bike suddenly and inexplicably flipped and he landed on his head. He apparently fractured some of his vertebrae after which he donned a neck brace and rode on for another seven days.

In *Hell on Wheels* you can see the moment when, unable to keep up in the Pyrenees, he finally gives up, stops on the side of the road, abandons his bike and crawls into the Broom Wagon. It has the same aura of Dickensian tragedy as watching a kitten drown.

He made a similar appearance in the opening stage of the 2008 Tour. I missed out on seeing most of that first stage because my band was playing a show and I was out getting drunk. About half way through the show, I messaged a friend to ask for updates. He messaged me back to say Casper had already crashed. I wasn't surprised.

In 2008 I think he got away with some minor grazes. His best crash was in 2007 when, riding for the Unibet team in the mid-season classic Ghent-Wevelgem, he entered the descent of the Kemmelberg, a short, violently steep road still paved in the rough cobbles of the late 19th Century. He was deep within the full *peloton* until he, once again, inexplicably flipped and landed on his face. He broke his collarbone, a wrist, some ribs, and his jaw. Better yet, he ripped his lip so badly he needed sixty stitches and tore his tongue. The final insult was that when they reset his lip they did it wrong and he had to have it redone. And then his team lost their sponsor.

I still remember the 2008 Tour fondly. It was the first one I watched after the Furniture Removalist had left me for Germany, so I had the right volume of heartbreak to make for an especially high grade of personal epiphany. It was also the first Tour since 1995 won by someone who wasn't subsequently embroiled in a doping scandal. Suddenly cyclists who'd always been passed-off as 'also-rans' began to win. The eventual winner, Carlos Sastre, had an overall average speed of 40.92 km/h, making it a little more believable than Armstrong's 2005 record of 41.654 km/h. In 2011, when Cadel Evans won, the average speed was down to 39.788 km/h. There was still the occasional doping conviction, notably Bernard Kohl, but their expulsion had the ring of 'the system is starting to work' about it. It felt less like watching the cartoon victory of Landis on his way to Morzine.

Sitting up late that year, I spent a lot of energy finding metaphors for personal renewal and regeneration. I remain a fan of Carlos Sastre and Cadel Evans, both of whom seemed slightly grumpy, somewhat eccentric, and marked more by consistency of effort than regularity of success. But it was Jimmy Casper who I really found myself following. His 2008 Tour was far less glamorous than his 2006 adventure. After struggling along, he was finally dropped on Stage Seventeen's decisive ascent of the Alpe d'Huez, failed to make the time cut and was forced to leave the race. More dramatically, he also tested positive for corticosteroids, although he was later cleared on the grounds that the test pertained to an asthma medication for which he'd failed to gain the adequate medical clearance. It marked his gradual descent into the lower ranked Continental teams and a few years later he was shuffled into retirement after being unable to secure a contract.

Casper's innocuous decline only made his victory in the opening stage of the 2006 Tour seem all the more valuable, offering one shining moment amid a sea of unrewarded effort and terrible crashes. It also, to me at least, marked a turning point in the race itself. By 2008 the Tour had shifted from the spectacle of Armstrong's brutal supremacy and Landis's unbelievable attacks. Instead, it became a story of persistence and endurance over the previous Superman heroics — a story in which I see Casper's lone Tour stage win as the forerunner. In between that one glittering win and his exit from the 2008 race, the Tour's meaning changed fundamentally.

A BRIEF OVERVIEW OF THE TOUR DE FRANCE

Strangely, a lot of people consider 2008 the most boring Tour in recent memory. I suppose if you were only watching the TV highlights, there were fewer displays of godlike panache. My theory is that, devoid of hardcore blood doping, things returned to a style of racing that was slightly more traditional, a narrative designed to be written about, as opposed to being televised.

The history of the Tour de France is at odds with the modern notion of sport. You notice this as soon as you attempt to explain the rules of a Grand Tour to a friend versed in better-known sporting pursuits, such as football, tennis, or basketball. Most modern spectator sports are designed to take place in a format accessible to live and, from 1950 onward, televised audiences. Because of this, most of them run for a specific period of time, after which a clearly defined winner becomes evident. By contrast, cycling, and its three Grand Tours of Italy, France, and Spain in particular, were designed in an age when the printed page held greater sway than televised images. The written coverage of the Grand Tours saw them roll out as sagas and, even today, cycling makes more sense when read about than watched.

A friend once described test cricket to me as 'sport's eccentric uncle', and much the same thing could be said about cycling. The first time I went to the cricket was with my lawyer. It was the second Test of the 2011 Ashes, held at the Adelaide Oval, and he explained to me that the Australian side was 'playing for a draw' and 'betting on rain ending play early'. This was as a result, he explained, of the first Test, which had been a draw, combined with a dreadful first innings by the Australians. I didn't really understand but I liked the way the context of the game spanned out over days and you had to follow it like the convoluted chapters of a Tolstoy novel. For my part, as we sat in the stands I tried to explain the difference between the points system for cycling's polka dot jersey, the place of stage victories, and their relationship to the yellow jersey for best overall time. Neither of us fully understood what the other was talking about. Rain ended play early and we devoted most of the afternoon to drinking Pimms.

Cycling races, and the Grand Tours in particular, were devised for commercial ends, and commerce works in strange and mysterious ways. The Tour de France, it should be remembered, was founded to sell copies of the sporting magazine *L'Auto* in much the same way that 20/20 cricket was designed to sell television advertising. As such, the Tour de France was intended to fuel a written narrative that kept people buying papers over the better part of a month. It makes more sense when you remember this. You can sell a certain number of newspapers writing about a single day race, like Paris–Roubaix, but you can sell a lot more if that race lasts for three weeks, involves multiple characters and subplots, and each stage has a cliff-hanger ending. To that end, while only one rider will complete the narrative of the yellow jersey, every single rider has the capacity to generate copy for journalists by taking part in breakaways, winning stages, or just crashing horribly.

From there, it should be understood that the narrative being told about cycling needs to be more than just 'so-and-so won, and so-and-so lost' because no one is going to buy a paper just to read that the breakaway stayed away for sixty kilometres, got caught, then there was a bunch finish and the yellow jersey stayed with whoever had it yesterday. Like great literature, great sports journalism must hint at the profound, and the journalist must therefore read profundity into the otherwise mundane act of a group of men riding bicycles over prolonged distances.

To achieve this, the narrative being told has to trigger comparison to a wider cultural milieu, which is why cycling creates a particular brand of fanatic. Its narratives share more in common with Greek mythology than football or basketball journalism. The Tour is an epic, rather than a sporting competition. When Henri Desgrange founded it in 1903, both he and his assistant, Geo Lefevre, wrote about it in a deliberately grandiose style. They re-named the riders with titles such as 'The Prince of Mines' and 'The Terrible

Butcher from Lens'. Benjo Maso's wildly underappreciated masterpiece *The Sweat of the Gods* cites a particularly flowery passage from Desgrange:

> The steepest mountains, the coldest and blackest nights, the sharpest and most violent winds, constant and unjust reverses, the most difficult routes, never-ending slopes and roads that just keep going on and on – nothing has been able to break the determination of these men.

Desgrange was what could be politely referred to as 'a character', which is a euphemism for jerk. He's also nicely indicative of the era in which he lived and his ascent from setting the hour record in 1893, to founding the Tour ten years later, weaves through the complex relationship between commerce, nation building, identity, and sport that occurred at the start of the tumultuous modern era in which we live.

The birth of the paper Desgrange ran, *L'Auto*, was, at least according to popular myth, a side effect of the Dreyfus Affair. This is one of the most famous Affairs ever and is too complex to summarize adequately here. In brief, it involved a Jewish officer in the French army, named Dreyfus, being framed for treason by anti-semites. The case against him was pretty obviously false and the trial became a focal point to argue about the relationship between the law and religion.

The Dreyfus Affair produced the kind of irreconcilable, deeply personal controversy capable of inducing bitter arguments among close friends. Among the vigorously anti-semitic was aristocrat and factory owner Albert de Dion, patron of a cycling magazine called *Le Velocipede*. The magazine's editor, Pierre Giffard, was of the exact opposite persuasion. They had a fight, Giffard declared Dreyfus innocent, Dion probably said something anti-semitic, one thing led to another and Dion pulled all funding out of the

Velo and started a new paper called *L'Auto*. To run it, he hired the equally bigoted Henri Desgrange.

Desgrange had a background in cycling, both as a rider and as a journalist, along with the benefit of a fairly forceful personality. Shortly after starting the paper, he decided he needed a media stunt to attract readers and in 1903, following the advice of his sub-editor Geo Lefevre, he started the Tour de France.

In 1903 France had no definite national road network and parts of the country still spoke their own unique dialects. Degrange's idea was to produce a spectacle of human endeavour so immense and unbelievable it would utterly enthral the entire French nation and, in doing so, significantly increase his sales. Thus begins the unique mix of crass commercialism and mythological spectacle that continues to provide the Tour's appeal. It sits somewhere between *The Iliad* and one of those natty Nike advertising campaigns.

The first race featured stages of three hundred kilometres, starting at five in the morning. Most of the early competitors were members of the lower end of the socio-economic spectrum. The first winner was a five foot, three inch chimney sweep called Maurice Garin. The next year, despite winning the race a second time, Garin was denied victory after Desgrange decided he'd cheated. Desgrange decided quite a few people had cheated and, indeed, quite a few of them had. A number of riders caught trains rather than ride the substantial distances contained within each stage.

People seem to forget this about the Tour de France. It has always been suspect and corruption and cheating are part of its fibre. If it was just a matter of winning and losing, this would probably ruin its appeal but, given the scope of the narrative a three week Tour produces, the ambiguous degree to which rules are respected and abused becomes emblematic of the manner in which suspicion, cheating, and corruption are inherent to the human condition.

The problem these days, particularly after the commercial success of the Armstrong Era, is that people expect the Tour de France to be a sporting event, which means they expect winners and losers and, more to the point, they expect believable winners and losers. In the wake of Armstrong's conviction by the US Anti-Doping Authority there's been much debate as to who 'won' the Tours from 1999 to 2005. To my eye, Armstrong won them by virtue of having the best overall time, but won them like a Shakespearian villain; through corruption and skulduggery, like Claudius in *Hamlet*, proving 'that one may smile and smile and be a villain', or at least it may be so on the Tour. Consequently, when judging the victory of a race, 'let every eye negotiate for itself and trust no agent', particularly if that agent is Bob Stapleton.

To someone used to watching ninety-minute football games, the narrative of a Grand Tour is too subtle and the doping too overt to stomach. It undermines the usual story of who won and who lost and its logic is harder to plot than the post-game narrative of who kicked which goal in what minute. When you read about the Tour, each stage produces a chapter within a wider, complex narrative that has nothing to do with winning and losing and everything to do with producing a spectacle of humanity at its best and worst. Doping, cheating, crashing, and failure roll across the page just as well as victory and fair play.

This was largely how I became a Jimmy Casper fan. Whenever his name came up it was in reference to an array of terrible accidents far superior to his modest victories. Casper's grim persistence is indicative of a quintessential theme within the roots of professional cycling. When the sport began in Europe it was ensconced in selling bikes to the working classes, for whom life was rough. Journalists dubbed the first Tour winner, Maurice Garin, 'The Little Chimney Sweep' because he was actually a chimney sweep. Other titles, like 'The Prince of Mines', captured the degree to which the human fodder of the professional cycling industry, both fans and riders, did actually work in mines, sweep chimneys, and farm the land through which bike races ran. It was not a life in which hard work inherently meant reward. Hard work just went 'on and on', like Desgrange's roads and the 'unbreakable determination' his riders gained within the pages of *L'Auto*. His coverage celebrated the 'will to keep going' rather than the 'will to win'.

With the advent of the Armstrong era, cycling has been globalised and is now more akin to the 'new golf' than a working class sport but we occupy the tail end of the same era of modernity Desgrange documented in 1903 and his themes remain relevant. Hard work and personal virtue are nice but they don't necessarily get you anywhere. You can strive like a champion and still be just another pleb working in the HR department while the Hand of Fate lays out the cards of bad luck, lack of opportunity, or an inbuilt absence of intellect, talent, or skill.

In the aftermath of the Neo-Liberal Eighties, there's still a myth we can all be winners. Perhaps the recent rise of cycling as a popular sport in the English speaking West is a delayed response to that. Maybe cycling has come back into vogue because we've recognised the obvious fact that we can't all be champions but it gives us the consolation that carrying on regardless has its own virtue. When I look at pictures of Jimmy Casper, with his mangled, battered face grinning laconically, this is the lesson I see.

STAGE 2

July 4th, 1953
Metz to Liege

FRITZ SCHÄR WINS THE FIRST GREEN JERSEY

The traditional object or tool … was not in any way 'wedded' to human forms; what it wedded was human physical effort and human gestures – indeed, the human body imposed itself upon that tool in order to carry out a material task. Today the human body would seem to be present only as the abstract justification for the finished form of the functional object […] Man's technical power can thus no longer be mediated, for it has no common measure with the human being or the human body.
— *Jean Baudrillard*

One of the problems with a three-week Grand Tour is that inevitably there are points when nothing much is happening. To counteract this, the Tour's organisers decided early on that it would be necessary to provide secondary 'races within the race', forcing the riders to do something journalists could write about even though nothing substantial was happening. Accordingly, over the years the yellow jersey was supplemented with a series of secondary jerseys and contests; intermediate sprints, an award for 'Most Combative Rider' decided by a jury of experts and, moreover, a polka dot jersey for the 'King of the Mountains' and a green jersey for the most consistent sprinter, both awarded using a system of points.

This is a bit like the way Leo Tolstoy built his epic *War and Peace* around five families of Russian aristocrats. By mashing their collective stories into one bewildering, lengthy tale interspersed with constant asides, he produced so many randomly intersecting plotlines that you can zone out while reading and, when you start paying attention again, something will probably be happening.

The green jersey is absolutely essential to the first week of the Tour, during which the race traditionally runs over a series of long, flat stages before entering the mountains. Strategically this is vital; the contenders for the yellow jersey will fight to conserve their energy, struggling to control the pace of the *peloton* and keep out of the wind. Unfortunately, energy conservation rarely makes for exciting sport. To be honest, I tend to sleep through most of the opening stages of the Tour. I'll doze off on the couch and wake up as the race nears its final kilometres. These lapses rarely result in missing anything important. If it weren't for the green jersey I wouldn't bother watching at all.

The sprinters' competition or 'Points Classification' was introduced to the Tour in 1953. The jersey is green because it was originally sponsored by a lawn mower company. These details are telling. During the Fifties, the Tour's audience began to shift from primarily newspaper readers to radio listeners and, slowly, viewers of newsreels and television. In the written age, it had been fairly easy to conceal how dull the opening stages were by filling column inches with gossip on race favourites, grandiose language, and general information on the stages to come. But with radio and television, things got harder.

You can still see this struggle today. During the opening stages of the Tour there's extensive televised helicopter footage of local landmarks and interesting sculptures constructed out of farmyard detritus. The race commentators are issued with a book identifying local landmarks and will spend significant amounts of time reading out paragraphs on the history of a chalet because there's essentially nothing else going on.

Then, in the final half hour of the race, things will suddenly kick into gear and the *peloton* will go from being comparatively placid to a writhing mass of competitive aggression. This is the battle for the green jersey, which is so hotly contested that entire teams are constructed to prioritise it over its more famous yellow equivalent. It is one of the greatest inventions of the Tour in the post-war era, decided on a system of points awarded for high placing in particular stages. On the opening flat stages, anything up to forty-five points might be awarded for a first place finish, down to a mere one or two for a fifteenth placed rider.

The points system itself is quite old, originally used to calculate overall victory in the early Tours, back when they couldn't keep track of the times properly. When it was re-introduced in 1953 it was titled the Grand Prix du Cinquentenaire. Beyond ensuring something happened in the first week, it had another, equally practical purpose. Many big name riders suited to the Classics and shorter stage races would pull out of the Grand Tours when it became obvious all they could do was squabble for minor stage victories. As the withdrawal of a big star impacted on audiences and, in turn, sponsorship dollars, the sprinters' jersey was designed to keep them, and their fans, involved in the race.

It worked a treat, creating a whole new breed of Tour stars. The first winner was the Swiss cyclist Fritz Schär, who took the opening stage of the 1953 Tour, along with Stage Two, had a brief stint in yellow after Stage Nine, and took sixth place overall. For a rider who pulled off such a solid Tour, he's weirdly unrecognised today. In part that might be because he played second fiddle in his team to two of the greatest Swiss riders ever; Ferdi Kubler and Hugo Koblet, who won the 1950 and 1951 Tours respectively. The sprinters' competition gave him a chance to shine in his own right.

After Schär, the green jersey was consistently won by some of the biggest names in cycling. In 1955 it went to World Champion Stan Ockers, who won it again in 1956 shortly before dying in a motor-paced track race. André Darrigade and Jean Graczyk traded it back and forth between 1958 and 1961. Darrigade won a total of twenty-two stages in the Tour and took the green jersey before going on to become World Champion in 1959, while Graczyk won no less than four stages in 1960, along with the Super Prestige Pernod Award for the year's best overall rider. After that, German tough guy Rudi Altig took it in 1962.

After that came 'Emperor' Rik Van Looy, who was World Champion in 1956 and 1957 and a winner of Milan-San Remo, Fleche Wallone, Paris-Brussels, and the Tour of Flanders twice each. He also won Ghent Wevelgem and Paris Roubaix three times. Then Dutch great Jan Janssen won it in 1964, 1965, and 1967 before taking the yellow jersey in 1968. After that Eddy Merckx took it, winning the yellow, green, and polka dot jerseys in 1969.

With that lineage, the green jersey has gradually become the focus for an entire discipline of road cycling, in which riders better suited to the Classics and one day races will devote themselves wholeheartedly to the Tour de France, despite having no hope of winning overall victory. By the mid-1980s entire teams were being constructed to focus on it, beginning with riders like Jean-Paul van Poppel and the SuperConfex team and culminating in the late 1990s with the testosterone fuelled machismo of Mario Cipollini. He turned the moment of the sprint into a passionate, emotive release; a sudden explosion of energy that, like his pink lycra body suits, permed hair and flamboyant mannerisms, was loaded with overt Freudian undertones.

After Cipollini, there's been a recognisable period in which the final sprint serves as a flurry of passionate activity after two hundred kilometres of nothing much, with a select number of fervently masculine, specialised sprinters hurling themselves towards the line like eccentric conductors competing to guide an orchestra through its crescendo. This kind of competition was established only after the creation of the jersey; in essence, a mechanism to provoke journalistic copy has, since Schär in 1953, became the goal of an entire discipline of athletes.

A BRIEF HISTORY OF THE BICYCLE

Naturally, there's more to the green jersey than just the purely commercial aims of sponsors. Sprinting is a very old discipline, dating back to the sport's origins. Unfortunately, professional track sprinting has declined substantially over the years, initially due to growing crowds for football, rugby, and tennis. It retained its popularity right up until the 1950s, even in English speaking countries, when stars like Reg Harris drew huge crowds and big money. The popularity of Belgian Six Day races and the Japanese Keirin circuit are remnants of this era. While its popularity has declined, sprinting still contains a particular epiphany deeply embedded within cycling, and the green jersey is the strongest expression of this.

The mixed fortunes of sprinting can be attributed to the rise of the automobile after the Second World War. This took away one of the things that made it so spectacular. We forget this today but, for a while, the bicycle was the fastest machine on the planet. The idea that an ordinary human could move at speeds in excess of 60km/h was mind-boggling in a world where most people travelled on foot. To that end, the sprint is an ode to the bicycle's capacity to amplify human power to degree once thought impossible.

It's worth remembering that the bicycle was not intended as a sporting accessory. It was originally designed as machine to enhance the energy of its rider and make it easier to get around. It achieves this by distilling the wattage produced by the cyclist's legs and dispelling it through the rear wheel with an efficiency far beyond that of walking or running. The display of this efficiency is most evident during sprints, when the maximum burst of energy is exploited for the maximum speed.

Sprint prodigy Mark Cavendish once commented on his advantage over his rivals:

> I'm a little bit different to the other sprinters. You look at them, most of them are big powerhouses. They're big guys like Thor Hushovd, [Alessandro] Petacchi – they put up nearly 2,000 watts, 1,800 watts in a sprint and just power themselves to the line. Now, I can put up to about 1,600 watts – that's when I'm training. Naturally I put about 1,300 watts out, which is 25% less. But I'm incredibly efficient. I've got tiny little short legs. I'm able to save a lot of energy during the stage because I'm smaller and hide in the wheels.

In his own unique way, Cavendish is explaining quite a complex piece of physics. At a technical level, the relationship between a cyclist and their bike is about the efficiency of their power to traverse through their legs, through the pedals, through the chain, and into the back wheel. When you think about it, this is a marvellous feat of engineering, more so when we recall all that energy has to be released at the exact right moment, at high speed, while balancing on two thin little wheels.

But when you look at the faces of the sprinters, it's also about the containment and then sudden release of a violent emotion. Their faces look like they're having some sort of extremely painful orgasm. The controlled and clinical nature of the build-up to the final sprint develops a sense of suppression and suspense before embodying a sort of extreme emotive energy, bursting out from the rider into their machine, with the bicycle amplifying the physical force of the human body. The sprint celebrates the rider's capacity to select precisely when to invest all of their energy into one spasm of effort but also the power of the bicycle to amplify the effort of its rider in a way otherwise unattainable.

This link between the emotive display of the sprinter and the efficient expression of physical energy is, I'd argue, part of the bicycle's appeal. The prototypes of the bicycle began in the 1770s, based around a desire to produce a human powered carriage. The aim was to free people from the tyranny of distance. By amplifying our energy, the bicycle quite literally expanded the human world. A bike ride of fifty kilometres might take less than two hours. In 1770 it was a long day's walk.

The prototype of the bicycle was produced by a German Baron named Karl von Drais who, suitably, named it after himself. His 'Draisine' was essentially a board of wood suspended over two iron wheels, propelled by pushing your feet against the ground. It's been referred to as a running machine, because it allowed you to accumulate momentum while running by effectively storing it in the wheels. In that respect it was definitely a prelude to the bicycle, although it lacked the finesse of later machines.

The Draisine was relatively successful but mostly used as a novelty among the owning class, being too expensive and impractical for regular use. People tinkered with the design, playing around with hand-cranked wheels and tricycles until, in 1867, a Parisian blacksmith called Pierre Michaux designed a two wheeled machine with pedals attached directly to the front wheel. The theme caught on quickly, particularly in England where the Industrial Revolution produced two major breakthroughs — the technological capacity to make fairly strong, relatively light frames out of steel and the spread of a national network of reasonably well maintained roads.

From there, Michaux's basic bicycle began to be used for longer trips and rapidly gained the attention of sportsmen, who have a natural propensity for novelty. A lot of the early competitive cycling events built off an earlier tradition of pedestrian races, which essentially involved walking long distances. These included things like walking one hundred miles in twenty-four hours and thousand-mile walks. The simple act of covering a long distance without the aid of a horse or a steam engine was considered a feat unto itself. Accordingly, the novelty of someone on a bike covering a couple of hundred kilometres in a day had the same appeal as a forty-five minute trans-Atlantic flight might have today.

However, the machine didn't emerge fully formed. As the invention of the bicycle pre-dated the invention of the bicycle chain, in the early days the pedal remained attached to the front wheel hub. Those of a competitive bent discovered that if the front wheel was made larger, then each time your feet rotated the pedals you'd move further. This is the origin of the Penny Farthing, which was the pinnacle of transport technology in the latter part of the Nineteenth Century.

Thanks to their leading role in the Industrial Revolution, the British transformed the bicycle in those years, producing lighter frames, introducing ball bearings to moveable parts, and developing the first spoked wire wheels. Sometime in between about 1875 and 1885, the technology required to produce the first bicycle chains appeared, resulting in the Rover Bicyclette, which featured a chain driven rear wheel, although still with the Penny Farthing's distinctive single metal bar frame and oversized front wheel.

Then, around 1894, the first of the 'safety' bicycles appeared, most notably the Rover, produced by the company that would later become renowned for its four-wheel drive motor vehicles. The 'safety' bike is what we'd now simply call a bicycle. The term 'safety' differentiates it from the Penny Farthing in that the use of a chain and cogs meant you no longer had to have a huge front wheel to move at high speed, bringing you a lot lower to the ground and making riding a lot less dangerous.

This is a delightfully simple piece of engineering. The pedal connects to a large cog that moves a chain, which turns a smaller cog attached to the back wheel. The different size between the two cogs means turning the large cog once makes the small cog turn multiple times, rotating the wheel with it. Additionally, by varying the size of the two cogs, one could change the 'gear' of the bike, using a heavier gear if you were on flat ground and wanted to power along, and a lighter gear if you wanted to ride up hills.

Commercially, this wasn't an immediate success. The safety bike competed with a growing number of tricycles (apparently the UK still had societies of tricycling enthusiasts in the 1950s) and the Penny Farthing (or Ordinary) until Safeties eventually gained dominance in the 1890s. By this point John Dunlop had invented a tire with an inner tube, and the diamond frame, still common in nearly every bicycle today, had become standard. For the most part, after the diamond shaped frame, the chain, and the inner tube were developed, the basic design of the bicycle had reached completion.

People did tinker with the details and developed methods of better energy efficiency, most notably the freewheel and, later, variable gearing. The freewheel, which first appeared in the 1870s, is the thing inside the hub of the wheel that means the wheel can keep turning when the pedals are stationary. They became more common on safety bicycles around the turn of the century and were first used in the Tour de France by Leon Georget in 1907 on the Col de Porte. Despite losing time on the climb, he regained it and won the stage on the descent because freewheels make it possible to coast, and coasting is a big part of a good descent.

This created some controversy, giving birth to the first generation of fixed wheel purists. Henri Desgrange was one of them. I forget how the story goes exactly but sometime around 1910 he made some comment about how the fixed wheel made the riders stronger by ensuring they had to use their legs all the time, even on the descents. One of the riders apparently responded that the only people getting stronger were the ones who hadn't crashed and ended up in hospital while trying to descend on a fixed wheel.

I think Desgrange also objected to the use of variable gears on the same principle, although riders did use a 'flip flop' hub – which meant the back wheel had one size of cog on one side, and another on the other. Traditionally, one side would have a freewheel and the other wouldn't. The idea was that when you were pushing along on the flat, you'd be riding a heavier gear 'fixed' to the wheel and then, when you got into the hills, you'd flip the wheel around and ride a smaller gear with a freewheel so you could coast downhill. Flip flop hubs have started reappearing as companies try to cater to the fixed/single-speed craze.

If I remember correctly, gearing first started with hub gears in around 1902. A hub gear involves an additional set of cogs inside the hub of the wheel itself, as opposed to more standard gears, in which the chain is dragged across different sized cogs attached to the back wheel by a derailleur, which literally derails the chain and then 're-rails' it on a different sized cog.

By 1909 three-speed hub gears built by the British company Sturmey-Archer were appearing on high-end bikes. Hub gears are still pretty common, particularly on bikes designed specifically for short distance commuting. The Furniture Removalist's bike had hub gears and, when I was growing up, my mother had a three-speed hub gear on her Peugeot folding bike that I thought was terribly advanced and technical.

The more widely used derailleur system first appeared in primitive form in the late 1880s, pioneered in France by Paul de Vivie. In 1914, a mechanic named Joanny Panel revised his invention with a two sprocket shifter and by the 1930s the modern derailleur was in place, complete with four sprocket rear gears and front chain rings, which gave a much greater variety of gearing than any hub gear. Derailleurs began to reach perfection in the forties and fifties with companies like Simplex and, most notably, Campagnolo.

The materials used in making the frames also began to change. In the 1930s the first aluminium bikes began appearing, relying on breakthroughs in the use of aluminium in the aviation industry. Bike frames have borrowed a lot from aviation. The use of titanium (my dream frame, the

Bianchi S9 Matta is made of titanium) started in, I think, the 1970s after trickling down from its use in aeroplanes, and I'm pretty sure carbon fibre (the current frame material of choice) has the same origin.

Things continue to change and if you read any bike magazine you'd think major breakthroughs were being made every week. But basically the design of the bicycle was cemented by 1900 with the advent of the diamond frame, chain, and gears. Other changes have been, pretty much, icing on the cake, primarily to either lighten the bike or increase the variety and reliability of the gears.

On the whole, the ultimate aim hasn't changed. The bicycle was designed to amplify the force of human muscle and that's what it continues to do. It gave people the power to traverse distances that had previously been unimaginable, enabled them to move faster than they'd ever been able to move before, and to achieve a freedom of movement never before experienced.

Perhaps this capacity to overcome otherwise insurmountable distances triggers off some subconscious instinct for strength and freedom. Perhaps there's something about the bicycle's amplification of the rider's own physicality that addresses a phobia of helpless weakness buried deep within our reptilian brains. This might explain why cycling holds such fascination and creates such euphoria which, in turn, might explain the expressions of painful orgasmic release that grip the faces of the sprinters as they surge towards the line. Either way, the bicycle continues to bring the expenditure of human energy to its pinnacle of efficiency in a way no other machine has replicated.

28 June, 1923
Cherbourg - Brest

HENRI PÉLISSIER AND THE CONVICTS OF THE ROAD

*The mountains seemed to sink lower, sunk by the victorious thrust
of his muscle.*
— *Henri Desgrange, on Henri Pélissier*

Stage Three of the 1923 Tour de France was won by Henri Pélissier. He would win two more stages before taking the overall victory in Paris. It was the pinnacle in a career that lasted more than a decade but also the high point in a tumultuous life. Pélissier was to become one of the Tour's first major doping stories and one of the great tragic figures of the sport, dying at age forty-six, less than ten years after he retired from the sport.

The 1923 Tour was a mammoth affair of 5386 kilometres, more than 1700 kilometres longer than the edition Landis would win in 2006. It was divided over just fifteen stages, with Stage Three alone consisting of more than four hundred kilometres. Of the one hundred and thirty-nine starters, a mere forty-eight would finish, with a time gap of two whole days separating the first placed Pélissier and last placed Daniel Masson.

At the age of thirty-four, Henri was one of a limited number of riders who had been racing professionally before the First World War, having started his career in 1911 with a win at the Giro d'Lombardia. He'd already started the Tour de France four times before, but finished only once with a stunning second place in 1914, just before the outbreak of war. Returning in 1923, he was at the head of an impressive team sponsored by the cycling manufacturer Automoto. Alongside him was his brother Francis, who had already won a stage of the 1919 Tour and the 1921 French national road race championship.

Their teammates included future Tour winners Ottavio Bottecchia and Lucien Buysse, as well as Hector Heusghem, who had lost the 1922 Tour only after falling foul of one of the numerous petty rules on bicycle maintenance. But it was Henri and Francis who made the race, attacking on Stage Three to cross the line in first and second place. Their teammate Bottecchia was in the yellow jersey, the first Italian to ever hold it, but this didn't seem to count for much. With help from his brother, Henri kept himself within striking distance of the race lead right up until Stage Ten, where he attacked over the Vars and Izoard. The next day he attacked again on the Galibier to secure a gap of a half an hour over Bottecchia, which he would hold all the way into Paris.

In the Tour of 1923, Stage Three had marked Henri Pélissier's first attack. In 1924, he quit the race on the same stage, outraged over the treatment of the riders and embroiled in a clash of wills with Henri Desgrange. The Tours of the

Twenties were notoriously long and difficult. This was a commercial consideration as much as a sporting one; sponsorship was hard to come by and the race was growing more extreme in an attempt to attract more readers. The stages were longer, the rules more convoluted, and the expectations on the riders ever more extreme. Perhaps unsurprisingly, it was in this context that cycling had its first major doping scandal, initiated by Henri Pélissier himself.

Halfway through Stage Three of the 1924 Tour, Henri, Francis and another rider called Maurice Ville quit the race. Henri was in a foul mood, having argued with Desgrange, who had lectured him for throwing away a spare jersey. Desgrange had a habit of inventing new rules at will and, that year, throwing away a jumper was forbidden lest it outrage the sponsors who had provided it. That afternoon the Pélissiers and Ville gave a now infamous interview to journalist Albert Londres of *Le Petit Parisien*. Published under the title 'Convicts of the Road', it captured the reality of life as a professional cyclist:

> 'You have no idea what the Tour de France is,' Henri said. 'It's a Calvary. And what's more, the way to the Cross only had 14 stations — we've got 15. We suffer on the road. But do you want to see how we keep going? Wait …'

> From his bag he takes a phial. 'That, that's cocaine for our eyes and chloroform for our gums …'

> 'Here,' said Ville, tipping out the contents of his bag, 'horse liniment to keep my knees warm. And pills? You want to see the pills?' They got out three boxes apiece.

> 'In short,' said Francis, 'we run on dynamite.'

With no stages under two hundred and seventy kilometres and five over four hundred kilometres – including a colossal four hundred and eighty kilometre stage from Les Sables d'Olonne to Bayonne – the 1924 Tour was even worse than the 1923 edition. Since its beginnings in 1903, the race had almost doubled in length, with twice as many stages, heading over substantially harder terrain. Desgrange's original intention of producing a spectacle large enough to astound readers into buying his paper had intensified progressively over time. Each Tour pushed the bar higher. While that made for thrilling stories in *L'Auto*, the spectacle of superhuman strength was, as Londres found, possible only through inhuman suffering and powerful drugs.

The results weren't just physically destructive. Henri Pélissier is renowned as one of cycling's great depressives – one of many. His endless griping and complaints prompted Desgrange to declare he 'didn't know how to suffer'. While his 1923 Tour win was the pinnacle to a highly successful career, it didn't seem to have made him any happier. Indeed, things got substantially worse after his retirement in 1927. In 1933, his wife shot herself and he subsequently entered into an abusive relationship with a woman significantly younger than him. Two years later, while he was trying to stab her, she shot and killed him using the same gun his wife had used in her suicide. By today's standards, one would think he'd provided Desgrange with ample fodder for tabloid tales of suffering and woe.

Of course, cycling has high standards for tragedy and drama. The first suicide by a Tour winner was in 1907, when René Pottier hanged himself just six months after winning the race. Legend has it he was found dangling from the same hook he used to store his bike. This set a precedent for the 'Icarus myth' among Tour champions, repeated by Hugo Koblet's suspected suicide in a motor accident, Luis Ocana's shotgun suicide, and Marco Pantani's cocaine-fuelled death alone in a hotel room.

Notably their deaths all occurred after retirement. In Pélissier's case, he never really seemed to recover from having lived out the dream of becoming a great champion. Once he'd reached the summit of the sport, spiralling out of control became almost inevitable, and his dramatic decline left a sort of mythological legacy within cycling.

ON THE NUANCES OF SPONSORSHIP

In the wake of the First World War, one might have expected Henri Desgrange to become more humane but instead he focused his energies on making the Tour borderline lethal. His aim, after all, was to produce an event that pushed the barriers of what was thought humanly possible and to use those stories of superhuman endurance to sell newspapers and make money. Every time a barrier was broken he had to push it out a little further.

It was this attitude that led Pélissier to quit the 1924 Tour and give his notorious interview to Londres. By this point, the two men had an established antagonistic relationship. Pélissier had formed one of the first cyclists' unions to successfully contest Degrange's attempt to prescribe how much each rider could eat during the Tour. Desgrange, in turn, penalised him for having a second glass of wine at a reception, leading Pélissier to quit the 1919 race in outrage. In 1920, Pélissier quit again after Desgrange penalised him for leaving a flat tire on the side of the road.

Their fight in 1924 began when Henri threw away a sponsor's jersey rather than carrying it with him as the rules required. On the surface of it, this seems like a petty and pointless regulation. Desgrange had introduced it in 1920, after striking an arrangement with the sporting goods manufacturer La Sportive, who provided all that year's jerseys. This followed one of his most successful brainstorms in 1919, when he introduced the now iconic yellow jersey for the overall leader of the race.

This was partly a promotional gesture. Yellow was the colour of paper used by the Tour's parent publication, *L'Auto*, which Desgrange continued to edit. However, there was another, more practical consideration. In 1919 Europe was recovering from the War, and there was a shortage of dye, so all the riders wore grey jerseys. Dressing the race leader in yellow allowed spectators to identify him as the Tour passed by.

As for the rule on discarding jerseys, when Desgrange signed the sponsorship deal with La Sportive, Europe was in a post-war recession. The French bicycle manufacturers who traditionally sponsored the Tour were all cash-strapped, bankrupt, or bombed out. Several major French bike companies, including Peugeot, Alcyon, La Française, Automoto, and Gladiator, formed La Sportive as a consortium, partly to keep the sport alive but also so they could collectively block foreign companies from cutting in on their turf.

Desgrange's relationship with these big French bike companies was simultaneously symbiotic and competitive. In the depression that followed the First World War, he needed them to survive, which is why he introduced rules to protect their products. It wasn't that he particularly cared what Pélissier did with his jerseys but a champion throwing away a sponsor's product tends to devalue both the product and the sponsorship contract behind it. Desgrange couldn't afford to risk such a thing. The French cycling industry was too fragile, and he was almost entirely reliant on their backing.

Now that the Tour is sponsored by so many different industries it's easy to forget that, right up until the 1950s, bike companies were overwhelmingly the major source of revenue. This changed as cars became more affordable but, for half a century, bicycles were the most affordable form of personal transport available, so the market was immense and competition among manufacturers fierce. Desgrange's canny salesmanship meant the Tour quickly cemented itself as the best way to get their product in front of potential buyers.

The relationship was always complex. In the Tour's early years Desgrange found the larger manufacturers could afford to buy up all the best riders, give them the best quality equipment and mechanical support, and then maintain total dominance. This produced a conundrum, in that he needed their sponsorship but, if he didn't control their influence, the Tour would quickly become little more than a contest between bike companies, not a contest of superhuman heroism. Unfortunately, no one buys a paper to read about a bike company.

To keep the right equilibrium, Desgrange was always tinkering with new and frequently bizarre rules to limit their influence without losing their sponsorship. At one point, he introduced a secondary category for those riders who rode the entire Tour on a single bike and performed all their own repairs. The idea was to reward the riders for their perseverance, not the quality of their equipment or the skill of their mechanics. This also offered an advertising coup for the bike companies, who could boast endlessly as to the quality of their machines, provided they didn't fall apart too badly.

Sometimes these rules were decidedly unusual. For example, in 1913 Desgrange banned freewheels, declaring them 'decadent', 'infernal' and arguing they 'seriously threatened' the integrity of the Tour. That year he sent the race over the Tourmalet, one of France's steepest peaks. Half way up, 1912 victor Odile Defraye was so tired from wrestling with his fixed wheel he abandoned. Coming down the same mountain, Eugène Christophe was in the lead, until he crashed and broke his front fork. With mechanical support banned, he had to lug the bike to the closest forge and weld the broken fork back together. Famously, he was penalised for asking the smith's apprentice to pump the bellows while he beat the forks back into shape.

Christophe's visit to the blacksmith is one of the Tour's most famous mechanical incidents. For Desgrange, it was the perfect outcome. The injustice of it filled column after column in the sporting papers, while also highlighting the importance of a reliable and well-built bicycle. It was a brilliant combination of sporting and sponsorship interests, with the only loser being the hapless Christophe.

In 1923 Desgrange began trialling a new approach. He divided the race into three categories of rider: professionals, a second division of semi-pros, and *touriste-routiers* or amateurs. The latter was something of a gimmick to attract more readers and help sell more cycling products in a sluggish market. The presence of non-professionals suggested it wasn't just superhumans like the Pélissier brothers who could complete the Tour. The man-on-the-street could too, provided he was willing to fork out the cash for a decent Le Sportive bike.

Viewed through a purely sporting lens, many of Desgrange's rules make little sense. Certainly, the idea of amateurs racing the Tour today seems farcical. Yet the notion of commercially sponsored sport was still relatively new and its boundaries were unclear. Consider what Desgrange was trying to achieve from a different perspective. The Tour gained part of its income by providing a sporting spectacle great enough to attract readers. It gained further income because those readers believed bikes, jerseys, tires and equipment played a role in making ordinary men capable of extraordinary achievements.

When Pélissier threw away his jersey in 1924, Desgrange's response was simply, 'You can't throw away your sponsor's material.' This begins to make sense if you consider the Tour as more than a sport. If you're trying to sell people hammers based on the notion that Mighty Thor uses them to create lightning, or winged shoes on the premise that Mercury wears them to zip around the world, it doesn't help if Thor throws away his hammer and uses a spoon, or when Mercury runs just as fast in Dunlop Volleys.

In theory, it should be obvious that buying a hammer won't make you Thor, nor will fancy shoes make you Mercury. As Armstrong once noted, it's not about the bike. But unless the Tour glorified La Sportive's products, La Sportive wouldn't sponsor the Tour, so Desgrange took a particularly protective attitude to their equipment. Of course, this is the most ingenious paradox that Desgrange, pirate king that he was, created within the Tour. Pélissier was right. The Tour was a Calvary but a Calvary in which the cross was sponsored. This doesn't make the suffering any less real but it does add an entirely new dimension.

July 7, 1999
Laval to Blois

MARIO CIPOLLINI, POSTER BOY FOR TESTOSTERONE

Machismo is disappearing, I can't find it in Contador. Contador has the anonymous face of a surveyor or an accountant.
— Mario Cipollini

The 1999 Tour de France is famous as the first of seven consecutive Tours won by Lance Armstrong but it was also the first edition after the Festina Affair, the doping scandal that would define the following decade. Just before the 1998 race began Willy Voet, a masseuse and general dogsbody for the Festina cycling team, was caught carrying a veritable pharmacy of performance enhancing drugs across the border between Belgium and France. Festina was home to major stars, including France's Grand Tour hopeful Richard Virenque, who would soon become famous for crying in court.

Somehow Virenque and his teammates still made it to the

starting line, racing until Stage Six, when media attention became so intense race director Jean-Marie Leblanc expelled them. By that point, French police had already arrested the Festina team's director and their doctor. They also raided the hotels of the other teams, arresting staff from the Dutch TVM squad.

In the face of overwhelming public scrutiny over doping, the entire cycling profession responded by proclaiming it was being victimised and going on a stubborn defensive. Riders staged strikes on Stages Twelve and Seventeen, sitting down in the middle of the road, riding slowly, and letting members of the disgraced TVM team take a stage win. The response from the sport's governing bodies was equally poor. Following a somewhat half-hearted crackdown on drugs, they ran a publicity campaign to declare the Tour de France 'clean'. The 1999 edition was dubbed 'The Tour of Redemption' although business continued much as usual.

Even if we ignore Armstrong's victory, that year's race still has a deeply dubious undertone. This is especially true of Stage Four, from Laval to Blois, which set the fastest ever speed for a Tour de France stage, at 50.4km/h over 194 kilometres. Not only was it a record speed, but it was also the first of a record four consecutive stage wins by the flamboyant macho sprint icon Mario Cipollini, led-out by his Saeco teammates.

Cipollini is one of the great characters of cycling, renowned for his antics and dress sense as much as his victories. Throughout his career he was fined by the UCI for turning up to races in novelty lycra outfits. The 1999 Tour was no exception. After partying through the first rest day, his entire team decided to celebrate Julius Caesar's birthday by dressing up in Ancient Roman themed kit, much to the disapproval of the race referees. Yet he was still a great athlete, with a career lasting almost twenty years and stage wins in all three Grand Tours.

In 1999 he excelled, arriving at the Tour with an entire team devoted towards dragging him to the line so fast no one could stay on his wheel. Certainly his victory at Blois wasn't due to the same kind of explosive sprint you'd expect of his descendents, such as Mark Cavendish, André Greipel, or Peter Sagan. It's more like watching a drag race, with his rivals simply falling off the pace. Like the 1999 Tour more generally, it's a little hard to watch in retrospect. Cipollini has gone on to criticise the Tours of the Contador era for their lack of 'machismo'. I'm not sure about machismo, but you certainly get the impression there was more testosterone in the *peloton* in his day.

The speed with which Cipollini pulled the *peloton* towards Blois was remarkable enough to foster a sense of suspicion from Christophe Bassons, a rider on the FDJ team who was also writing for the French sports journal *L'Équipe*. Bassons had a reputation for riding clean, despite having ridden for Festina. Indeed, two of the convicted dopers on that team, Armin Meier and Christophe Moreau, declared to the French police that Bassons had been the only clean rider in the entire squad, having reputedly turned down a substantial pay rise awarded only on the condition he agreed to take EPO.

When the Festina Scandal broke out, Bassons had hoped cycling was actually going to reform. After Stage Four, with speeds reaching record levels, he began to suspect his optimism was misplaced. That suspicion became evident in his columns, especially when he wrote that the *peloton* had been 'shocked' by Armstrong's strength. His fellow cyclists responded by shunning him completely. On Stage Ten the entire *peloton* deliberately slowed the pace in protest against him. Angry, he rode away from them. They chased him down, making a point of glaring as they rode past him in a collective show of disapproval. In an interview with the BBC, Bassons recalled:

And then Lance Armstrong reached me. He grabbed me by the shoulder, because he knew that everyone would be watching, and he knew that at that moment, he could show everyone that he was the boss. He stopped me, and he said what I was saying wasn't true, what I was saying was bad for cycling, that I musn't say it, that I had no right to be a professional cyclist, that I should quit cycling, that I should quit the Tour, and finished by saying **** you.

Bassons retired from the sport shortly after. While this was the first show of both Armstrong's capacity as a Grand Tour winner and his capacity to bully his opposition into silence, what's most interesting in hindsight is how few people questioned any of it; the high speeds, the unbelievable performances, or the *peloton* openly attacking its whistle blowers in the middle of the largest race in the world.

Instead, Armstong won four stages and the Tour was declared renewed. That's possibly due to simple economics. His victory opened up the US market, bringing hundreds of millions of dollars into the sport. But it's probably also because the Armstrong story was so good. The fable of a poor boy from the US, who overcame cancer and went on to win the Tour de France, is pretty alluring, far more so than Basson's claims of continued doping. James Joyce once said Catholicism was a 'lie but a beautiful lie', and the almost religious belief in Armstrong springs from similar origins. Even if you didn't personally believe him, the amount of people that did made it better to pretend. As for Cipollini, he crashed on Stage Nine on the descent of the Col de Montgenèvre and withdrew from the Tour.

ON CHEATING FATE, OR
MAYBE THE FRENCH JUST LOVE LOSERS?

When doping allegations first emerged against Lance Armstrong in the French media it was argued that the French simply resented being bested by an American at their own national game. To be fair, the French have an unusually ambiguous attitude to consistent winners, regardless of their nationality. They weren't too fond of Eddy Merckx and even their own five times Tour winner, Jacques Anquetil, was more respected than loved.

The clash seems to have a more ideological than national undertone. As cycling has been adopted by the English speaking world, it has met an audience accustomed to sports in which people win, such as football, baseball, and basketball. There's something distinctly Protestant about these sports, with an ideological foundation that hard work will produce reward, preferably within a fixed time period. By contrast, cycling has its origins in Catholic Europe, especially Spain, Italy, Belgium, and France, where martyrdom plays a greater role in the national psyche, and loss and struggle are virtues unto themselves.

One reason the French loved Louison Bobet, the first person to win the Tour de France three times in a row (1953, '54 and '55), was because he lost it a few times first; coming fourth in 1948, third in 1950, and a lowly 20th in 1951. He also cried the first time he rode it, in 1947. Similarly, the French had a great affection for Raymond Poulidor, known as 'The Eternal Second' because he came second in the Tour three times, and third five times but never won it.

Maybe the French just love losers but also perhaps the fabric of the sport is just better suited to stories of struggle and adversity? Too much winning goes against the grain.

By contrast, the popular tradition of ball sports in the Anglo world has a much clearer story of conquest: you see the ball go over the line, you see the athlete throw his hands up in victory, and you experience a vicarious joy at this triumph. This was what Armstrong brought to cycling. He only really raced once or twice a year and conspicuously won both stages and the Tour overall. Millions of viewers in the English-speaking world could see a guy crossing the line first to beat the Old World of Europe, with its dodgy Italians, swarthy Spaniards, and snooty Frenchmen.

Of course, Armstrong had predecessors, most notably three-time Tour winner Greg LeMond and Giro winner Andy Hampsten. Yet the Texan had the added narrative of having beaten cancer as well. His wasn't the story of someone who competed, struggled, and failed. He had defeated death through sheer force of will and, it seemed, that same will to win was now focused squarely on the Tour de France. He made victory and defeat seem like moral choices. Failure was a sign of moral weakness.

David Walsh who, along with Paul Kimmage, was one of Armstrong's most hated journalists and persistent critics, discussed this in an interview with *Velocity Nation*:

> I do believe that (Armstrong) had an insatiable desire to win … And I think when he realized that he couldn't win in this sport as it was, by the mid 90s, before he got his cancer in late '96, he realized that he couldn't do it without a serious doping program, hence the decision to go to (doping doyen) Michele Ferrari in late '95. But it was that desire, a guy who just couldn't accept losing…

That sort of 'victory at all costs' approach makes sense in a normal sport, where all you have to do is kick a ball over a line to win and the match ends after ninety minutes but, when you're following a sport that's akin to a Greek tragedy on wheels, it jars slightly. In cycling, you expect a bit more *rota fortuna* — the wheel of fate that lifts you up one day but will inevitably throw you down the next. On the flat stages, the sprinters might win, waving their arms and pulling that grimace they pull but in the mountains they'll be struggling just to stay in the race. If a cyclist wins too often it seems like they've cheated fate.

Some see the angry grimace of a victorious sportsman as emblematic of the moment they cement themselves as one of life's winners. I see it as a fleeting instance of pride and vanity before the wheel turns and the gods wreak their terrible vengeance. Traditionally, cycling has always celebrated that old adage *sic transit gloria*, or glory is fleeting. One of the reasons Armstrong had so many detractors, even before he was caught, was the sense that he was somehow cheating Fate. His glories came too easily and too consistently.

The potency of the Grand Tours in particular is the spectacle of watching mortals battle against Fate to assert their agency, and their luck, both good and bad, is a key part of that. The sheer length of a great bike race exposes the riders to so many variables, so many factors beyond their control and so many unexpected twists. It is like an odyssey, and this is why we can relate to it. It speaks to the great journey and unexpected fortunes that make up our own lives. Embellishing one's fortunes with EPO would be a bit like Odysseus catching an express flight home from Troy.

STAGE 5

June 26th, 1965
Châteaulin – Châteaulin

RAYMOND POULIDOR WINS BUT STILL LOSES

*What a piece of work is a man! How noble in reason, how infinite
in faculty! In form and moving how express and admirable! In action
how like an Angel! In apprehension how like a god! The beauty of the
world! The paragon of animals! And yet to me, what is this quintessence
of dust?*
— *Hamlet*

There are some on whom Fortune never smiles and life is
one long saga, with the gods thwarting each and every
step. In cycling, the epitome of this is Raymond Poulidor.
Over the course of his seventeen-year career, he came second
in the Tour five times, and third a further three times, but
never once held the yellow jersey. His legend is born out of
winning just enough to show a prodigious talent, strength

and persistence, but still losing at vital moments in ways that spoke of poor luck and human weakness. Poulidor spent his career in combat with two of cycling's undisputed gods, Jacques Anquetil and Eddy Merckx, and his fortunes were, like Odysseus, beset with numerous trials and tribulations at the hands of forces beyond his control.

Stage Five of the 1965 Tour was probably the clearest example of this. After a one hundred and forty-seven kilometre road race in the morning, the riders embarked on a second stage that afternoon; a 26.7 km individual time trial around Châteaulin. Poulidor won it by seven seconds, placing himself comfortably in the top five overall as the Tour prepared for its first forays into the mountains. It was a strategically perfect position, ahead of all his serious competitors. A little known Italian neo-pro named Felice Gimondi held the yellow jersey. He'd taken it after a lucky breakaway on Stage Three and managed to keep it after coming in second in the time trial. Poulidor didn't see him as competition and, to be fair, no one else did either. He was only twenty-three, had never raced a Grand Tour before and was certain to fall away in the mountains.

As far as the fans were concerned, Poulidor was destined to win in 1965. His great rival, Jacques Anquetil, had chosen not to race after securing his fifth and final victory the year before. Eddy Merckx had only just turned professional and it would be four more years before he began his reign as the most successful professional cyclist of all time. Poulidor's legacy was ultimately shaped by these two immortals but, for that one year, the throne was vacant and many saw him as the rightful heir.

Anquetil's place at the top of the sport had been unassailable for years and his absence changed everything. It wasn't just that he was physically strong but calculating and cunning. He won with a consistency afforded by outfoxing his opponents and controlling the *peloton* so effectively the race seemed decided long before the finish line. The 1964 Tour had been the first time he'd ever looked really vulnerable. Just before the race a psychic in the employ of a newspaper declared he'd die on Stage Fourteen and, being somewhat superstitious, that threw him into a bit of a panic.

He didn't die but something almost as bad did happen. Poulidor dropped him on the ascent of the Port d'Envalira, gaining a time gap of almost four minutes. Anquetil was on the cusp of giving up until his team director, the seasoned Raphaël Géminiani, drove alongside him, screamed at him and handed over a bidon full of champagne. Shortly after, Poulidor crashed and Anquetil beat him to the line, rattled but unbeaten. On Stage Fifteen, things got worse when Poulidor attacked again on the Portet d'Aspet, winning the stage and dragging himself within ten seconds of Anquetil.

On Stage Seventeen Anquetil used all of his considerable skill and strength to win the forty-three kilometre time trial and seize the yellow jersey. Poulidor came in second, just thirty-seven seconds behind him. With no one else posing serious competition, the race was now about the two of them; the aging but undefeated king and the pretender to his title. The race hinged on its final mountain stage, ending with a summit finish on the colossal Puy de Dôme. The Spanish climbers Federico Bahamontes and Julio Jimenez had gone ahead for the stage win, leaving Poulidor and Anquetil alone to battle for the yellow jersey. The two men rode up the mountain side by side, jostling against each other. Everyone else fell away behind them. They were both exhausted but it was the final moment in which a decisive victory could be made. Poulidor knew it was his last chance and threw himself at it entirely, attacking time and time again. Each time Anquetil found the strength to respond until, with less than a kilometre to go, he finally broke. Poulidor pulled ahead to gain forty-two seconds. It was enough to prove that Anquetil could be beaten but not quite enough to take the yellow jersey. After a final time trial in Paris, Poulidor lost the Tour by less than a minute.

For Anquetil, the damage was done. His immortality was thrown into doubt. The relationship between the two riders was a bit like Poseidon and Odysseus. When a God is beaten by a mortal, it provokes a particular sense of ire. For both Poseidon and Anquetil, they adopted the mantra 'If you can't win, then you can at least ensure the other guy loses.'

In a sport that's very good at creating rivalries, the Anquetil/Poulidor conflict is, to my eye, second only to the great rivalry between Italian legends Bartali and Coppi. And, like Bartali and Coppi, their antagonism took on values that tapped in to some greater point of contention within the national psyche. Anquetil personified French metropolitan sophistication and faultless modernity, with his penchant for slick cars, a beautiful wife, a taste for Champagne, impeccable dress sense, and a somewhat cold and mercenary approach to racing. His long time *domestique* Vin Denson recalls a race in which Anquetil sent him off to fetch food and drinks, standard chores for a *domestique*, but in this case he was asked to find white wine to go with an omelette — all to be consumed on the bike. He also used to carry around a comb so Anquetil could look his best when he crossed the finish line.

Poulidor, by contrast, was emblematic of rural France — wholesome, likeable, honest, and continually thwarted by his snobbish metropolitan rival. People joked that when he won a race he used the prize money to buy another cow for the family farm. The fact that Anquetil kept beating him over and over again just added to his popular appeal, in the same way you root for Odysseus over Poseidon when reading

The Odyssey. The French might have respected Anquetil's calculated cunning but Poulidor's place as a country boy struggling against the odds provoked a deep-rooted sense of empathy. As professional cycling is driven by what sells as much as who wins, Poulidor frequently got better sponsorship dollars — something Anquetil couldn't abide.

While Anquetil won his fifth Tour victory in 1964, Poulidor had cemented his reputation as the most deserving contender. He'd come third in 1962, eighth in 1963, and second in 1964. His strength grew as Anquetil's waned and the older man knew it. The best he could hope for now was to retire unbeaten. Anquetil's former *domestique*, Vin Denson, writes in his biography:

> I think that by 1965 he knew he was past his best as a Tour rider. What's more, he was really worried about the possibility of being beaten by Poulidor. ... As I came to discover, it often seemed that all Jacques cared about was making sure Poulidor didn't win, or at least didn't finish ahead of him. I remember at the end of that season [1964], coming up to the Tour of Lombardy, he asked me what form [British rider Tom Simpson] was in. Tom had just become World Champion and he knew we used to train together. I told him that he was absolutely screaming. But at Lombardy he instructed me to sit on Poulidor. So I said to him, 'Poulidor's no danger; it's Tom you need to be worried about.' 'Don't worry about Tom,' he said. 'You sit on Poulidor's wheel. Mess him about.' The result? Tom won, Poulidor finished behind Jacques, and Jacques was happy with his day's work.

This makes sense from a sporting perspective but the fans hated it. From their point of view, Anquetil's era had always been somewhat problematic. In 1961 he'd taken his second and most decisive victory, announcing beforehand that he intended to win the yellow jersey on day one and retain it all the way to Paris. He did just that, taking yellow by five minutes in the opening time trial and winning overall by a whopping twelve minutes. After that, he built a team strong enough to dominate the *peloton*, planned, plotted, and developed an uncanny capacity to avoid making mistakes. His Tour victories were almost mathematical and his superiority was perceived as somewhat inhuman.

His third victory, in 1962, was also the first year the Tour was televised on a daily basis. This is one of those points at which the Tour reveals itself as a commercial spectacle as much as a sporting one. In 1958 the organisation behind international football, FIFA, made their first innovative and highly successful attempts to have the World Cup televised. Suddenly, cycling had real competition for its audience.

The first televised World Cup just happened to coincide with an extremely strong Brazilian team who played in a spectacular style that enthralled viewers. This partly explains why football is so popular today; it was one of the first sports to understand the new medium of television. In comparison to cycling, it's far better suited to the small screen, with a playing field that's easy to film and a definite ninety-minute time span.

The Tour's managers knew their sport needed to make the transition to television if it wanted to keep attracting sponsors. So, following football's lead, in 1962 they arranged for daily broadcasts. Viewers across France tuned in to watch the Tour live for the first time. And what they saw was Jacques Anquetil and his team keeping the entire *peloton* together in a closely packed bunch, riding a steady tempo, unremarkably and without interruption, for hour after hour.

Within the *peloton* itself, Anquetil's dominance was incredibly complex; cutting down breaks before they could get off the front, holding everyone together, and enforcing his superiority. As a written summary, you can make a stage like that sound interesting. On television it was like watching paint dry.

On the final stage in 1963, when Anquetil rode into the Parc du Princes velodrome, the crowd actually booed and sales of the sporting papers began to drop. Yet while Anquetil's calculated racing style didn't translate to television at all, Poulidor's doomed attacks did. He might have lost but he looked better doing it.

When Anquetil decided not to race the 1965 Tour de France, it was something of a relief. That year, television audiences watched with bated breath as Poulidor looked set to seize what many saw as his birthright. When he won the Stage Five time trial the fans saw the opening gambit of their new champion. It was a solid, sensible victory, putting him within striking distance of yellow as the race headed into the mountains, yet staying just far enough away to avoid the pressures of leadership.

This is a fairly common tactic in the race's opening weeks. The Grand Tour contenders will aim to stay in the top ten but allow a lower ranked rider to take the lead and, with it, the burden of leadership. Poulidor had left the yellow jersey to Felice Gimondi, certain that the inexperienced young Italian would lose time as the race progressed. Instead, Poulidor focused his energies on the rider seen as his most dangerous rival, the Spanish climber Julio Jiménez. He planned to limit his losses to Jiménez in the mountains and then take the lead in the final time trials, on Stage Eighteen and in Paris, thereby avoiding the pressure of riding with the yellow jersey too early in the race.

The problem was that Gimondi, unlike most neo-pros who fluke a yellow jersey, didn't lose time in the mountains and went on to win both of the final time trials, taking the overall victory by two minutes, forty seconds. The 1964 Tour was meant to be Poulidor's but he'd lost it again, to an unknown Italian no less. Oddly, it didn't do his reputation any harm, particularly given he was gracious in defeat. With a last ditch attack on Mont Ventoux, he'd secured another spectacular and noble defeat. Indeed, coming second in both 1964 and 1965 strengthened his status as a folk hero. He never did go on to secure a Tour victory, earning the nickname of 'The Eternal Second' after facing the onslaught of Eddy Merckx a few years later. Yet he remains one of the most loved and famous cyclists of his generation. The British cycling scholar Tim Hilton writes that,

> In so many rural farmhouse kitchens there were three icons on the walls: the Virgin Mary, a reproduction of Millet's Angelus and a photograph of Poulidor that had been cut from a newspaper.

FEAR OF CRYING

One of the things I like least about the Armstrong era is that it wiped away the legacy of Poulidor by making failure unpopular and defeat ignoble. Armstrong had the quintessential 'second is the first loser' attitude to racing. This is probably as much the fault of his own eternal second, Jan Ullrich, as Armstrong himself. After winning in 1997, Ullrich came second on no less than four occasions but his legacy has been undermined by implication in the Operation Puerto drug scandal. On top of that, he's also had a few less than glamorous busts for recreational drug use and is remembered almost as well for his fluctuating off-season weight as his sporting prowess.

Psychologically, I think 2011 winner Cadel Evans took up Poulidor's place as the Eternal Second, although I might be biased given that, like Evans, I'm Australian. That said, 'Cuddles' (as he was quickly nicknamed) is an unlikely Australian sporting hero precisely because, like Poulidor, he loses more spectacularly than he wins. There's a nationalist influence in the way the two riders are perceived.

Australia sees itself as a superpower in the making, with the coal, natural gas and uranium reserves to prove it. We expect our athletes to affirm this ascendant spirit when they compete on the international stage, giving the Old World grief like a wisecracking teenager egging on a grumpy old man. Evans doesn't really fit that bill; he lacks the cursing, drinking machismo of a Shane Warne or Pat Cash. For years, we waited for him to finally become an aggressive, domineering champion who'd sink a pint of lager on the podium and say something controversial. Instead, even when he finally won the 2011 Tour, he just kept looking like that awkward kid in primary school who cries in PE and accidentally calls the teacher 'mum'.

By contrast, Poulidor's regional French fans tended to see him as a bastion of old-fashioned regional values holding out against the cynicism of the modern, metropolitan world — a bit like the plot of an *Asterix* comic played out on bikes. Poulidor was racing during an era when French power was declining and he served as metaphor for the slow fade of better days. Evans rose to fame as the Australian dollar climbed to an all time high and our economy boomed shamelessly in the face of the Global Financial Crisis. For the French fans, Poulidor was emblematic of their national identity, whereas Australians found it hard to make sense of a guy who cried on the podium while hugging a stuffed lion.

A while back I found myself talking to a French expatriate

who, as a teenage girl, had seen Anquetil and Poulidor race. She was a big Evans fan, telling me that the French had taken to him, albeit not to the same degree as Poulidor, because after years of Amstrong's calculated, suspiciously robotic but unspectacular victories, he was so openly emotive and awkward. Certainly his ungainly riding style, slightly hangdog expression, and penchant, even when not actually crying, to sound as if on the verge of tears, marks him as a different type of man to the chemically enhanced super athletes of the Armstrong era. The French were, according to my ex-pat friend, just waiting for someone like him to appear. After all, one of their greatest champions, Louison Bobet, used to cry all the time and lost multiple times before his three back-to-back wins. They love that sort of thing.

Certainly, Cuddles does personify something quintessential to the sport. He always looks like he's in pain, he loses regularly, but he's always struggling onwards. He's marked against the Armstrong era by his fallibility. Yet, the lesson he leaves isn't some feel good truism that it's okay to lose, or that grown men can cry. Tears and loss, Evans suggests, are inevitable. In this respect, he's a lot like Poulidor, in that their appeal lies in how they offset the spectacle of effortless, mechanical victory personified by Armstrong and Anquetil, with an 'everyman' aura of perseverance in the face of somewhat fickle fortune.

Oddly, Evans began to gain greater respect as the Australian dollar started to drop, the mining boom slowed down, and the unemployment rate crept up. Maybe we just hit a point where the chest-beating bravado of the Armstrong years stopped reflecting the boom times we'd been living through. Like Poulidor, Cadel Evans has always had his faults and failings. His 2011 win was good but it isn't what defined his career. Like his predecessor's battles against Anquetil and Merckx, it was Evans' persistence that gave his efforts meaning. As Armstrong's endless sequence of victories grew harder and harder to believe, the appeal of the Australian's undoubted mortality grew ever more pressing.

June 30th, 1959
Blain to Nantes Individual Time Trial

ANGLADE, ANQUIETIL, AND RIVIÈRE

There is no such thing as society.
— *Margaret Thatcher*

Raymond Poulidor wasn't Jacques Anquetil's first major rival and 1964 wasn't the first Tour de France to showcase the complex relationship between French fans and their champions. In 1959, two years after his first Tour victory, Anquetil rode into the Parc du Princes to hoots of derision. The French national team had spent most of their time racing against each other and, in the process, allowed a Spaniard to take the yellow jersey. The fans were outraged.

In 1959 the Tour was still being raced by national, rather than trade, teams. This seems unthinkable today — the Tour is so entangled with its sponsors that you're more likely to know who rode for Garmin or Discovery Channel or Rabobank than you are to know their nationality. But in the late Fifties, cycling's major source of income was newspapers, whose sales rely on a common language and a geographical, rather than corporate, identity.

To that end, the 1959 Tour played on its readers' sense of national pride. There were teams representing Belgium, Italy, and Spain, a mixed German-Swiss team, another of Dutch and Luxembourgers, and a team of 'Internationals' who didn't fit anywhere else. As it was their race, the French fielded no less than four separate squads. Three of them were drawn from second tier regional riders — Paris-North East, Centre-Midi and West-South West. Above them all was the French national team, containing the crème de la crème of their cycling stars.

This top tier French squad was mind boggling in its supremacy, consisting of Jacques Anquetil, Louison Bobet, Raphael Géminiani, Andre Darrigarde, and Roger Rivière. However, as Bobet was racing his last Tour, Géminiani was about to make his step from the bike to the team car, and Darrigarde wasn't a Grand Tour contender, French victory all came down to Anquetil and Rivière. This created a bit of a problem as they had a well-established rivalry. The rest of the year they were captains of their own trade teams and neither wished to play second fiddle just because they were racing under the same flag at the Tour.

French media coverage made it seem like virtually no one else was racing. Anquetil had won the race in 1957 aged twenty-three and, after a patchy couple of years, was back in form and looking to take up Bobet's mantle as the best cyclist of his generation. While Rivière had yet to win a Grand Tour, he had beaten Anquetil twice to become World Pursuit Champion on the track, broken his World Hour Record by more than a kilometre, and was showing both the form and the brilliance to cement himself at the top of the heap.

When both were given joint leadership over the French

national team, it fell to manager Marcel Bidot to reconcile them. He failed. In the lead up to the Tour, Anquetil announced,

> For the rest of the year, I race against Roger. Today, we're asked to be teammates. The organisers and Marcel Bidot are insisting on it but I will still race against him.

At first it didn't really seem to matter. The competition was no match for either Anquetil or Rivière. Luxembourger Charly Gaul, winner in 1958, had a weak team and lacked time trialling ability. Spain's eccentric team leader, Federico Bahamontes, was almost exclusively interested in the polka dot jersey. Indeed, in 1954 he'd made a lone breakaway to gain mountain points but gave up a potential stage win by stopping at the summit to eat an ice cream while he waited for the *peloton* to catch up. The Italian team was relatively weak and its captain, Ercole Baldini, lacked panache on the climbs, while the squads of Belgians, Dutch, Luxembourgers, Germans, and miscellaneous ex-pats didn't even register.

The French, by contrast, were so rich in talent that even their own national champion, Henry Anglade, had been knocked back into the second tier Centre-Midi team. And herein lay the spark of the 1959 Tour de France. Things started as everyone had expected; the French big guns dominated the race with André Darrigade sprinting to victory in the opening stage, and Robert Cazala taking both the stage and the yellow jersey on Stage Three. Neither Darrigade nor Cazala threatened the Tour aspirations of their teammates Anquetil and Rivière. They were merely proof of France's superiority.

And then came Stage Six, the first individual time trial of the Tour, raced over forty-five kilometres between Blain and Nantes. The inclusion of a time trial towards the end of the first week of the Tour always feels like the moment when the first real shots are fired. Up until then, the potential Tour contenders seem fairly anonymous, marked less by clear success than any hint of failure; a crash, a break missed, or a poorly timed mechanical problem. In the first time trial, the time gaps are produced which will define the race as a whole, dictating who has to attack in the mountains and who simply has to stick with the lead group.

Both Anquetil and Rivière were time trial specialists, and both knew their performance on Stage Six would shape which of them could demand team support. The course suited both equally, a slightly undulating route of forty-three and a half kilometres, through uninterrupted fields and hedgerows. It was long enough that they could gain time on their opposition, tucking down over their handlebars to maintain the metronomic cadence that had made both of them champions on the track. At the end of the day, they'd secured first and second place. Yet, despite Anquetil's reputation as both a previous Tour winner and a time trial specialist, Rivière easily outran him, gaining a fifty-eight second lead and winning the stage.

Rivière also proved that he could easily outrun any of the other contenders. After the time trial, the 1958 winner, Charly Gaul, was down by one minute, thirty-six seconds and Bahamontes, two and a half minutes. It was now clear that even if they managed to distance him in the mountains, they'd have to build four or five minute leads to insulate themselves from a repeat performance on the seventy kilometre time trial on the penultimate day.

Rivière's time trial victory utterly shaped the following two weeks. It meant that he merely had to limit his losses. His competitors would have to 'make' the race, attacking and trying to drop him. Beyond that, it also gave him leverage over Anquetil in claiming leadership over the French team. Unsurprisingly, Anquetil didn't accept this position in the slightest. On the contrary, his pride clicked into gear and his focus shifted towards proving he was better than Rivière at all costs.

In the hubbub, no one noticed that Henry Anglade, French national champion and head of the second tier Centre-Midi team, had also snuck in a solid time trial, a respectable two minutes eleven seconds behind Rivière. On Stage Seven, from Nantes to La Rochelle, he made it into a break that won a further five minutes and entered the top ten overall. Meanwhile, Anquetil and Rivière's clash began to split the French national team apart. On Stage Thirteen, from Albi to Aurillac, Anquetil attacked with the aim of dropping his teammate and seizing team leadership. He succeeded in gaining time over Rivière but was beaten to the line by Anglade who, while his supposed superiors argued, seemed to be creeping further and further up the rankings.

On Stage Fifteen, things became further complicated over the twelve kilometres of an uphill time trial on the Puy de Dôme. The Spaniard Bahamontes won brilliantly, leaving both Anquetil and Rivière more than three and a half minutes adrift. Anglade, however, put in a stunning performance to take third place. He was now the highest ranked Frenchman, with a very comfortable margin over his more famous compatriots.

Suddenly it became obvious that the feud between Anquetil and Rivière had backfired. By racing each other, they'd failed to take adequate time over their rivals and the Tour was now, almost inexplicably, a race between the Spanish eccentric Bahamontes and, worse, the second-tier Frenchman Anglade. Anquetil and Rivière were horrified.

Beyond the shame of losing, there was another factor to

consider. Both Anquetil and Rivière shared an agent, Daniel Dousset, who also represented their Spanish competitor, Bahamontes. Anglade, by contrast, was represented by a rival agent, Roger Piel. At this time, agents controlled a 'stable' of riders and would use the collective prestige of their stable to leverage higher appearance fees during the all-important post-Tour criteriums. These were a major source of income, on par with the Tour itself, so it became in the economic interests of both Anquetil and Rivière to ensure Bahamontes won. They promptly shifted from fighting each other to attacking their fellow Frenchman Anglade.

Things came to a head on Stage Eighteen which ascended the Galibier, the Iseran, and the Petit Saint-Bernard; one of those three-summit stages that usually serve as the setting for legendary Tour moments. Anglade crashed twice on the first descent and his countrymen made a break for it, dropping not only him but also Bahamontes and Gaul. Once they had a big enough gap, they figured the overall lead was in their grasp again and went back to racing each other. Unfortunately that mindset kicked in long before either of them had actually finished the stage and, while they wasted time trying to outfox each other, the lead group of pursuers caught up with them.

Not only did it catch them but Anglade, Baldini, and Gaul overtook them, leaving Anquetil and Rivière bickering while Bahamontes rode along in their slipstream. As the gap opened, it became clear that Anglade had gained enough of an advantage to win overall.

Anquetil and Rivière, unwilling to be shown up by a second-tier French rider or to undermine the financial interests they shared with Bahamontes, actively chased down their countryman. In the eyes of French fans, attacking Anglade after he'd crashed was bad enough. But chasing him down was even worse, particularly because in doing so they towed Bahamontes back into contention and essentially gifted him the win. The Spaniard had already taken the overall lead in the mountain time trial a few days earlier, and the unexpected support from Anquetil and Rivière solidified his place at the top of the General Classification. He cruised in to Paris in yellow, the first ever Spanish winner.

In effect, by pacing Bahamontes back to the lead group on Stage Eighteen, Anquetil and Rivière had undermined a French victory to protect their own interests. For the French people it said a lot about modern France; individualism and commercial self-interest overriding unity and national honour, with a regional champion betrayed by the personal interests of two big names from Paris. From the Stage Six time trial onwards, a contest had been expected between the two French stars, but ultimately a clash of individuals had led to national disunity and defeat. For post-war France, it had a particular resonance.

LOSING IN THE MODERN AGE

There's no inherent link between the affairs of sport and those of the public or political realm. Ultimately, the clash of Anquetil, Rivière, and Anglade had little direct relevance to France's socio-economic welfare or the fortunes of its people, yet their disunity became a sporting moment embedded within the nation's collective memory. Post-war France was a deeply fractured place, and the 1959 Tour served as its mirror.

Consider France's international affairs after the Second World War. Where once it had been a great empire, now its colonies revolted against it. Following the Battle of Dien Bien Phu in 1954 (the second year Bobet won the Tour), the French had been ignominiously kicked out of Vietnam, which they'd controlled since 1887. It was akin to the English withdrawal from Singapore in 1942; one of the key points at which the Old World's strength simply buckled.

By 1959 France was losing the very last jewel from their imperial crown, with Algeria in a state of revolt. The resulting war split France down the middle, dividing those who abhorred the brutality of colonial ambition from those trying to resurrect the glory of their former empire. In this light, the division within the French team in that year's Tour fed into a simmering anxiety about national identity. Money and the desire for personal glory had taken precedence over national unity or honour and it was hard for the French not to read the actions of their sporting heroes as a reflection upon themselves.

Of course, it's not like a French win in the Tour could have won the war in Algeria, or even that a stage victory might spark some spirit of harmony. But a sporting event like the Tour is a powerful source of metaphor, if only because the sheer volume of people watching make it a common touchstone. On top of that, there's the mass of journalists writing about it, keen to make the most of that capacity for metaphor.

This is as true now as it was then. Consider, for example, how easily you can read the Armstrong years as a mirror for the rise and fall of the US in a modern, globalised economy. He was born in September 1971, just a month after Nixon tore up the Bretton Woods agreement, detached the US dollar from the gold reserve, and triggered the end of the system of financial management that had underpinned the international economy since 1944. That economic reform created the economic moment of Globalisation, which linked to the birth of Neo-Liberal politics in the US.

Armstrong came of age in the 1980s and his career pursued the ideology of hyper-individualism associated with the Reagan era. He won his record fifth tour in 2003, the same year the US ignored criticism and launched a war in Iraq without UN backing. His fall, also fittingly, occurred against the backdrop of the Global Financial Crisis, with his comeback to cycling happening roughly in synch with the sub-prime loans crisis in 2008.

It's easy to see Armstrong as symbolic of his time. It's not too difficult to link his rise to a period of US economic strength and military success, ultimately undermined by a sort of moral crisis. Perhaps he's just a guy on a bike who won a lot and then turned out to have cheated, but his rise and fall take on a broader significance very easily. Naturally, I'm not suggesting cycling shapes the fortunes of nations but with such a wide audience its cultural influence will, inevitably, allow it to transcend a purely sporting context.

The contest between Anquetil, Anglade, and Rivière occurred at a point of breathtaking and incomprehensible change in France. In the space of a single lifetime, France had gone from a nation of peasants to an industrial superpower, seized and then lost an empire and been invaded twice. World War One alone killed almost four percent of its population. When peace finally came the legacy of Vichy and collaborators loomed large. Almost seven thousand people were declared traitors and sentenced to death after the Second World War, and a further fifty thousand formally punished for betraying the nation. In 1956, when rebellion erupted in the French colony of Algeria, it triggered the drafting of a new constitution and the formation of the Fifth Republic, led by Charles de Gaul. Barely six months later, the Spaniard Bahamontes won the Tour while the French national team squabbled. The fortunes of nations are complex, convoluted and far beyond the control of any one person. Perhaps sport doesn't shape them. Perhaps it means very little at all, but in the face of that complexity it's easy to see how it might give people some collective tool to reflect upon themselves. It is, after all, easier to comprehend the contest of three men on bikes than the interwoven fortunes of a nation of individuals.

July 7th 1937
Aix-les-Bains - Grenoble

GINO BARTALI AND BENITO MUSSOLLINI TRY TO WIN THE TOUR DE FRANCE

The inner nature of the whole nation as well as the individual man all works unconsciously.
— *Goethe*

When it comes to blurring the lines between sport and politics, the Italians take the cake. The first Italian Tour de France winner, Ottavio Bottechia, won the race in 1924 and 1925 but was found dead on the side of the road in 1927. He was rumoured to have been murdered by Fascists who took issue with his critique of dictator Benito Mussolini. When the second great Italian Tour champion, Gino Bartali, first raced it in 1937 he was much more cautious as to how he engaged with Mussolini's dictatorship. The Fascist government took their sport extremely seriously indeed.

Italy had always been a great cycling nation, but their champions usually focused on their own race, the Giro d'Italia. Like the Tour de France, it had been founded to sell copies of a sporting paper, *La Gazzetta dello Sport*. Gino Bartali had won it with aplomb in 1936, only his second year as a professional. He also won the Giro d'Lombardia and the National Championships, propelling his family out of rural poverty and himself into the position of national hero.

A week after the 1936 Giro finished, Bartali's younger brother Guilio, also a cyclist, died while racing. So the story goes, he was descending when a car, having ignored the race's road closures, drove into him. Seriously injured, he died in hospital after a failed operation, holding his older brother's hand after blood loss left him too weak to speak. Gino, heartbroken, almost gave up cycling and retreated heavily into his Catholic faith. When he came back, he declared he was going to win both the Giro and the Tour de France in the same year.

However, Bartali's 1937 season started badly after he got stuck in a storm during a training ride and contracted pneumonia. He still managed to win that year's Giro, but his health was poor. His doctor warned him against racing the Tour, and his parents worried they would lose a second son to cycling. Heeding their wishes, Bartali announced he was pulling out of that year's Tour de France.

Unfortunately for Bartali, by that point the Fascist propaganda machine was already running his Giro/Tour double as an inevitable victory — proof of the incredible physical might of the Italian people. It was both a big call and a bit premature but Mussolini had a well-developed sense of how to link sport, media, and nation building and it didn't involve half-hearted gestures.

When Bartali tried to back out of the Tour, the *Il Popolo d'Italia* newspaper (founded by Mussolini himself) went to town. They ran a series of opinion pieces pressuring him to race on patriotic grounds, declaring, 'In the land of France, it is a matter of going to defend our flag'. When Bartali still wouldn't take part, they claimed he was just holding out for a higher appearance fee and cared more about money than the national good. They then proclaimed, 'Bartali is called to represent our sport, our youth, our strength, and all our eyes are on him, many of them rather ill disposed.' Eventually, the head of the Italian cycling association, who also happened to be a general in the army, paid him a visit. Bartali agreed to race.

The 1937 Tour was a bit of an event. The governments of Western Europe knew war was looming and were using sport as a proxy for impending combat. Henri Desgrange had instituted the shift from trade to national teams in 1930, embroiling his event in the contest for national supremacy. In 1936 he became ill and passed the Tour's directorship over to his deputy, Jacques Goddet. It was a wise appointment. Goddet would go on to direct the Tour for the next fifty years. His first steps were to relax Desgrange's ban on the use of gears and, correspondingly, to increase the focus on the mountains. He then pushed thirty-one stages into twenty-six days, partly to increase the drama, partly to stamp his mark on the race but also to increase profits from selling stage starts and finishes to towns on the route. On some days, the riders had to ride three separate stages. On the fifth day, for example, there were two stages ending in sprints, and a thirty-four kilometre team time trial.

Over the first few days, Bartali lost time. Then, on the fourth stage, between Metz and Belfort, the race entered the mountains, where he flew over the Balon d'Alsace as the rest of the field thinned. While the German, Erich Bautz, took the victory, Bartali shot up the rankings, having distanced both of his major competitors, 1936 winner Sylvère Maes, and the leading French rider, Roger Lapébie. With Bartali now clearly the favourite, the Italian press went crazy. After a couple of flat stages and a team time trial, the Tour entered the Alps. Bartali attacked over the Aravis and Tamié climbs in the Bauges mountain range, with the race coming back together only towards the end. Gustaaf Deloor took the victory and Bartali gained yet more time over his key rivals.

On Stage Seven, he delivered what seemed to be the knockout punch when he took his first Tour stage victory. With the route crossing both the Galibier and the Telégraph, Bartali attacked again. In a brilliant show of force, he broke away as the *peloton* moved through the mountains. He crossed the summit of the Galibier alone while the once proud French team splintered behind him. Two of their key riders dropped out as he set a blistering pace over the Telégraph, winning the stage, putting eight minutes between himself and Maes, and a whopping sixteen minutes back to Lapébie.

It was the first time he'd taken the yellow jersey and, with a lead of nine minutes eighteen seconds, he looked unbeatable, positioning himself as easily the best climber in the race. Even the French, via *L'Auto*, declared, 'Bartali will never be caught … on the contrary he will increase his advantage on every mountain stage.'

The next day, on Stage Eight, while chasing down a breakaway, he and his *domestique*s, Guilio Rossi and Francesco Camusso, were racing over a small bridge in light rain when Rossi's wheel slipped. Bartali dodged to miss him, hit the bridge parapet, and flew three metres down into the river below, hitting his chest on a rock. He managed to finish the stage although he lost the lead to Maes.

Battered and bruised, he continued on over the next four stages but without his former panache. Then the Italian team withdrew him from the race altogether, with the team doctor declaring he was too ill to continue. Bartali was outraged. The injury had set him back but he knew his form was good and he could come back as the race rolled into the Pyrenees. To his eye, the decision was made because the Fascists felt they couldn't risk a loss. For propaganda purposes, it was better to drop out under the banner of poor health.

The race itself continued to suffer amid nationalist arguments. Having taken over the lead, Sylvère Maes and his Belgian team dropped out as well, criticising the French for some dodgy decisions favouring their lead rider, Roger Lapébie. With both Bartali and Maes gone, it was Lapébie who won in 1937 but Bartali continued to blame his loss on the Italian Fascists.

Bartali was a staunch member of the left-leaning Catholic Action, which was in continual conflict with the Fascists for placing God before nation. It made him an awkward national sporting hero, even after he came back to dominate the 1938 Tour, winning by almost twenty minutes. Then, at the height of his power, the professional cycling calendar was thrown into turmoil by the outbreak of war. Bartali continued to ride whenever he could. Moreover, he began a covert war against Fascism, working with the church to help smuggle jews out of the country. When the Fascists were finally defeated, his efforts made him a national hero, something further cemented when he won the 1948 Tour de France. Yet he remained angry about the Fascist intervention in his bid to win the 1937 race. Victory would have made him the first cyclist to win the Giro and Tour in the same season. It would have been the jewel in the crown of a career gutted by the Second World War. Instead, it remained an unfulfilled dream.

MORE ON SPORT AND POLITICS

Fascists understood sport in the 1930s. They understood that it wasn't just about running around in circles or riding a bike or swimming very fast. It was about millions of people believing one guy running or riding or swimming meant something greater. This came to a head at the Berlin Olympics in 1936, when Hitler set a new template for the use of sport as a form of nation building.

In addition to building a gigantic new stadium, the German government invested heavily in mass media, including some of the first forays into television and substantial support for live radio coverage. Leni Riefenstahl, whose infamous propaganda film *Triumph of the Will* had been commissioned by Hitler in 1934, was hired to make a new film, *Olympia*, for the occasion, applying the same Wagnerian overtures to the Games that she had previously applied to the Nazi rallies in Nuremburg. Incidentally, Frenchman Robert Charpentier won that year's Olympic road race. The French team also took out the team time trial and the pursuit.

While the Berlin Olympics are remembered as a pinnacle in the use of sport for propaganda, they had a precursor; two years earlier Benito Mussollini had brought the newly established FIFA World Cup to Italy. It had set him back 3.5 million lira but the rewards were worth it. Mussolini had a strong interest in sport. He'd spent substantial time working as a journalist and had an excellent feel for his audience, which translated into his capacity to run a dictatorship for eighteen years. As editor of the socialist party newspaper *Avanti!*, he'd lifted circulation from twenty thousand to one hundred thousand. When he was expelled from the party, he founded *Il Popolo d'Italia* to act as the mouthpiece of his new political aspirations. Less than ten years later, he controlled all of Italy.

Mussolini's politics were an odd mixture. Abandoning his earlier socialist leanings, he scrapped all respect for egalitarianism. In its place, he developed a belief, fuelled partly by Plato's *The Republic* and Nietzsche's *The Will to Power*, in rule by an elite, grounded in a concentrated sense of nationalism. He began developing sports policy almost immediately after seizing power in 1922, shutting down the YMCA and sports clubs run by the Catholic church, and replacing them with his own state-run institutions and inserting sport into the school curriculum. Part of this was a pragmatic attempt to improve the health of a nation suffering from malnutrition and poor living conditions. Beyond that, he knew a nation that could be unified through sport would have the kind of cohesive, semi-fanatical sense of patriotism he needed to maintain control.

In their book on Bartali's life during the Second World War, *The Road to Valour*, Aili and Andres McConnon describe Mussolini's use of sport:

> Adults were strongly encouraged to dedicate their leisure time to a government-sponsored network of national sports and recreation clubs. Millions of Italians joined, and in just seven years the number of sports complexes in the country grew tenfold. [...] A maxim of Mussolini's printed in large letters on the wall of a boxing club in Florence said it all: 'I don't want a population of mandolin players. I want a population of fighters.'

The physical strength of Italian sportsmen came to represent the physical superiority of Italians over those nations they competed against and a justification for Mussolini's leadership of the Body Politic. As the McConnons continue:

Absent a war, sport was one of the most convincing ways the Fascists could promote their ideology outside of Italy. It was a 'calling card for the nation abroad,' as one historian described. And so, in the physical culture of Fascism, athletes could no longer be just athletes – they were 'blue ambassadors', charged with displaying 'glorious actions in sports struggles against the strongest representatives of other races in the world.

When Italy hosted the 1934 World Cup, they put those theories into practice, building a series of new stadiums, a new trophy, and bribing a Swedish referee to swing the matches in their favour so they could get the biggest possible propaganda return. When they inevitably won, Mussolini's old newspaper declared the victory was 'in the name and in the presence of the Duce.'

At the next World Cup, he reputedly sent the players a message right before the final; 'Win or die'. With that motivation, Italy beat Hungary by four goals to two, after which the Hungarian goalkeeper declared, 'I may have let in four goals, but I saved their lives.' Mussolini's influence on Italian football is still strong, with his favourite team, SS Lazio, still openly attracting a strong Neo-Fascist fan base.

After the war, sporting victory continued to hold a significant place within the Italian national psyche. In 1948, ten years after his first win, Bartali returned to the Tour de France, aged thirty-three, once again heading the national team after having spent much of the war working as a clandestine courier for the Catholic resistance. He returned to racing across a vastly different landscape. Aside from the physical damage caused by the war itself, with ongoing food shortages, collapsed infrastructure, and a failed economy, the Italian political system without Mussolini was deeply fractured.

In April 1948, as Bartali trained to contest the Tour, Italy was approaching its first meaningful election since *il Duce* had seized power twenty years earlier, with the vote split between the Catholic centrist Christian Democrats, led by Alcide De Gasperi, and the Italian Communist Party led by Palmiro Toggliati. The election was tense enough but to make matters worse it was caught up in the festering beginnings of the Cold War, with the CIA running covert campaigns to support the Christian Democrats and the Communists receiving support from the USSR. Even after the Christian Democrats took power with just under 70% of the vote, the political environment remained heated.

By June, tensions were so high that even the Italian parliament would sporadically erupt into mass brawls. Things came to a head on July 14th 1948, when the Communist leader, Toggliati, was the victim of an assassination attempt. Shortly after leaving the parliament, he was shot three times at close range by a twenty-four year old who just happened to be carrying a copy of *Mein Kampf*. The Tour was just entering its second week, with an on-form Louison Bobet in the yellow jersey.

Toggliati went into a coma and the country slipped into turmoil. Conspiracy theories took off and the thinly contained conflict between the Communists and Christian Democrats exploded. The Italian General Confederation of Labour called a General Strike, the military were mobilized, partisans began making attacks in regional areas, and at least fourteen people died in riots. The country was on the cusp of ungovernable chaos.

The assassination attempt had occurred on a rest day for the Tour de France. Bartali had spent it in a foul mood. Amid a host of new stars, the media had written him off as over-the-hill. Despite having won three stages, his supremacy in the mountains was no longer as crushing as it had been and he languished in eighth-place overall, more than eighteen minutes behind the new French star Louison Bobet. The race looked to have been decided against the aging Italian.

In the foyer of his hotel Bartali was approached by a group of journalists. He'd grown weary of answering their questions about what it was like to be old and promptly started yelling at them. He was stunned when they told him Toggliati was in a coma and Italy was on the brink of collapse. That night the Italian Christian Democrat Prime Minister Alcide De Gasperi rang him and, so the legend runs, asked him to win the Tour because it was the only thing he could think of that would draw the Italian nation back together. Bartali said he'd try.

And try he did. He won the next three stages in a row, all in the mountains, took the yellow jersey, won a fourth stage on the flat and took the race victory overall by twenty-six minutes and sixteen seconds. When the news reached Italy that he'd taken the lead, the Italian parliament was busy working up to another fist-fight and Toggliati remained in a coma. Reputedly one of the parliamentarians ran into the Chamber of Deputies and yelled, 'Great news! Bartali has won the stage and maybe the yellow jersey! Long live Italy!' The entire parliament erupted into cheers. Shortly thereafter, Toggliati's doctors announced he'd survive. When he emerged from his coma, the first thing he asked was an update on Bartali's standing in the Tour. It's a romantic story and doubtless something of an exaggeration. But, romantic or not, Bartali's victory in 1948 certainly helped prevent Communists and Catholics from killing each other in the streets — an interesting outcome for a bike race.

July 5, 1971
Nevers to Puy de Dôme

LUIS OCAÑA, BLOOD, MUD, AND THE YELLOW JERSEY

Goodbye to the Old World …
— *Motörhead*

The Fifties and Sixties are known as cycling's 'Golden Age', home to its greatest champions and the biggest crowds. Eddy Merckx would later write of the era,

> It was a magical time to be a boy and a cycling fan. From the despair and pain of a war only a few years past, cycling was a sign that life and society were re-emerging, that everything was going to be okay.

This may have been true for Belgium, France, and Italy but in other nations the trauma of the war years lingered on. Germany, obviously, remained in a state of disarray and was absent from the Tour until 1960. Spain, the only country to survive the war with its ultra-nationalist dictatorship still intact, was even more complex.

Spain's dictator, Generilissimo Franciso Franco, not only survived but retained power until his death in 1975. He'd risen to power in the vacuum after Spain's monarchy collapsed in 1931. When the country went to the polls in 1936, a coalition of left-leaning Republicans took power. Franco, aligned with the ultra-nationalist right, was embroiled in a coup, which quickly exploded into a short but bloody civil war. By April 1939 he'd defeated his opposition to seize control. Six months later, World War Two began. Franco, ideologically aligned with Hitler and Mussollini, declared Spain's neutrality. When peace finally came, the Allies left him to his own devices. Under his rule, the country provided a glimpse of what the world could have looked like under Fascism; dissenters were purged, perceived traitors garrotted, and the economy collapsed.

Spain had always been riddled with ethnic and regional rivalries. Like Mussolini, Franco attempted to use the national race, the Vuelta a España, to bring some sense of cohesion. It didn't work. In the Basque Country, a province with its own language and history, separatist guerrillas saw the Vuelta as an unwanted incursion by oppressors. Their threats against it were so fierce the race didn't enter the Basque Country until a ceasefire was finally struck in 2011. Spain did field teams in the Tour de France, and produced some brilliant climbers, most notably Federico Bahamontes but also Bernado Ruiz and José Serra. Yet they were mostly used for internal propaganda, rather than as ambassadors on the international stage.

It wasn't until Franco's power began to wane in the early Seventies that Spain produced an undisputed international champion. Luis Ocaña's career was as disturbed and inconsistent as the country he'd grown up in. He was born in 1945 in the town of Cuenca, which had been a hold-out of the left-leaning Republicans during the Spanish Civil War. After almost two decades of repression, his father gathered up the family and fled to France in 1957, hoping to find a better life as refugees.

A decade later, the young Luis returned to his homeland to win his first major professional title, the Spanish national championships. Legend has it he rushed home to present the national jersey to his father, who was dying. The old man was outraged, asking, 'How dare you bring me this jersey with Franco's flag on it.' Luckily, Ocaña never had to ride for the Spanish national squad at the Tour de France. Goddet had finally done away with the national team format by the late Sixties and Ocaña spent the best years of his career riding for a pen company, Bic.

This was how I first encountered him. I'd developed a fixation with retro cycling kit and, wading through the catalogues of my favourite cycling retailer (Prendas Ciclismo) I came across a jersey emblazed with the iconic Bic orange and yellow logo. Looking for more information on the team, the first thing I encountered was a picture of Ocaña in a Bic branded yellow jersey, laying in the mud, screaming in pain. It looks more like a photograph from a war zone than a bike race. With medical staff crouched over him in the pouring rain, he looks like he's been shot.

The image comes from the crash that ended Ocaña's bid to win the 1971 Tour de France, a race he'd dominated with a series of stunning alpine attacks. He did eventually win the Tour in 1973 but his loss is better remembered. To understand why you need to understand that Ocaña was the only rider to challenge the undefeatable Eddy Merckx. The Belgian was at the peak of his powers, in the middle of a career that remains the most successful of any professional cyclist. He'd burst to fame at the Tour in 1969 when he won, not only the yellow jersey, but also the green and polka dot jerseys along with a total of six stages. In 1970 he returned to win a further eight stages and a second yellow jersey, having already won that year's Giro d'Italia.

On top of that, Merckx was winning almost everything else as well. He'd won Paris-Nice (three times), the 1967 World Championship (the first of three World victories), Milan-San Remo (three times), Paris-Roubaix (twice), the Tour of Flanders, and Liege-Bastogne-Liege. He was only twenty-six and would go on to win the Tour and the Giro five times each.

In his native Belgium, Merckx is afforded the kind of prestige normally given to statesmen. He was awarded the title of Baron in 1996, chosen as 'Sports Person of the Century' in 2000 and has a train station named after him in Brussels. Even the parochial fans of other cycling nations are generally willing to accept he's the most successful professional cyclist ever. He was given a personal audience with the Pope when he visited Italy and even gained a spot in the iconic French comic *Asterix in Belgium*, where he features as a 'fast runner'. Merckx simply won everything he entered. By 1971 his opponents believed he was unbeatable and had simply given up. He'd won the 1970 Tour by twelve minutes and there barely seemed any point in racing.

His flawlessness as an athlete produced two very big flaws in the eyes of cycling fans. The first was that he never seemed to suffer. His victories looked easy in a sport that feeds off adversity, struggle, and failure. This came to a head in the 1975 Tour when an enraged spectator punched him on the ascent of the Puy de Dôme, injuring him badly enough that it cost him his sixth Tour victory. Merckx was a great sportsman but in a sport that operates beyond the simplicity of winning and losing, that didn't inherently make him a great cyclist.

The second problem was that Merckx had no great foil; no Poulidor to his Anquetil, Coppi to his Bartali, or Ullrich to his Armstrong. Ocaña was the only true rival he ever had and the 1971 Tour was their most heated contest. The two men made perfect opponents. Merckx was calm, methodical, and seemed beyond pain. Ocaña was passionate, irrational, and seemed to do nothing but suffer. Like many of the great climbers, Ocaña's talents had a bipolar quality, flailing wildly from sublime to miserable. He's remembered alongside Henri Pélissier, Charly Gaul, and Marco Pantani as one of sport's most famous manic-depressives. Unlike the devotedly competitive, single-minded Merckx, Ocaña was in a permanent state of internal conflict; brilliant and triumphant one day, miserable and inept the next.

Most significant of all, unlike his colleagues, Ocaña refused to believe Merckx was unbeatable and went into the 1971 race determined to win. He'd even purchased a dog and named it after his rival so he could get into the habit of ordering at least one Merckx about. His campaign began in earnest on Stage Eight, which ran for two hundred and fifty-seven kilometres from Nevers to end with a summit finish on the Puy de Dôme, the site of the 1964 Poulidor vs Anquetil battle. It was the first of four mountain stages and Ocaña launched his offensive with dramatic aplomb. Merckx's team had controlled things right up until the final kilometres. Then Ocaña jumped away up the final climb. Behind him, Merckx, shadowed by future Tour winner Joop Zoetemelk and mountain specialist Joaquim Agostinho, couldn't respond. The Spaniard began to gain time.

Footage of the stage shows Ocaña in a rhythm all his own, spinning and bobbing his way through the crowds and cars, sliding up the hill as if producing his own gravitational pull.

The race coverage cuts to the top of the mountain, with the run-in to the finish line shrouded in fog. Ocaña emerges from mist, slowing just before the line to collapse over the handlebars. He had pushed himself so hard he had to be taken away in an ambulance. After a long pause Merckx appears, driving ahead with a painful, stubborn display of brute force to stumble over the line fifteen seconds down, still in the yellow jersey but robbed of his aura of invincibility.

This was Ocaña's first shot and, with it, he proved not only that Merckx could be beaten, but beaten decisively. The second shot came on Stage Eleven on July 8th. Ocaña leveraged his discovery that a well-timed attack could break Merckx's rhythm and attacked again on the Col de Porte. The ever-verbose Phil Liggett describes Ocaña's performance as, 'The fluid rhythm of a fearless man in the form of his life.' Watching the footage, he simply glides away from the sport's best climbers, Agostinho, Van Impe, Zoetemelk, Thévenet, and Merckx himself. His attack had started only just out of Grenoble on the Côte de Laffery, where he quickly gained two minutes. By the time Merckx hit the summit, the gap had widened up to five minutes. It kept growing. Ocaña arrived at the finish line into Orcières-Merlette, eight minutes and forty-two seconds before everyone else. His lead seemed virtually unassailable. Merckx's comment at the finish line revealed a somewhat shocked recognition that he could be beaten, 'For the first time, I was dictated to by a rider stronger than me. Now it's all over... I am incapable of attacking.'

Having hit one extreme, the nuances of Ocaña's personality meant he was inevitably destined to hit another. His problem was that the extremities of his character struck up against the solid, consistent, and indefatigable personality of Merckx. Evidently there was a difference between beating Merckx, and causing Merckx to ride like he'd been beaten, even if he claimed that he was 'incapable of attacking'. The following day, the 9th of July, was a rest day, but the Belgian spent it with his Molteni teammates practicing sections of the next stage. It was mostly a flat route but began with a descent back down from Orcières–Merlette, where Ocaña had cemented his victory the day before.

When the race resumed on July 10th, Merckx ignored the niceties of an informal neutral zone and had his entire team attack as soon as the flag went down. The race hadn't had time to string out yet and the entire *peloton* found itself descending en masse down a steep descent at high speed. In the chaos that followed, the Belgian and his Molteni team got away and raced the entire 250km stage like a time trial, arriving at the finish line so far before the expected arrival that the Tour's entourage hadn't set up the podium yet. In that one stage he clawed back two minutes and twelve seconds. He was exhausted but Ocaña had suffered even more after spending the entire stage in a panicked chase.

The next day, Merckx pulled back another eleven seconds in a sixteen kilometre time trial but he was still more than seven minutes behind Ocaña as the race headed back into the mountains. Still, Merckx proved incapable of conceding defeat. On Stage Fourteen, the Tour went over the Col du Portet d'Aspet and Col de Menté. Merckx made a few attempts to break away over the first climb but Ocaña simply sat behind him. Then he attacked again with greater gusto on the second climb, hammering away with a sense of renewed vigour when he noticed Ocaña wasn't eating and seemed stiff. Then it started to rain. As they approached the summit the rain turned to thunder and lightning and a full storm broke over them. Against the advice of his teammates, the Spaniard kept matching every move Merckx made no matter how pointless.

Unable to get away from Ocaña on the ascent, Merckx

attacked on the descent, shooting away down storm-drenched roads. Ocaña followed every move. When Merckx crashed trying to take a hairpin bend on a saturated road, so too did Ocaña. Merckx got back up and kept riding while Ocaña, fumbling to get back on his bike, was struck by the fast-descending Zoetemelk and Agostinho. In the resulting carnage he was so badly injured he collapsed on the side of the road screaming in pain. After being airlifted to hospital, he was forced to abandon the Tour, while Merckx took to the podium at the end of the stage.

That was the last time Ocaña seemed a real threat to Merckx. In the 1972 race he pulled out with bronchitis. When finally he did win in 1973 it should have been conclusive proof of his brilliance, he had an almost sixteen minute lead over second-placed Bernard Thévenet, but Merckx didn't race the Tour that year and, without that counterpoint, the victory rings a bit hollow. Ocaña was always going to be a great rider but his near victory in 1971 suggested he was better than great; no one else had ever pushed Merckx to his limits before. No one else had such a capacity for extremes. The cycling journalist Philippe Brunel writes,

> Luis lived his life at the extremes and that was why he became the only person to challenge Merckx, because you had to be extreme to take on Eddy Merckx.

Ocaña's propensity for extremes had allowed him to break away on Stage Eight to secure one of the finest victories of his career but it was a difficult quality to control. Had Ocaña remained calm on the descent of Stage Fourteen it's almost certain he would have won the Tour but that wasn't in his nature. He was at his best when he was at his limits. Unfortunately, this would become all the more obvious when he could no longer channel his energies into his sport.

MONEY CHANGES EVERYTHING

Ocaña seemed destined for extremes. As a refugee from a war-ravaged, disjointed nation, he was the product of an age in which the Old World had torn itself apart, dissolving the regional and national identities that had grounded Europe for centuries. In place of tradition, Ocaña's great feats were performed in the service of a pen company.

Suitably, his eventual victory in the 1973 Tour occurred the same year Franco finally stood down. Even after that win, he was never really at peace. This becomes obvious in contrast to the middle class Merckx — consistent, indefatigable, and certain. After retirement their respective fates became even more disparate. Merckx launched a successful bike company and the grateful nation of Belgium granted him the title of Baron. Ocaña retired to the still divided, economically depressed Spain, where he turned heavily to drink, destroying his liver and contracting Hepatitis C. Later he was diagnosed with cancer and shot himself in 1994, aged forty-nine.

In a brilliant article for *Rouleur*, Carlos Arribas interviews Ocaña's son, Jean Louis, who says of his father, 'He couldn't live in today's world. He wouldn't understand anything, just as no one in this world understood him'. It's an apt analysis. Talking to his friends and relations, Arribas found few of them had expected Ocaña to die of old age. He had what could be politely referred to as a 'romantic' personality and was almost Quixotic in his approach to racing with grandiose attacks underlined by wild collapses and tantrums. That attitude served him well as a professional cyclist but not so much as a normal human being.

Coming from the only nation to remain Fascist after the Second World War, Ocaña had entered the modern world as a refugee. He'd begun his career at the start of the era in which commerce, rather than nationality, defined the Tour de France but, back in his homeland, rabid nationalism was still in vogue. Outside of Spain, the world had undergone a major ideological shift after Second World War; whatever the faults of liberal democracy and global capitalism, it seemed preferable to the fascist governments it had just defeated. Sure, global capital might disband traditions and provoke the occasional economic depression, but it didn't gas six million jews, bomb civilians, and torture dissenters.

When the Tour shifted to trade teams in the Sixties, most of Europe had lost its taste for national fervour. It's an interesting contrast. Twenty years earlier, Mussollini had been pressuring Bartali to win the Tour de France and threatening to kill the Italian football team if they lost the World Cup finals. But by the late Sixties, with Franco still bludgeoning Spain into submission, Ocaña was racing for Bic.

Of course, it wasn't just that the war had made pen companies look more appealing than the Fatherland. After the war, the Tour's major source of sponsorship had changed from bicycle companies seeking to advertise in what were essentially regional newspapers, to large corporations trying to get their name out in the increasingly dominant mass medium of television. Alongside this, the automobile began to replace the bicycle as the most common form of transportation. Beyond a mere technological advance, this marked a profound shift in people's understanding of space.

Today the car is so ubiquitous we forget that its arrival was unique to our modern world and the change it brought was cultural as well as mechanical. Compare the modern Tour with its origins and we begin to see the impact. When it was first raced in 1901 the idea of a human being traversing the whole of France was unheard of. Before the war, France, like most of the world, still had distinct regional identities, histories, and dialects and, unless you lived in the capital, information on the outside world was rare. In less than a generation, the tyranny of distance virtually dissolved. Where once a nation's border was something distant and insurmountable, now one could drive across all of Europe in a matter of days.

Cycling author Robert Dineen pins the change down to one specific year:

> In 1959 Ford produced its first Mini, trebled the production of its Anglia and played the leading role in transforming young people's attitude toward personal transport. Previously, they could only afford a bike, but now, through the coincidence of an improved economy and the availability of relatively cheap small cars, they could afford something much more convenient, fashionable and, for men, attractive to the opposite sex. '

Dineen goes on to quote cycling historian Roger St Pierre:

> Everybody used to go to work by bike. In pictures of the '50s you see a flood of bikes emerging from factories. By the '60s it was, 'Why are you riding a bike? Can't you afford a car?' It became a reverse status symbol. It was a symbol of no status. If you rode a bike, you were a pleb.

As bike sales plummeted, bike companies simply couldn't supply sponsorship anymore. Where once they'd boasted their capacity to free the average man from geographical isolation, now they were nothing more than a sporting accessory.

This immense cultural shift occurred in less than the space of a lifetime. Before the war, cycling's Grand Tours had been a display of men traversing great nations through Herculean effort. After the war, it meant something else. It wasn't just that people now rode for a corporate rather than national identity. After all, no one wants to watch a pen company take a great victory or suffer a gruelling defeat.

So what was Ocaña riding for? A decade earlier Bartali had been asked to ride for Italy. Ocaña never rode for Franco's Spain. There was something more personal he was chasing. Whatever its end point, it drove Ocaña to extremes and struck a chord with of fans who watched, enthralled, as he made that first attack on Stage Eight of the 1971 Tour. It was the spectacle and allure of this chase that Bic was sponsoring. The bike might have been the medium but Ocaña's message went beyond the national identities of the pre-war world and far beyond the promotion of Bic stationary. He spoke to the promise and the threat of the new world, in which the borders that had shaped life before the War had dissolved.

STAGE 9

July 10th, 1989
Pau to Cauterets

THE LAST DAYS OF STEPHEN ROCHE

Tread softly because you tread on my dreams.
— *William Butler Yeats*

As the Tour became more commercialised through the Seventies and Eighties, its reach started to expand beyond Western Europe. There had always been cycling fans in the English-speaking world, particularly in Britain and Ireland, but, right up until the Nineties, following the sport had meant waiting for imported copies of French language magazines like *L'Equipe*. Local English language papers simply didn't see the merit in covering cycling. When British great Beryl Burton won her second (of five) pursuit world championships in 1960, her local paper, the *Yorkshire Post*, gave it three inches of coverage, about half the amount of attention it lavished on a local athletics meeting.

Oddly, competitive cycling had originated in Britain but had been left to decay while the European field grew.

The main reasons for this were a distinctly British disdain for professional athletes and an extremely risk-averse attitude within the sport's governing body, the National Cyclist's Union (NCU). In 1892 the NCU was so powerful it organised the first attempt at a world championship. Working with newspaper editor Henry Sturmey, it had formed the precursor of the UCI, the International Cyclists' Association, as a conglomerate of national cycling bodies. This early dominance collapsed after the NCU banned all professional athletes from its events in an attempt to protect the 'noble amateur' from the ravages of grubby professionalism.

By then, it had already sown the seeds of its demise. In 1890 a woman fell from her horse after it was startled by a group of cyclists. Fearing censure from the police, the NCU banned groups of riders from racing together, effectively outlawing road racing. Over the next decade the Tour de France would see European cycling boom. In the United Kingdom, the sport had been deliberately stunted. For the next century, British cycling remained dominated by local clubs, who mostly raced amateur time trials and track races. As the NCU's rule spread throughout the British Empire, it produced generations of English-speaking cyclists who saw the European professional *peloton* as an elusive and exotic dream, filtering across the Channel in last month's imported magazines and the occasional radio broadcast.

When the Tour shifted from national to commercial squads in the Sixties, anglophone cyclists finally began to seep into the ranks of professional teams. This included riders like Brian Robinson, Tom Simpson, Vin Denson, and Barry Hoban, and the Irishman Seamus Elliot. In the Seventies and Eighties, a host of English speaking riders followed their tracks, including Australians like Alan Piper, Shane Sutton, and Phil Anderson; New Zealander Steven Swart; Americans like Greg LeMond,

Andy Hampsten, and Davis Phinney; the Canadian Steve Bauer; and the great Scottish climber Robert Millar.

In 1986, a US registered team sponsored by Seven Eleven made their first Tour appearance, while the American Greg LeMond, riding for La Vie Claire, became the first English-speaking winner of the Tour. The next year saw the first British registered trade team, managed by a wildly overweight transport baron called Tony Capper. The team, ANC-Halfords, disintegrated horribly after scoring a wildcard invitation but proved there was a growing taste outside of Europe for professional cycling.

And then there was Stephen Roche who, in 1987, won not only the Tour but also the Giro and the World Championship, becoming the only cyclist other than Eddy Merckx to win the sport's Triple Crown. Roche had the additional benefit of being cheerful, eloquent, and smart, attracting media attention across the Channel. One of his biggest fans was Paul Kimmage, just three years his junior and quick to follow him over to France. Kimmage, now better known as a sports journalist, rode as a *domestique* to his hero in the 1989 Tour. That year, unfortunately, was a disaster for the Irish champion.

The 1989 Tour de France is considered one of the greatest editions of the race. It had been pegged as an open contest, with former winners Greg LeMond and Laurent Fignon both back with a vengeance after years of poor luck. Pedro Delgado, winner in 1988, looked capable of a repeat performance. Stephen Roche had been in poor form through the previous year but had ridden well at the Giro and his fans were hopeful. When Delgado missed his starting time in the opening day's prologue by almost three minutes, the race became a tight contest between Fignon and LeMond. Roche, by contrast, struggled along, a shadow of his 1987 form.

His decline in 1989 says almost as much as his win two years earlier. After a perfect season in 1987, the following year was written-off by recurring problems with a knee injury. In the 1989 Giro he'd come ninth, and looked to be resuming his earlier brilliance. He went to the 1989 Tour with high expectations.

Unfortunately, that optimism was unfounded. His race fell apart completely on Stage Nine. Twenty kilometres before the Col de Marie Blanque, the *peloton* had picked up speed after the Fagor rider, Robert Forest, broke away. As the pace increased Columbian climbing icon Luis Herrera went on the attack. Behind him, Fignon and LeMond sent their teams to the front in an attempt to wear each other out. At the summit the lead group came over, a minute and fifty seconds behind Herrera, with both LeMond and Fignon sparring wildly. Roche struggled along behind them. The injured knee that had written off his previous season had returned.

The pace increased again on the approach to the next summit, when Delgado sent his young teammate Miguel Indurain off the front. At age twenty-five, Indurain was already an experienced Tour rider, having ridden it four times, including as part of Delgado's 1988 winning team. He would go on to win the Tour five times. That attack marked the turning point in his career. It was strategic; the idea was to take the pressure off his teammate and force LeMond and Fignon to control the race. Yet, while it was a turning point for Indurain, it was a death knell for Roche. The speed increased to the point he could no longer keep up.

The Irishman came in fifteen minutes late, exhausted and in pain. Nursing him through the stage was Paul Kimmage. Also from Ireland, he'd followed Roche's path into the professional ranks, albeit with far less success. Kimmage was one of Roche's biggest fans and was now one of his most devoted *domestique*s.

He was there at the exact moment things fell apart:

> We had ridden about twenty kilometres and were
> approaching the first Col, Marie Blanque, when Stephen's
> hand went up. I dashed to his side immediately. It's a great
> thrill having him in your slipstream, weaving in and out
> of the team cars after he has punctured. But this time it
> wasn't a puncture. It was his knee, the weak knee that he'd
> damaged in a six-day race in Paris in the winter of 1984.
> Suddenly it was giving him fierce pain, and we called the
> race doctor. The spray can was produced but we all knew
> that the solution was not to be found in aerosol. He was
> cooked, it was over.

Roche quit that night. In the 1990 Tour, he turned up late
to the start of the team time trial and was eliminated for
failing to make the time cut. He managed to win a stage of
the 1992 Tour de France but he was never again at the head
of any major race and retired in 1993. For Kimmage, the
fallout was even worse. With his champion gone, he climbed
off half way through the long but otherwise unremarkable
twelfth stage between Toulouse and Montpellier. It was a
harsh introduction to the professional *peloton* and one that
Kimmage never fully digested. More than that, it was the
end of the era in which professional cycling was never more
than an exotic and distant dream to the anglophone world.
The dream was now a reality and, as Kimmage found, it held
truths far harsher than the fantasies he'd held as a boy riding
around Dublin.

PAUL KIMMAGE AND THE PROMISED LAND

By the time he climbed off his bike in 1989, Kimmage had already given up on cycling and decided to pursue a career in journalism. The next year his book, *Rough Ride* was published, becoming the first insider account of the sport's reliance on drugs. By today's standards, the amphetamine use detailed in *Rough Ride* is quite tame but at the time it was extremely controversial. Kimmage highlighted both the endemic use of performance enhancing drugs and the willingness of the authorities to turn a blind eye to it. Moreover, it was deeply personal; not a lament for a stain on the national character but a blow to his very personal hopes and dreams. Looking back to the start of his career, he wrote:

> Before all this, I had looked at the sweaty faces of the stars on the television screen and in photographs and seen only glory. And now what do I see? I see dilated pupils and unnatural spots. I study not what they eat but what they swallow. Where once I applauded muscle, I now question its fabrication.

The thing I find fascinating about Kimmage is that his professional career as a cyclist only lasted three years but his profession as a pariah journalist, crusading against doping has lasted close to three decades. He's spent far more time questioning the 'fabrication' of glory than he spent chasing it.

There's an argument that its just naïve to enter into professional sport and expect it to be a utopian realm devoted to physical perfection and a code of honour. After all, a pro cyclist is paid to attract a crowd large enough to ensure commercial sponsorship. The idealism and morality of an athlete isn't inherent to that process, as Armstrong's success would later prove. That said, in the same way Ocaña rode for something greater than the glory of Bic Stationery, Kimmage believed cycling had some higher purpose and had hoped turning pro meant something more profound than amphetamine abuse. Looking back to the start of his career, he lamented:

> The promised land was not what I had dreamed it would be. It strangely resembled the world I was trying to escape. It was hard, desperately hard. It was also dirty and corrupt. I wanted to leave but realised that leaving was almost as hard as getting there.

When you watch cycling, you know it's hard. But then so is sitting in an office, bored out of your brains for eight hours a day. Of course, you don't expect a normal job to be 'the Promised Land'. When I started working in an office at age twenty-one, I hadn't spent my childhood dreaming of being there so, if I'd found out my colleagues were taking performance enhancing drugs to help with the filing, I probably wouldn't have been that disappointed.

Working in an office is generally pretty horrible. I've done a lot of it over the years and it's left me with a messed up back, a paunch, and ruined eyesight. The work isn't physically hard but the drain of being painstakingly bored for eight hours a day sure is. A few years after I finished my doctorate, I worked on a research project looking, oddly enough, at doping in professional cycling. One of the professionals we talked to had tried to go back to normal work and couldn't hack it. Talking about why he left the sport, he remembered:

> I used to hate it because I thought it was hard and there was no real reward for it, – I thought that I should be doing other things. Where now all that's erased. I don't think it's hard anymore, I think it's easier than a normal

life. Because I've experienced normal life, worked very hard for eighteen months, working two different jobs as a normal person, forgot about the bike and I realised that's a lot tougher than what riding is.

I've never been a professional cyclist but working in an office doing data entry for eight hours a day was hard in the sense that doing anything obviously pointless is hard. Much of my working life has felt akin to being anaesthetised against my will.

Cycling was the antidote to that; whether through the rush of the wind, the thump of my heart, or the sudden adrenalin provoked by idiotic bus drivers. Riding becomes an immense panacea to the entrenched blandness of the kind of jobs most people have. It's extremely liberating to ride a bike and the idea that there are people who do it for a living is very appealing. Whatever the realities of professional sports, to the spectator it's wonderful to believe that somewhere, beyond the dullness of daily life, there's a promised land one might ascend to where one spends one's days gliding through sun drenched valleys and climbing winding roads through thick forest, while thousands of adoring spectators scream encouragement at you. It's unrealistic but, then, that's the point of dreams.

To this end, Kimmage opens his book with a quote from William Butler Yeats that sums things up nicely:

I, being poor, have only my dreams;
I have spread my dreams under your feet;
Tread softly because you tread on my dreams.

Watching professional cycling, you know it's a job and a profession. The advertisers' logos emblazoned on every available surface remind you of that. But you don't see it, just as you don't really see the Bic logo on Ocaña's chest. What you see is a dream.

For Kimmage, that dream turned into a reality and then it turned suddenly and violently sour. I'm glad I was never in that position because, paradoxically, the doping scandals never really dented my enthusiasm for the sport. I could understand why people were so desperate to ride their bikes for a living that they'd cheat to be there. I figured out while I was still quite young that normal work was painful and pointless and, quite frankly, if someone had told me I could escape it with a good doping regime I would have been severely tempted.

STAGE 10

July 4th, 1952
Laussane to L'Alpe d'Huez

FAUSTO COPPI BECOMES A GOD

Thou art a symbol and a sign
To Mortals of their fate and force.
— Lord Byron

Angelo Fausto Coppi was born in 1919 to a peasant family in the Piedmont region of Italy. His life is now so embroiled in myth that it's hard to pick the truth from the fiction but his rise began with the gift of a bicycle by his uncle and namesake. The elder Fausto was a merchant sailor and devout cycling fan who was thrilled to discover his sickly nephew's love of riding. Returning home from the sea, he gave the young Coppi the money to buy a quality racing bike. His nephew was fifteen, thin, fragile and pale, yet he won the very first race he entered, taking home a small cash prize and a salami sandwich. He won his second race as well, dropping the field to win alone. This time he was awarded an alarm clock.

In between working as a delivery boy for the local butcher

and helping with the family farm, Coppi would train and race alongside the locals but it was obvious there was something different about him. He came from a poor peasant family, yet looked oddly regal. Physically, he was gaunt with gangly limbs but he rode with an elegance and strength that set him apart.

One day a limousine turned up in Coppi's village. From the back seat there emerged a heavy-set man wearing dark glasses. His name was Biagio Cavanna, a former boxer driven into retirement when he became blind. He had since become a master masseuse, coach, and sporting savant. Visiting the Coppi family home, he asked young Fausto to lie on the table, where he felt his ribs, listened to his heart, and massaged his legs. When he was finished, he declared Coppi would become the greatest cyclist of all time.

Throughout the Forties and Fifties Fausto Coppi's victories were so plentiful it seemed impossible to explain them without constructing myths and legends. He won five editions of the Giro d'Italia, two of the Tour de France, Milan-San Remo three times, and the Giro di Lombardia five times, as well as Paris-Roubaix, the 1953 World Championship and, to top it off, he also set an Hour record.

It wasn't just that he won but that the victories were so emphatic. In 1949 he became the first rider to win both the Giro and the Tour. In 1952 he repeated the feat, winning the Giro by almost ten minutes and the Tour by almost a half an hour. Had the Second World War not interrupted the best years of his career he would almost certainly have won more.

Eddy Merckx would later usurp his place as the most prolific winner within the sport of cycling. Yet Coppi had something Merckx lacked; a character both sublime and tragic formed through the mixture of sporting brilliance and personal misfortune. His name itself captures this contradiction — Angelo, like an angel, and Fausto, like the fable of a man who sold his soul to the devil in return for greatness.

His career began when he won the Giro d'Italia in 1940. It was his first year as a professional and, at just twenty years of age, he remains the race's youngest winner. He'd started as a *domestique* for Gino Bartali on the Legnano team but, when Bartali crashed, Coppi was given leeway to ride for himself. On Stage Eleven the Giro moved over three peaks in the Apennines. A storm settled over the *peloton*, smothering the race with snow and lightning. Coppi attacked, disappearing into the fog. By the finish line he had an unassailable lead.

It marked the start of a bitter rivalry with Gino Bartali. The war interrupted both of their careers and, when peace resumed, they fought viciously for the title of Italy's *Campionissimo*, or 'Champion of Champions'. Bartali, five years the elder, was a staunch Catholic, conservative and patriotic. Coppi, bordering on atheist, showed little respect for the old order. Indeed, he was censured by the Pope after leaving his wife to father a child with his mistress. Their rivalry became emblematic of a cultural division in post-war Italy. Writer Curzio Malaparte compared the two:

> Bartali belongs to those who believe in tradition … he is a metaphysical man protected by the saints. Coppi has nobody in heaven to take care of him. His manager, his masseur, have no wings. He is alone, alone on a bicycle … Bartali prays while he is pedalling: the rational Cartesian and sceptical Coppi is filled with doubts, believes only in his body, his motor.

Their differences came to a head whenever they were expected to ride together. Coppi sat out the 1948 Tour after Bartali was given captaincy of the Italian national squad. When both were assigned to ride the World Championship the same year, they spent the whole race chasing each other, leaving the overall victory to the Belgian Brik Schotte, with French riders taking the second and third steps on the podium.

The Tifosi, Italy's rabid cycling fans, were outraged to see personal ambition put ahead of national honour. Both men received three-month suspensions from the Italian Cycling Federation. More importantly, the public sense of disgrace began to translate into a loss of appearance fees. With that threat, the Italian national coach, Alfredo Binda, managed to sign them both for the Italian 1949 Tour de France squad. They spent the first part of the race fighting with each other until it looked like they would both lose. Then, facing another barrage of public hostility, they agreed to cooperate.

Coppi paced Bartali up through the mountains on Stage Sixteen and then let him take the win and the yellow jersey to celebrate his thirty-fourth birthday. They repeated the feat the following day on the two hundred and fifty-seven kilometre stage to Aosta, climbing over the Tour's highest peak, the Col d'Iseran, and the Grand St Bernard. This time, Coppi drifted away to win alone with such aplomb he came into Paris ten minutes ahead of the second placed Bartali and more than twenty minutes ahead of the third placed rider, Jacques Marinelli. As Geoffrey Wheatcroft writes of Coppi's win:

> Cool as ever, Coppi won the time trials, and then annihilated the field on the Alpine passes, not so much climbing the Vars, Izoard and Galibier, it was said, as flying over them. He left Bartali for dead below the Izoard to win the stage by twenty minutes and then raced over the Galibier, past a memorial to Desgrange that had just been unveiled there in the presence of Andre Leducq. Coppi crossed the line at the Parc on a comfortable 10'55" ahead of Bartali... In a newspaper column describing the victory, Coppi was at his most laconic. It was perfectly easy, he said: 'We all have two legs.'

Having already won the 1949 Giro, Coppi completed a goal Bartali had coveted but never accomplished; winning two Grand Tours in a single year. He was the first cyclist to achieve this and it made him a superstar unlike any the sport had seen.

Having ascended to the pinnacle of the sport, he descended into misfortune. In 1950 he crashed, breaking his pelvis and losing most of his season. In 1951, his brother died in a crash while racing the Giro del Piemonte. Grief stricken, Coppi still participated in that year's Tour but lacked the heart to truly compete.

By 1952 his luck had returned. He won that year's Giro so decisively it was barely a competition. By July he was in superb form, with the experience afforded by twelve years as a professional. He also had something else; a quality afforded by personal tragedy and poor luck.

The 1952 Tour was particularly ripe for iconic moments. It included new forays into the mountains, most notably the Puy de Dôme and a summit finish in Sestrières, but there was one inclusion that would eclipse them all; the first ascent of the Alpe d'Huez. It's since become almost an essential part of the Tour, partly because of its difficulty, partly because its twenty-one hairpin bends produce a particularly good spectacle, and partly because Coppi's victory there left it with a reputation unmatched by any other summit finish.

That year's race began with a deceptively open field. The winners of the three previous Tours, Hugo Koblet, Ferdi Kübler, and Louison Bobet, were all absent. Vying to take their place were Stan Ockers (second in 1950), Raphaël Géminiani (second in 1951), Jean Robic (first in 1947), and Spanish climber Bernardo Ruiz. By Stage Nine, the yellow jersey had already traded hands six times. But the Italian team was unified behind Coppi. Among his *domestiques* was his old rival Gino Bartali, two times Giro winner Fiorenzo Magni, and his loyal *gregario* Andrèa Carrea.

Carrea is nicely representative of the devotion Coppi inspired. By the end of Stage Nine, he'd taken the race lead after an unexpectedly successful breakaway. When he was presented with the yellow jersey, he burst into tears, horrified at the thought he'd betrayed his team leader. On the morning of Stage Ten he posed for photographs in the yellow jersey shining Coppi's shoes. Such devotion was rewarded. The Italian team's combined might had hammered Stan Ockers back into eighth place, thirteen and a half minutes away from the lead. The Spaniard Ruiz was a further two minutes back, and Géminiani a minute behind him.

Yet Coppi was still five minutes down. After years of haphazard form, and at age thirty-three, his true potential was unknown. With the exclusion of his win on the Stage Seven time trial, he'd sat in the wake of his team, rarely showing any semblance of his ability. Since his win in 1949, the race itself had changed, with an increase in summit finishes and a decrease in time trials. It was a course designed to make alpine attacks a priority and increase the potential for upsets in the overall standings. Alpe d'Huez, with a climb lasting thirteen kilometres up to a total height of 1,803 metres, has a reputation for rupturing the General Classification. The road to the summit zigzags over twenty-one hairpin bends, disrupting any rhythm with a gradient that wavers between seven and twelve percent.

As the riders began Stage Ten, the weather was hot, forcing a slow, laborious ascent through the winding roads towards the Alpe. Coppi continued to sit in the slipstream of his *domestiques*, watching his competitors but never seeking to force a move. At the first hairpin, Jean Robic attacked out of the saddle. The cantankerous Frenchman was determined to prove his 1947 win wasn't a fluke, throwing himself forward in the hope of a stage victory and a podium finish. It was the kind of explosive, audacious attack Robic was renowned for and he quickly distanced himself from the *peloton*. The only rider who could go with him was Coppi.

Yet while Robic hurled himself forward in a tumult of energy, Coppi remained seated, climbing gracefully with a high cadence. The Frenchman had pushed himself two minutes ahead of the *peloton* when Coppi simply drifted past, ascending towards the summit with such ease that everyone else became mere spectators. Watching from the sidelines, former Tour winner André Leducq remarked:

> Coppi had rosy cheeks, bright eyes, and supple legs. Everyone else looked like they were suffering. It must be a wonderful feeling to soar like that, to have everyone at your mercy.

He arrived at the summit one minute, twenty seconds ahead of Robic, and a further three minutes twenty-two seconds over third placed Stan Ockers. He had taken the stage win and the yellow jersey.

After that Coppi became untouchable. On Stage Eleven, the French team launched a series of attacks to claw back time but he dropped them all to ride over the Croix de Fer, Galibier, Montegenèvre and up to the summit to Sestrières alone. Over the following days he took a further three stages and a lead of more than twenty minutes. His superiority was such that the Tour organisers had to double the prize money for second and third place to keep the rest of the *peloton* racing in the final week. By the time they reached Paris, Coppi was twenty-eight minutes ahead of Stan Ockers, having taken one of the most immense victories of the Tour's modern age.

It wasn't just the fact he won but the manner in which he attained his victories. It was as if the rest of the *peloton* didn't exist; as if Coppi was simply riding for himself and in a realm of his own. He hadn't so much defeated his competition as made them irrelevant. He went so far beyond merely winning it was as if he'd transcended sport altogether.

In 1949 he had become the first person to win the Giro and the Tour in the same year. Repeating this feat in 1952 had looked impossible, yet he had not only achieved it but done so with huge time margins over his competition. There are a handful of other cyclists who have, over the years, achieved greater results — Anquetil, Merckx, and Hinault would all complete double Grand Tour victories. At a purely sporting level, their *palmarès* are more extensive. Most notably, Eddy Merckx would take a 'Triple Crown' in 1974, winning the Giro, the Tour and the World Championship all in a single year. But Coppi offered something else entirely. With a career half lost through war, ill-fated injuries, his brother's death, and his rise from rural poverty, his victories held more meaning.

In 1953 he won the World Championship and the Giro d'Italia. They would be his last major victories, although his career dragged on for another six years. He never entered the Tour again and couldn't finish the 1956 Giro. He entered his last Grand Tour, the 1959 Vuelta, at the age of thirty-nine. He was the first to be dropped each day and didn't reach the finish line but his legacy continued to grow. The image of his faded greatness still drew huge crowds. It was as if they flocked to see something inherent to the man himself, a quality that remained present even as his athleticism disappeared.

There was a sense that he'd found a sort of perfect rhythm that allowed him to perform at a level beyond the merely mortal. Perhaps he'd lost that power as he grew older but the trace remained. Whatever lows he plunged to in his later career, he had reached a pinnacle most of us will never attain. As his greatest rival, Gino Bartali, put it, Coppi was 'a god on a bicycle, fluid form in motion.'

WHY THE BRITISH LOVE CAMPAGNOLO

In September of 1958 Fausto Coppi flew to England to race at Herne Hill, England's oldest and most prestigious cycling track. By then he was well and truly past his prime and audiences were waning for track racing. Yet the stadium was packed, with crowds flocking from across the British Isles to watch the aging champion in mock competition against the local stars. One of the spectators at the 1958 Hearne Hill race was local cyclist Brian Redfern:

> One thing I can recall is that most of the riders used 'Eau de Cologne' which could be smelt every time they passed us, not usual amongst British cyclists at that time!

The presence of Eau de Cologne is telling. Especially among a generation of older cyclists, Coppi is still described as less of a sporting phenomenon than an aesthetic one; sublime, graceful, and regal. His style embodied, not so much sporting success, but an ideal that couldn't be fully articulated. Like art or music, he expressed something that couldn't be described in words.

Coppi was the first professional cyclist whose popularity went beyond continental Europe. Indeed, there's a uniquely British obsession with him. Even during the war years, before his Tour victories, he embodied something greater than athletic competition. English solider and cycling fan Len Levesley became a minor celebrity after a chance encounter with the Italian champion. Levesley was stationed in Tunisia, where Coppi had ended up as a British prisoner of war assigned to menial tasks. Levesley, sitting down for a haircut, was shocked to find the 1940 Giro winner acting as his barber:

I'd only seen him in cycling magazines but I knew instantly who he was. So he cut away at my hair and I tried to have a conversation with him, but he didn't speak English and I don't speak Italian.

With television still a decade away and only scant English radio coverage of professional cycling, Levesley's knowledge of Coppi came from a mix of sporadic newspaper reports and images in imported magazines. It left a lot of room for interpretation.

For a whole generation of young British cyclists, like Levesley and Brian Redfern, their knowledge of the European *peloton* had been defined by imported French sports magazines. Beyond the edge of their pages, they imbued Coppi's image with the glamour and intrigue lacking in their own lives:

> At that time most of us could only read about the cycling stars of the day in the cycling magazines and especially the *Miroir Sprint* and *But et Club* bought at newsagents in Soho. In the 1950s there also being practically no TV or newspaper coverage of any cycling events. So for us racing cyclists the chance to see Fausto Coppi and the other stars live was a fantastic opportunity and couldn't be missed.

In pictures, Coppi always looked the epitome of grace and, in an imported magazine, written in French and purchased in Soho, that glamour must have been amplified. When he arrived at Hearne Hill, he wasn't just a faded athlete, he was a mirage from a world more glamorous and refined than the drudgery of post-war Britain, with its sooty skies, manufacturing towns, and ever-growing suburbs. Into the gaps left by their haphazard French, English-speaking cyclists inserted their own, ideal version of what Coppi meant. By dousing themselves in Eau de Cologne, they sought to reach the level of sophistication he represented.

To understand the appeal of someone like Coppi and the exotic world that he represented, it's worth remembering that post-war Britain was a less-than-exciting place. While it lacked the turmoil of its neighbours on the Continent, the stability was grey, grim, and increasingly suburban. In 1937 John Betjeman had written, 'Come, friendly bombs and fall on Slough/It isn't fit for humans now' while, two years later and on the cusp of war, George Orwell wrote even less generously:

> It's a thing that makes you laugh inside to walk down the streets of these inner outer suburbs and to think of the lives that go on there... Just a prison with cells all in a row. A line of semi-detached torture chambers where the poor little five-to-ten-pound-a-weekers quake and shiver, every one of them with the boss twisting his tail....

As the country rebuilt after the war, those 'poor little five-to-ten-pound-a-weekers' couldn't help but dream of something better than suburban life. To head into Soho and see images of the exotic, graceful Coppi atop his celeste Bianchi, or milling around the winner's podium in a double-breasted suit, had an obvious allure. It suggested a mysterious world just across the seas as glamorous as anything out of Hollywood.

Paul Smith, the British fashion mogul and cycling fan, recalls wading through old copies of *L'Equipe* in the late Fifties and becoming a Coppi fan based purely on the photos, 'I chose Coppi ... he was very stylish off the bike. He wore beautiful double-breasted suits and overcoats.' Another of those who saw him race at Hearne Hill was cyclist Tony Hewson, who later described Coppi's arrival:

> An unassuming black car edged its way on the square and two men got out... Suddenly there was a groundswell

of sound like a rustling prayer – 'Il campionissimo' and people hurried from everywhere. I didn't know what to expect: something fabulous, justifying his fame; a luxury sports car, police escort, army of minders, fanfare, choir of angels! There was nothing, just these two men and a modest black car with the crowd swarming around them. Yet so powerful was the Coppi mystique that his humble presentation seemed merely to enhance his glamour.

Whatever the truth about him and whatever his actual athleticism, myth and fable outstripped it. Owen Mulholland writes that:

> Coppi's impact on the sport went far beyond an impressive list of victories. He may have been born in poverty, but he had the appearance of an aristocrat […] His tall, almost feline body was crowned by a face that would have made a Roman senator proud. And his appearance was just the beginning of those elevated sentiments.

For a generation weaned onto cycling with images of the graceful champion, it hardly mattered that Coppi had barely won a race in years, and that the organisers of criteriums would deliberately cut down the length just so he could make it to the finish.

Pierre Chany, whose articles appeared in the imported copies of *Miroir Sprint* so prized by British cycling fans, wrote of his final years that he was a

> Magnificent and grotesque washout of a man, ironical towards himself; nothing except the warmth of simple friendship could penetrate his melancholia.

It was this that the British cycling fans flocked to see at Hearne Hill in 1958, not his capacity to ride a bike. Coppi was no longer a successful athlete, but he was cycling's equivalent of Lord Byron or Shelley; a romantic icon with his forlorn expression, drooping smile, and penchant for dignified decline.

Of course, Coppi wasn't riding at Hearne Hill for the sake of mythology and romance. He was there at the end of his professional career and he needed to make money. The immensity of his myth allowed him to do that even when he couldn't really compete. That becomes particularly obvious when you look at the fortunes of his two major sponsors, the bike company Bianchi and component makers Campagnolo. Fifty years after his death, he remains central to their advertising.

Coppi rode for the Bianchi team from 1945 onwards, winning both his Tours, four Giros, Paris-Roubaix, and the World Championship on their frames. Campagnolo, who took over his sponsorship from Simplex after the war, promptly released their 'Paris-Roubaix 1002' after his 1950 victory in the cobbled classic. When a British cycling fan finally tracked down those imported magazines in the Fifties, they would have seen Coppi on a Bianchi with Campagnolo parts. In the English-speaking world, he was synonymous with the distinctively non-English blue-green of Bianchi's frames and the elaborate, curling silver style of Campagnolo derailleurs.

British cycling journalist Graeme Fife remembers the lustre those brands took on in Britain in the Sixties. As a youth he laboriously saved for Campagnolo components:

> Campagnolo had something of the Grail about it and still does. It was the way the Campag rear mech, apparently made of goblin silver, was so compact, instantly recognisable from the ubiquitous Huret, and the elegantly slim tongue-shaped levers, speckle-edged with tiny embossed detail, shimmering with the kind of classy superfluity that whispered excellence.

Coppi cemented his legend by dying a tragic, romantic death before his time. After a hunting trip to Africa he contracted malaria. Flying back to Italy, it was misdiagnosed. By the time the doctors figured out what was wrong with him, it was too late and he died on the 2nd of January, 1960, aged forty. Possibly it's the tragedy of an early death that fueled his legacy. He lived out cycling's ever popular Icarus narrative by dying before his time. It made him something of a martyr; both an icon of the modern age but also one of its victims.

Certainly, his allure still remains strong. In 2010, fifty years after his death, British cycling outfitters Rapha staged an exhibit in his honour. Cyclists visited it like a shrine, gasping at antique Bianchis and photographs of an era gone long before they were born. In one of their numerous essays on sartorial elegance and cycling, Rapha's copywriters captured Coppi's charm:

> His style was fluid and light and while his engine roared, the Campionissimo's pedal turns echoed the elegant strokes of a bird in flight. His demeanour was always debonair, even when he was clearly suffering. Style and class personified.

Arguably, this is global capitalism going about its business; the commodification of a great champion to sell expensive Italian cycling goods to the otherwise under-tapped market of the English-speaking world. On the other hand, the dreams those young Paul Smiths and Graeme Fifes found in their imported magazines and Campagnolo components weren't necessarily cheapened just because they had to pay for them.

Whatever myth Coppi came to embody, it struck a chord beyond the purely commercial. Perhaps this is the difference between the gods of the Old World and those of Modernity; the former stayed in their Pantheon and dished out plagues and poxes, albeit for free. By contrast, you had to spend money on imported magazines and bike parts to worship Coppi but then, if you were lucky, you also got to see him in the flesh, racing around Herne Hill.

July 18th, 1955
Marseilles – Avignon

AN AUSTRALIAN ON VENTOUX

In the case of the car, the physical efforts – the 'micro movements' – used to negotiate space are minimal, producing a desensitized effect.
— *David Bell and Azzedine Haddour*

The 1955 Tour de France was the third and final victory for the French champion Louison Bobet. It was also the first to host a German team since the end of the Second World War and almost became the first to feature a doping related death. Jean Malléjac, runner-up in the 1953 Tour, collapsed on Stage Eleven's ascent of Mont Ventoux. When the Tour's doctor arrived, he was unconscious with his jaws tightly clamped shut. He later claimed he'd been tricked into taking amphetamines.

On the final stage into Paris, one other notable oddity became apparent. Russell Mockridge was sitting at the back of the *peloton*, singing happily to himself, thrilled to have finished his first Tour de France. The twenty-seven year old had travelled all the way from Australia with his young family. Bespectacled and well spoken, he didn't fit the profile of a professional cyclist. In his autobiography, he would declare,

> If I could not win a race without artificial stimulation, I would retire from cycling tomorrow. Also, to me, one of the most appealing things about being a professional athlete has been that I could lead a clean, healthy life.

He was one of two Australians who'd started the Tour, along with John Beasley, and the only one to finish. Australian cyclists weren't entirely unknown in France. Iddo Munro and Duncan Kirkham had made the long voyage to Europe for the 1914 Tour. In 1928, there'd even been a joint Australian-New Zealand team, led by Hubert Opperman. Its fortunes were telling.

Arriving in France with just four riders, Opperman had planned to assemble a full ten-man squad by hiring six experienced Europeans. By the time the race started, he'd failed to recruit a single one. That year's Tour featured no less than fifteen team time trials and the tiny squad of antipodeans had to endure the humiliation of being overtaken by full squads of elite European professionals. Their failure was indicative of the barriers of distance, language, cost, and confusion faced by Australians on the Continent.

In 1955 Mockridge had been invited to ride for Charly Gaul's Luxembourg mixed squad. Although he won neither a stage nor a jersey, the young Australian had deeply impressed the French. Jean Bobet, younger brother of Louison, described him as 'the most extraordinary champion with whom I have rubbed shoulders.' Despite such glowing praise, Mockridge never rode another Tour. With his wife and infant daughter, he left the uncertainty of life as a European pro and returned to Australia later the same year.

Mockridge was indisputably the greatest Australian cyclist of his generation. If Coppi had seemed exotic to the British, the professional *peloton* seemed even further removed in suburban Melbourne. When he returned from Europe it was as if he'd ascended to the Pantheon of the Gods and then returned to tell the tale. He won the Australian Road Championships three times in a row in 1956, 1957, and 1958. In 1956 he also set a new record for the Warrnambool to Melbourne, Australia's most prestigious one-day race.

Despite his limited results in Europe, Mockridge was prolifically talented. Prior to turning professional, he had already raced two Olympic Games, coming 26th in the 1948 road race before taking two gold medals in the 1952 Games, and setting a record for the kilometre time trial. In his first foray to Europe, while still an amateur, he won both the amateur and the open division of the 1952 Grand Prix de Paris, beating the British track great Reg Harris and a host of other top professionals.

When he returned to Europe again in 1955 he had won the Paris Six Day and the Tour du Vaucluse. It was this that secured his spot in Charly Gaul's squad, where he helped the Luxembourger secure third place and the King of the Mountains title. When Mockridge finished the Tour, one Paris daily paper was so impressed it declared, 'Next year you will finish among the top ten.'

Much of the awed response to Mockridge was simply because he finished the 1955 Tour, despite all the odds. Of one hundred and fifty starters that year only sixty-nine had finished. The only other Australian in the race, John Beasley, had quit after three days. Both of them were riding for Gaul's team, where they were seen more as filler than potential contenders. As Mockridge later wrote:

Contrary to my expectations, there were no tactical discussions when our team gathered at meal times. Nicholas Frantz, our manager, obviously felt that John and I were only present to make up team numbers. We were a team only in that we wore the same colours.

The climatic moment of the 1955 Tour was Stage Eleven, running for one hundred and ninety-eight kilometres between Marseille and Avignon. The pinnacle was the 1912 metre climb over Mont Ventoux, the Giant of Province. First introduced to the Tour in 1951, it has a particular reputation, partly because of its gradient but also because, once the riders pass above the tree line, it becomes obvious that the mountain is a dormant volcano — devoid of trees, grey, windswept and, in July, often viciously hot, with the heat reflecting off the mountain's white stone.

The combination of Ventoux's heat and amphetamines almost killed Jean Malléjac that year and proved fatal for Tom Simpson on the same climb in 1967. In 1955 the mountain battered the field to pieces. Charly Gaul, for whom Mockridge was riding, was one of the supreme climbers of the era yet required medical attention at the end of the stage. Ferdi Kubler, winner of the 1950 Tour, had attacked early but ended up semi-comatose by the end, falling off his bike before stumbling over the line to declare 'Ferdi killed himself on the Ventoux!' He never raced the Tour again and retired the next year. Even Louison Bobet, who won both the stage and the race overall surmised, 'A day like that takes years off our lives.' That someone could appear from the distant outpost of Australia and ascend such a brute was an achievement in itself.

To cap it off, Stage Eleven on the Ventoux took place on Mockridge's twenty-seventh birthday. The heat was so extreme that he was struggling well before the climb had even started, dropping off the back of the *peloton* to cram sugar cubes down his throat and seek the charity of local farmers:

> I staggered into the kitchen of the small house and without saying a word the family went into action, like a team of veteran soigneurs. Madame sponged my face and the back of my neck with icy water while Monsieur fetched me a ladle of water to drink. They offered me some food but all I wanted was sugar loaf, as much as I could eat.

Refreshed, he made it to the finish, passing the collapsed Malléjac on the way, and later writing, 'Oh what a hellish way to spend a birthday.' But, despite that, Mockridge still made it to Paris, coming in sixty-fourth, more than four hours behind the victorious Louison Bobet. It was his perseverance that made him popular, with one French journalist writing:

> The Australian had all the disadvantages in the race, yet he stuck it out to finish while other riders – and several famous ones – gave up. We have adopted you, Russell, for good. You have proved yourself worthy.

Moreover, Mockridge's resilience impressed Louison Bobet himself, riding into Paris for his record third Tour de France win. On the final stage, Louison and his brother Jean had dropped back to visit the car of Tour director Jacques Goddet. After accepting his congratulations, they were making their way back to the head of the *peloton* when they encountered Mockridge cruising at the back of the group and singing to himself:

> We caught up with Russell Mockridge, who had dropped back by about 20 metres, the better to enjoy the moment, which was historic for him as well. I drew alongside him

and heard him singing, 'It's a long way to Prince's Park, it's a long way to go...' Up came Louison, and Russell Mockridge addressed him 'Bravo, Mr Bobet. It's a grand day for you! For me, too ... after the Ventoux.'

I was speechless. This Olympic track rider, the antipodean phenomenon, was rejoicing at being there, at the gate of the Parc de Princes. In his way he too had crossed the Ventoux, the Giant of Provence ... It seems the call of the Ventoux can be heard as far away as Australia.

It's unfortunate that Mockridge never rode the Tour again nor found a path to pursue a further career on the Continent. He returned to Australia the following year, where his experience put him head and shoulders above the local scene. He was killed in September 1958 while racing in the Tour of Gippsland in the outer suburbs of Melbourne. Heading through a crossing with a five-man group, a bus rode directly into them, crushing Mockridge's head, then backing up over his legs.

FEAR OF A BIKE PLANET

At the inquest following Mockridge's death, the court interviewed Robert Watson, the bus driver who killed him:

I saw a troop of cyclists travelling east along Dandenong Road at what appeared to be a very fast rate of speed and passing on the near of the kerb side of the stationary cars. They appeared to have their heads down.

Having seen both the riders, and the other cars parked to let the race pass, Watson then proceeded to drive straight into the middle of the group. At the civil trial that followed,

Watson's employer, the Clarinda Transport bus company was ordered to pay six thousand pounds, or the equivalent of about eighteen months work at the average wage. Mockridge's biographer, Martin Curtis, describes the trial as 'designed to paint the cyclists as careless and culpable.'

A shift was evident in the way Mockridge's death was handled that is specific to the post-war era. Prior to the war, cycling was a legitimate form of transport. After, it was reduced to a hobby, something to be discouraged on public roads where the increased presence of the automobile made the superfluous act of riding a bicycle an active risk to one's health.

The fear of death is a natural deterrent to would-be cyclists. Certainly, as a youth, I was discouraged from riding and with good reason. A child riding to a nearby school was killed in a hit and run, a classmate in high school lost a limb crossing the road, a friend's father was doored by a parked car while riding home from work. The corner of the door punctured his throat. The motorist drove off, leaving him near death in the gutter.

Anyone who commutes by bike will have their war stories and close encounters. Coursing down Magill Road on my way home from work I once had a four-wheel-drive pull out of a side street and stop suddenly in the middle of the road directly in front of me. As I frantically tried to manoeuvre behind it, the driver rolled backwards. I just barely scraped past but I don't think they even noticed they'd almost killed me. Another time, a car full of P-platers ignored a stop sign into merging traffic and came within centimetres of mashing me against another car. I remember the instinctive calm as I watched their car running up against my handlebars while I feathered the brakes and checked how far I could merge before going under the wheels of the car beside me. They sped off and I emerged miraculously unharmed and buzzed with adrenalin for a couple of hours after.

It's an interesting parable for the post-war city that urban design has focused increasingly on the flow of automotive traffic at the expense of everything else. Where once riding a bike or walking was considered normal, to do so now is almost seen as asking for trouble. The disincentives are built into the very fabric of our cities. As a kid, I grew up in a suburb where it was a forty-five minute walk to the closest shops. It was built in the post-war era on re-zoned market gardens, under the influence of 'Garden City' designers like Ebenezer Howard. The traffic focused, Modernist design of people like Robert Moses and Le Corbusier probably seemed like a viable alternative to the crowded, inner city slums of the Depression but, within ten years, 'urbanists' like Jane Jacobs were raising serious critiques of this approach to planning:

> Traffic arteries, along with parking lots, gas stations and drive-ins, are powerful and insistent instruments of city destruction. To accommodate them, city streets are broken down into loose sprawls, incoherent and vacuous for anyone on foot.

Certainly, being a kid in a suburb where you effectively couldn't get anywhere without driving, the world seemed 'incoherent and vacuous'. The popular youth hangouts were a footbridge by the high school and the car park outside McDonalds. When the place was designed in the Fifties, the planners laid out a 'green belt' running along a river into which they'd directed the gutters from all the local roads. Along its banks they'd even laid out a bike track; decrepit, cracked, and crumbled. As a teenager I'd ride it's length, a full seven kilometres to the local outlet, where all that gutter water spewed out into the ocean. By night, the green strip was home to the local drug dealers and strictly off limits.

There was a sort of psychology to growing up and living in a place like that; an idea that the outside world was inherently dangerous and could only be traversed by car, lest you were either attacked by the local hoodlums or struck down by a motorist whose momentum you'd foolishly impeded. Accordingly, I spent most of my youth at home watching television, growing steadily obese and miserable. With the only other transport option being rare and unreliable buses, there was nowhere much to go and it was nigh on impossible to get there anyway.

Against that backdrop, owning a car seemed like a passport to freedom, although when I finally started driving it turned out to be less liberating than I'd expected. As a nineteen year old, I worked as a delivery driver and the novelty of sitting in gridlocked traffic listening to the stereo soon wore thin, scraped away by the cost of repairs, petrol, and inexplicably expensive malfunctions. When I started riding regularly I found it wasn't just cheaper, it was weirdly exhilarating. Going back to driving always feels like entering into a sensory deprivation chamber; you can't feel the texture of the road, the wind, the weather and nor does there seem any inherent connection between the motion of the car and effort of the driver.

Driving a car is, after all, an essentially parasitic experience; all the energy is generated by the machine and even most of the cognitive decisions are made by traffic lights and road markings. This clashes substantially with the image of the automobile showcased in virtually every car advertisement, which portrays the experience as wonderfully liberating. The driver soars through picturesque countryside, the wind in their hair and their loved ones by their side. Rarely do they show you stuck in traffic while the engine overheats.

The author Charles Montgomery describes the effect of this disparity and its main product, road rage:

> The driving experience primes car drivers for meltdowns. They are conditioned by popular culture to see cars as symbols of freedom, yet city driving is a slow-motion trap that subjects drivers to constant restrictions on their movement. Drivers are thwarted from enjoying the promise of motion by traffic lights, by congestion – and yes, by cyclists – and they suffer the natural but impossible desire to escape and move forward. All this while being strapped to their seats!

After I started working in an office, I'd find myself stuck in gridlock every day on the way to work. Then I'd be stuck in the office staring at the computer for eight hours, after which I'd sit trapped in traffic again on my way home, whereupon I'd be so exhausted all I could do was sit and stare at the TV. The mythology argued that if I had the job to buy the car I could use the car to free myself with long, relaxing country drives. But, in reality, I used the car to get to the job, which paid for the car, and locked me in a vicious cycle of sitting in small spaces being driven to a frustrated rage.

You can see why motorists get so enraged by cyclists. Before or after a hard day of sitting in a cubicle watching a computer screen, you find yourself trapped in a tiny metal box staring at the traffic lights, knowing your end destination is another night of sitcom repeats. The existential angst of such a conundrum is much easier to vent upon the fool in lycra cavorting through the gridlock than it is on the complexity of poor urban design and an unsustainable work/life balance.

In this respect, cycling was, for me at least, a profound revelation. I was capable of propelling myself across the most immense distances, rolling through the jammed traffic and growing physically stronger while the increased blood flow and adrenalin rush provoked by near death encounters made my cognitive functions particularly sharp. In comparison to the sedentary lifestyle I'd become accustomed to, cycling seemed as much an aesthetic awakening as a physical one.

I'd suggest that this is because the bicycle is unlike most other machines in that it has an extremely direct relationship to your body. Where a broken car might leak oil or exude steam, a broken bike fills your legs with lactic acid, makes your heartache, and sucks the air out of your lungs. By contrast, a good bike is a sublime extension of one's strength, both physically and mentally. When I first started riding a bike it was like an explosion of rare, unconstrained feeling.

As a machine, the bicycle exploits one of humanity's greatest evolutionary achievements; the human leg is a marvel of energy efficiency. It passes power through the twitch muscles in the thigh, through the calves and, in a series of carefully timed triggers of muscle and sinew, out through the ball of the foot. The precision of this transfer makes us far more efficient over longer distance than the hoofed quadrupeds that have traditionally supplied our protein.

Running that energy through a pedal, out through the chain ring and cassette to the rear wheel not only amplifies the strength of the human leg but allows it to retain momentum. Such a system decreases the energy expenditure and the build up of lactic acid to a level sustainable over immense distances. A human might be able to walk at six kilometres an hour and cover fifty kilometres a day. The bike makes it suddenly obvious just how much power we are individually capable of generating and even an amateur cyclist such as myself can cover four times that distance in the same time.

Where the automobile expands human movement largely by replacing agency with mechanics, the bicycle amplifies the rider's own power to such a degree as to make them effectively superhuman. Particularly as our lives have grown less and less active, this amplification of our agency over our own movement makes cycling ever more enticing. Where once the bike replaced the physical burden of having to walk everywhere, now it provides an alternative to the physical repression of being forced to sit all day. It isn't just a replacement for physical effort, but a method of rediscovering one's own strength from the obscurity of a sedentary lifestyle.

To paraphrase Mockridge, one of the most appealing things about riding a bike is the potential to lead a clean, healthy life, rather than one defined by work, driving, and sitting still. As he noted in his autobiography:

> Sometimes when I set off on a training ride I think of others who are shut up in stuffy offices or noisy factories, and I am grateful that I can spend so much time in the open air… there are plenty of times I hated the actual competition. But my attitude to the whole business can be summed up if I say: I don't particularly care for being a competitive cyclist but I LIKE THE LIFE. I like the freedom that it gives me. The freedom to spend at least a little time enjoying the things that so many people can only enjoy in the few hours outside their working day.

This sense of freedom and the possibility of an alternative way of living drives the mythology of cycling. It makes perfect sense that those whose professional life is confined to an office should love riding bikes; it's the polar opposite to being stuck behind the computer, and the sense of reward one gets from a long ride is the perfect panacea to the hollow, albeit more financial, rewards one receives for writing a report, keeping the accounts in order, or delivering a good conference presentation.

The hostility directed at cyclists in the modern city is not only a rejection of lycra clad lunatics skipping through the traffic but a more profound rejection of the idea that there is a life, different and better than the one so many of us have found ourselves living. This hatred is a phobia drawn from the same source that makes the bike so appealing; that it suggests an alternate world to the sedentary one of the car, the office, and the couch.

Against the rhythm of the morning commute, the working day and the nightly television schedule, the cyclist suggests a different cadence, one simultaneously threatening to those who've worked hard to believe there's some justification for their sedentary world, and deeply appealing to those who seek a different rhythm. From the time we enter school as children, we are taught that the path to fulfilment is found by sitting still, being quiet, and working. Cycling throws this mirage to the wind. It speaks of a form of play, of an outdoor life devoid either of the car or the television. Cycling presents a justification for life found not in the purchasing power of salaried employment but in the rhythm of one's own heart, lungs, and legs.

STAGE 12

July 13th, 2000
Carpentras –Mont Ventoux

THE PASSION OF MARCO PANTANI

Hell is the rhythm of others.
— *Paul Fournel*

From 1991 to 1997 the Tour de France grew dull. To begin with, Miguel Indurain won it five times in a row by mixing dominance in the time trials with consistency in the mountains. Later Bjarne Riis and Jan Ullrich perfected this formula with the aid of good doping programs. From 1999 until 2005 Armstrong followed the same template, albeit with more showmanship. But, in 1998, there was one glorious year when the Tour displayed a level of grandiose melodrama not seen in decades.

This was the year Marco Pantani won with a combination of furious alpine attacks and impetuous audacity. It was the pinnacle of his career. Two years later, on the Ventoux, he would take his final Tour stage win and embark upon a violent decline, culminating in his death at age thirty-four in

2004. It's worth comparing his fortunes in the 1998 race to those of the 2000 Tour. They mark the final flourish before the Armstrong era.

By 1998 Pantani's flamboyant climbing, emotional fragility, and *enfant terrible* status had already put him alongside Luis Ocaña and Charly Gaul as one of the great manic-depressives of the sport. Like Gaul and Ocaña, he seemed to generate his own gravity and, like both his forbearers, when he lost control of that force it wreaked terrible results. He was utterly unlike his contemporaries Indurain, Ullrich, and Armstrong; all big men who dominated the Tour through a steady, consistent force. Pantani oscillated wildly, always struggling to bring himself into equilibrium. Watching him race, he seems to be in a constant state of metamorphosis; struggling to find a particular rhythm which, once attained, brought him into harmony with himself and allowed him to float away from his opposition.

In this respect, Pantani was extremely similar to Charly Gaul, who won the Tour in 1958 and the Giro in 1956 and 1959, as well as the mountains jerseys for both races and, over the course of his career, a colossal twenty-one Grand Tour stage victories. Roland Barthes insisted Gaul was capable of channelling something beyond the realm of mortal men:

> At certain moments, Gaul is inhabited by a god; his supernatural gifts then hang a mysterious threat over his rivals. The divine gift given to Gaul is lightness; by grace, elevation, and soaring (the mysterious absence of effort), Gaul suggests a bird or a plane (he perches lightly on the spurs of the Alps, and his pedals turn like propellers.)

Like Pantani, Gaul seemed to produce his own gravity, his pedals spinning like a centrifuge. Then, whilst the earth's pull weighed down on his competition, his velocity would increase. There was something mystical about it; as if he could elude the laws of physics to attain a state of grace unknown to those around him. When age robbed Gaul of this ability he not only retired but retreated into the woods of his native Luxembourg to live as a hermit. For almost three decades he seemed lost to cycling until suddenly reappearing, oddly enough, as an advisor to Pantani.

As cyclists, both men were small, light, and showed a remarkable capacity to accelerate, recuperate and then accelerate again, changing pace and speed with a versatility few riders could match. When they found that perfect rhythm they were unbeatable; their eyes seemed to glaze over, their impishness and manic-depressive personas became calm, and they'd cross the finish line as if awakening from a dream. After they left the sport they both struggled. Without the platform of the high mountains it was as if they lost their centre of gravity, spinning off course with disastrous results.

Pantani's climbing prowess had already put him on the podium of the Tour de France once, in his first appearance in 1994. When he raced it a third time, in 1997, his climbing was so good he set a record time up Alpe d'Huez, won the stage into Morzine, and finished third overall, behind Jan Ullrich and Richard Virenque. Still, many great climbers creep into the top ten with a few well-timed breakaways in the big mountains yet few of them go on to win in their own right.

At the start of the 1998 Tour, Pantani looked unlikely to return to the podium. He came one hundred and eighty-first out of one hundred and eighty-nine riders in the opening time trial. However, in the Alps he began to show his true form. After a few opening salvos in which he clawed back a minute or two, he launched a single, devastating attack on Stage

Fifteen over the Croix de Fer, the Telegraphe, Galibier, and Les Deux Alpes. By the end of the stage, his opposition was pulverized and Pantani held the yellow jersey with a margin of just under four minutes. Ullrich was left to limp across the line nine minutes behind him. Despite winning two more stages, the German couldn't reclaim the lead, coming into Paris in second place by more than three minutes.

Pantani's Tour victory combined with an equally spectacular win in the Giro d'Italia the same year to make him one of the few cyclists to complete a Grand Tour double victory in a single season. After a decade of big men winning Tours with grim consistency, he was just what the sport needed; an emotional, dramatic rider who won with attacks and audacity, rather than a dominant team and dull reliability.

Unfortunately, the Festina Affair cast a long shadow and both Pantani and the 1998 Tour are more famous for their association with doping than any sporting spectacle. The next year, while in the lead of the Giro d'Italia, Pantani failed a doping test after winning the penultimate mountain stage into Madonna di Campiglio. With only two stages left to race, he was removed from the Giro. In a single day, he went from being touted as the inheritor of Gaul's legend to being lambasted as a fraud.

After that, Pantani's life began rapidly spiralling out of control. It wasn't just the performance enhancing drugs. Pantani's personality seemed to thrive on extremes. Devoid of the rush of winning major races, he took solace in cocaine, which helped neither his emotional state nor his cycling. He didn't race again in 1999, devoting most of the rest of the year to a level of self-pity and erratic behaviour that would have made Ocaña proud. In a letter to his then girlfriend, with whom he had a particularly dramatic relationship, he wrote:

I isolated myself, the slave of a problem which doesn't make you strong but the slave of pain and I apologise to everyone. But above all to the people who believed that Pantani is great and who believe that I was honest in my goals like my rivals.

He was a walking disaster after his doping conviction. When he returned to competition he was desperate to prove himself a champion, mixing heroic but frequently doomed alpine attacks with a penchant for the kind of spectacular self-destruction usually associated with rock stars. My favourite picture of Pantani shows him shaking a policeman's hand, standing in front of his car, which is perched partially on top of another car. Apparently he'd been speeding the wrong way down a one-way street and crashed into no less than eight other vehicles.

Pantani's decline matched the corruption of the Tour itself. He missed the so-called 'Tour of Redemption' in 1999, still on a cocaine bender after his Giro scandal. He returned in 2000 to race what turned out to be his last ever Tour de France. Fittingly, his swan song contained two brilliant mountain stage wins. Pantani had entered the race an outside favourite but he proved no match for Armstrong and Ullrich. When he made his first serious attack on Stage Ten's ascent of the Hautacam, Armstrong not only caught him but dropped him easily. The Italian was perplexed, remarking, 'It isn't possible that, on all these climbs, he rides that much faster, given all the effort I make.'

As the race approached its Stage Twelve summit finish on the Ventoux, Pantani found himself off the back. The lead group contained a veritable who's who of future doping cases; Ullrich, Armstrong, the Spaniard Joseba Beloki, Richard Virenque, and the two Columbian climbing aces Santiago Botero and Roberto Heras.

Doping or not, Pantani knew how to ride the mountains. When the lead group moved away from him on the lower slopes of the Ventoux, he took the gamble and rode his own pace, keeping a steady, fluid rhythm and conserving his energy. While the rest of the group arrived, gasping and already exhausted, on the mountain's infamously lunar upper slopes, Pantani caught them with energy to spare. He then promptly attacked three times, drawing out the Columbians and Beloki. Armstrong, in yellow, simply sat in the group watching his competition drag the Italian back. Pantani's tactical nous was at its finest. Twice he let them catch him but, before they could recoup, he attacked again with more ferocity. Finally, after the third attack, there was no response as the group slumped, unable to follow.

Pantani's lead grew rapidly. Once he was out of sight he began searching for a steady rhythm, just fast enough to keep the pack at a distance. As he found his ideal cadence, the race seemed decided. Then, inexplicably, Armstrong jumped away from the other pursuers and began bridging the gap with alarming speed. Watching it ten years later, knowing about the doping, it looks ridiculous. In comparison to the fast, rhythmic flick of Pantani's legs, Armstrong seems inhumanly strong. Not only did he catch Pantani but the Italian had to sprint to keep up with him. As he pulled ahead, Armstrong pointed at his back wheel, to tell Pantani to sit in his slipstream. The two slugged up the hill, arriving at the finish side by side. With no discernable sprint, Pantani took the stage win while Armstrong increased his lead over Ullrich and Beloki.

With his typical ego, Pantani told the press pack at the finish line, 'I didn't like Armstrong's company. Armstrong's a great champion, but I'd have liked to have arrived alone.' Armstrong, ever the sportsman, declared he'd let the Italian win and responded, 'I don't know what Pantani's thinking but... he's just a little shit starter.' When Pantani won again on Stage Fifteen to Courchevel, Armstrong revisited the Ventoux stage, telling the media,

I let him win because he had ridden really well on that climb and I knew what he had been through. I was wrong to be generous, though.

Armstrong was saving face. Pantani's second win had caused chaos. He'd attacked, alone, one hundred and thirty kilometres from the line in an attempt to close his deficit on the lead riders and take the yellow jersey. His victory was spectacular, leaving the race scattered behind him in the style that had won him the 1998 Tour. Armstrong limped in a minute after him, while Ullrich didn't appear until almost three minutes later. The American later described the stage as 'the most difficult day of my life.'

Despite having pulled off one of the most astounding stage wins of his career, Pantani withdrew from the Tour the next day. That night he complained of stomach pains and left the race with less than a week to go. His manager, Manuela Ronchi, wrote of his decision to withdraw:

One of the side effects of the intestinal problems Marco was suffering from was a fluctuation in certain blood parameters and there was surely no point running the risk of more nasty surprises should he be blood-tested the following day.

The Italian media didn't swallow the story, dubious as to his mysterious stomach aliment and distrustful of his entourage. Under headlines like, 'The Night of Many Mysteries', his final victory on the Tour ended in suspicious ambiguity.

Pantani never raced the Tour again. When he appeared at the 2001 Giro, police raided his team hotel and found insulin in his room, leading to an eight-month ban. He returned to the 2003 Giro but this time his grandiose attacks failed to yield a result. The Tour didn't invite his team to race that year and he entered a psychiatric hospital in an attempt to deal with his substance abuse and anxiety. After he was released, he was dragged into court under charges of sporting fraud for his irregular blood values in the 1999 Giro, being acquitted only because there was no law active at the time against doping. He died in 2004, alone in a hotel room, of acute cocaine poisoning.

IN SEARCH OF PERFECT CADENCE

Raphaël Géminiani once described Charly Gaul by saying,

> Always the same rhythm. A little machine with a slightly higher gear than the rest, turning his legs at a speed that would break your heart.

He had a reputation not only as a great climber but, like Pantani, a 'little shit starter'. While leading the 1957 Giro, he'd stopped by the side of the road to urinate when a group containing the French Tour champion, Louison Bobet, rode past. Gaul hated Bobet and promptly 'made an indecent gesture with his organ of virility'. Bobet was outraged and led an organised attack, costing Gaul so much time he lost all hope of winning. In response, Gaul spent the rest of the race helping Italian outsider Gastone Nencini win, pacing him through the mountains to ensure Bobet lost.

The incident left Gaul with two nicknames; 'Cheri-Pipi' (roughly translated as 'Dear Little Piss'), and 'The Angel of the Mountains'. They capture the extremes of his personality well; just like Pantani, Gaul oscillated between athletic brilliance, nervous shyness, and childish egoism. Roland Barthes described him as the 'Rimbaud of the Tour', in reference to the precocious but unmistakably brilliant teenage poet who, having inspired the Surrealists, stopped writing by his early twenties and died before he turned forty.

Aside from their personalities, both men were physically similar, with small, light frames that gave them superb power to weight ratios. Both amplified this with a similar pedalling style, spinning small gears fast. It's a method that shifts the strain from the leg muscles to the cardiovascular system, allowing the rider to establish a rhythm that reduces lactic acid build up and generates a higher energy output over longer periods of time. Yet it is as much a psychological state as a physical technique. It requires the rider to find a perfect harmony between the rhythm of the lungs, heart, legs and pedals, or 'the perfect cadence'.

If that rhythm can be attained, the cyclist achieves the utmost energy efficiency. Accordingly, the quest for perfect cadence draws almost religious contemplation among cyclists. It represents a state of ideal physical and psychological unity. It's their capacity to attain this rare state that gives Pantani and Gaul their aura of greatness. On those occasions when they could harness the discordant elements of their personalities into a perfect rhythm, they were explosive and unbeatable. Beyond simple physicality, perfect cadence becomes a metaphor for knowing one's self.

Of course, in a merely technical sense cadence is just the speed and rhythm at which the rider spins the pedals and is simply a matter of physics. The mathematics of gear ratios is obvious — most road bikes will feature fifty-two teeth on the largest chain ring and maybe eleven on the smallest cog on the back wheel. This means every time you turn the pedal you cause the back wheel to rotate 4.7 times. Whereas, if you're using a smaller chain ring with, say, forty-two teeth and a bigger sprocket with maybe twenty-three teeth, every revolution of the pedal will only cause the sprocket to rotate 1.8 times.

This means more energy is required to turn a heavy gear of 52x11 than a light one of 42x23. The larger gear will make you go faster per pedal stroke but will create a greater drain on muscle and leg strength. A smaller gear will not carry you as far but will use up less energy. The idea is to find the point at which one's energy is being most efficiently utilised in correspondence with one's gears and pedal stroke. Beyond the mathematics, this requires the cyclist to know their body well enough to recognise the line between sustainable and exhaustive energy use.

Cadence is always important in cycling. It was once standard for road cyclists to spend time on the track or ride fixed wheels in training so they could perfect their rhythm, rather than rely on freewheeling to catch their breath. Track cyclists, particularly those who ride longer races, obsess about it because their bikes are devoid of both derailleurs and fixed wheels and so choosing the correct gear and developing the best possible cadence defines their entire discipline.

For those with a love of the mountains, cadence is an utter obsession; not just a physical equation but almost an additional sense on par with vision and feel. On a gradient, when the bicycle is robbed of its capacity to store momentum, and the drag of gravity is exponentially greater, the energy expenditure required for each pedal stroke becomes acute and the most efficient cadence is paramount.

Cyclists love to debate these issues and most books on bike maintenance will feature gear ratios, indicating how many inches worth of tire you'll turn for each pedal stroke depending on your gear. But in practice, the issue quickly transcends any rational discussion. Cycling is about finding a rhythm. This is what makes it so hypnotic and makes riding hills so addictive. On a steep climb, the rhythm of the pedals, of the heart and of the lungs, is so all-consuming it stops you thinking about anything else. As the road shifts, weaves, rises and falls, the rhythm of the cyclist will adapt accordingly.

My favourite cycling author, and established Ruskin expert, Tim Hilton, summarizes this emotion beautifully:

> There is nothing like the feeling of riding a bicycle at maximum speed, at dawn and alone. Concentration becomes meditation – or something else, beyond thought. It's unlike anything else in the world of physical effort.

Coming home from work, I used to go out riding in the foothills that surround my hometown on summer nights when the sun didn't set till late. I had a fifty-kilometre loop, up an initial 6% incline, on to a long, weaving false flat across the top of a low mountain range. Coming home, there was a seven kilometre descent followed by an ascent with a patch of road at 10%, ridden with the setting sun on one's back. With the exclusion of the Lance Armstrong fans frantically trying to prove their masculinity, most of the cyclists I saw up there had entered into the sort of comatose bliss usually only achieved with heavy sedatives. In my lightest gear I'd sway up the final ramps in a sustained, mild oxygen debt, to cruise along the crest of the hill in a state of serenity. I assume most cyclists who ride the hills experience this sensation. It's achieved because cadence isn't just about physicality, oxygen intake and lactic acid; it's about finding the perfect rhythm when the brain and the body enter into their utmost unity.

The great philosopher of cadence is, in my opinion, Paul·

Fournel, who writes:

> The cyclist is his own gyroscope. He produces not only movement but equilibrium. The faster he turns his legs, the more harmonious this equilibrium becomes: he's spinning.
>
> If your wheels spin round, your legs spin round; if your legs spin round your head will too.

Given that Gaul ended up a hermit and Pantani died of a drug overdose, this might seem a little idealistic. However, their lives fell apart when they no longer had the ritual of the Grand Tours to force them into finding that perfect rhythm. Pantani was at his best when racing for three weeks straight, working himself into the same sort of rhythmic fervour you'd expect from a Whirling Dervish. It was when that rhythm was interrupted, by Armstrong's growing dominance or bans on racing for his drug use, that he'd devolve into misery.

Fortunately, most of us don't reach those extremes. For most of us, good cadence comes down to understanding the rhythm between your bike and your body. If your cadence is good, your legs will not be in pain and you won't have to struggle for every pedal stroke. Over time, you'll enter into Fornel's sense of equilibrium. You spin and the sensation is akin to floating or drifting. To have a perfect cadence, a perfect speed, a perfect heart and lung beat, and to find your brain reacting to your surroundings with no conscious effort, is to enter into a state of Zen. All good cyclists will know this sensation. It is the sensation of perfect rhythm and it is at the heart of cycling as a philosophical, rather than purely physical, experience.

STAGE 13

July 13th, 1967
Marseille to Carpentras

TOM SIMPSON'S LAST WORDS

A man's reach must exceed his grasp, or what's a heaven for?
— Robert Browning

Of the many infamous cycling deaths, Tom Simpson's is the most iconic. His legendary, albeit misquoted, last words were 'Put me back on my bike', a mantra that would be comic if their origins weren't so tragic. Unlike the sport's other legendary fatalities, such as René Pottier (who hanged himself), Henri Pélissier (shot by his mistress), Bottecchia (beaten to death by Fascists), Ocaña (shot gun suicide), Pantani (cocaine overdose) or Hugo Koblet (suspected suicide by car crash), Simpson died at the height of his career and on his bike. In the middle of the 1967 Tour, he collapsed through sheer exhaustion, albeit helped along by a mix of amphetamines and liquor. Despite his cheerful demeanour, Simpson had a marked tendency to go well beyond his limits. It made him both the first truly successful British professional as well as a man capable of actually riding himself to death.

Tom Simpson was a star in Britain before his death and a legend after it. He was the first British cyclist to truly make it on the European professional circuit. As a kid, he joined his local cycling club, Harworth, and was nicknamed 'Four Stone Coppi', in reference both to his unashamed worship of the Italian champion and his diminutive size. By 1954, aged seventeen, he was fitting training around his work as an apprentice engineer and winning races against the seniors.

Simpson always had a reputation for sheer persistence and audacity. He'd tried to encourage Harworth to break away from the staid National Cyclists Union, which frowned upon road racing, and join the newly formed British League of Racing Cyclists. When they refused, he absconded to the Scala Wheelers, hoping to find something closer to the glamour of the European professional *peloton*. One of his fellow riders, semi-pro George Shaw, recalled that he was obsessed with the mystique of racing on the Continent:

> We read all the magazines, or rather looked at the pictures because we couldn't translate the French. We all wanted to ride the Tour de France, but really he wanted it and we dreamt it.

After that, Simpson managed to wheedle advice out of the recently retired track champion Reg Harris, wrote letters to Francis Péllisier (brother of former Tour winner Henri) asking for advice on improving his form, and tracked down Austrian trainer George Berger, who was living in England but well acquainted with French cycling. Using their accumulated advice, he qualified for the British team at the Melbourne Olympics in 1956, aged just eighteen, where he took a bronze medal in the team pursuit. After racing the 1958 Empire Games, and with the added incentive of dodging the national draft, he left for Europe intent on turning professional.

At that point, Brian Robinson was the only British professional in Europe and, along with Irishman Seamus Elliot, one of a very limited number of English speakers to make it on the Continent. In 1955 Robinson had been part of the first British team at the Tour in almost twenty years. Only two of them finished; Tony Hoar in last place and Robinson a very respectable twenty-ninth. Hoar's professional career only lasted a year but Robinson went on to win stages in both the 1958 and 1959 Tours.

When Simpson arrived in Europe, it was Robinson who helped him find his first contract, riding for the St Raphaël squad. Simpson quickly proved his worth. In his first major race, the Tour de l'Oust, he took out a stage sprint, a time trial, and only lost the leader's jersey after a puncture on the final day. In 1960, his first full year as a pro, Simpson made a forty kilometre solo escape in Paris-Roubaix, only getting caught five kilometres from the finish. It was the first time the Queen of the Classics was televised and the French lapped it up. Simpson played up to the media attention, dressing in bowler hats and suits to act out the role of the English gentleman.

After that he thrived, coming twenty-ninth in his first Tour despite riding for a weak English national team. In 1962 he became the first-ever English rider to wear the yellow jersey. The race had shifted to trade teams for the first time since before the war, allowing him a stronger roster of support riders than he could get in a purely British squad. He ended up finishing sixth overall. It was the first time anyone from the Anglo world had seemed like a real contender for a Tour de France victory.

For the most part, Simpson focused on one day classics and shorter tours; winning the Tour of Flanders in 1961, Bordeaux-Paris in 1963, and Milan-San Remo in 1964. In

1965 he took the Tour of Lombardy and, in another first for an Englishman, the World Championship. Back in Britain, the club scene he'd emerged from was ecstatic. One of their own had made it at the top level of the sport and, in doing so, proved dreams could come true. In his wake, a new generation of British professionals began to seep into the European circuit, including Vin Denson (later to become a *domestique-deluxe* to Anquetil), Barry Hoban (who went on to win eight Tour stages and Ghent-Wevelgem), and three-time Tour stage winner Michael Wright.

Like Mockridge's trip to Europe, Simpson's success struck a chord in the close-knit community of club cyclists in his homeland, most of whom came from lower middle class or respectable working class backgrounds and found their options limited to dead end jobs, interrupted only by a short stay in the national service. Tim Hilton, one of the generation of young cyclists for whom Simpson was a hero, recalls the careers of many of his fellow riders around that time — a pastry cook, a motor mechanic, a few police and firemen, market gardeners like Beryl Burton (whose autobiography is interspersed with stories of picking rhubarb), and a great many postmen. Simpson's success laid the path to a way out; leaving grim, drab work in grim, drab post-war Britain for the glamour of the European professional *peloton*. As Simpson's biographer, journalist William Fotheringham, writes, 'Cycling was a better way of earning a living than working in a factory in England.'

Simpson prepared for the 1967 Tour knowing he'd been a professional for eight years and his strength wouldn't last forever. His aim wasn't necessarily to win overall but to avoid ever having to go back to the life he'd known before racing. He told his roommate at the start of the Tour he thought his career had two more years and he needed to make another

£60,000 to set himself up for life.

To earn that sum, he knew he needed to perform well enough to attract bigger contracts and appearance fees in the post-Tour criteriums. Simpson's agent, Daniel Dousset, had told him he either needed a stage win or a top-five finish to get the fees he wanted. To spur himself on, Simpson went into a luxury car dealer and put down on a deposit on a brand new Mercedes, saying it gave him 'something to aim at'.

The 1967 Tour was, once again, raced by national teams, rather than the trade teams of the previous few years. Simpson's Great Britain squad was built around him but it lacked the strength or professionalism of his competitors. Aside from Brian Hoban, Vin Denson, and Michael Wright, the rest of the squad — Pete Chisman, Arthur Metcalfe, and Colin Lewis — had little experience outside their homeland. Lewis, who roomed with Simpson, remembers his team leader as meticulous and demanding, remarking, 'He had every right to be. He was going for the top three, with a makeshift team.'

Lewis suffered an early introduction to the scope of his captain's demands when, half way through a stage, Simpson demanded his hat. Given Simpson already had his own hat, Lewis asked why, to which his boss responded, 'Because I want to have a shit in it.' The two stopped, Simpson disappeared behind a lorry with the hat, and re-appeared, without the hat. Lewis, as his *domestique*, then faced the added indignity of towing him back to the body of the race.

After a season of good form, Simpson's plan in 1967 was to focus on three Tour stages, including the Ventoux, and ride conservatively when possible. With a solid prologue and consistent finishes, he made it through the first week in thirteenth place, ahead of many of the other favourites. He held on as the race hit the first batch of mountains, until Stage Ten when it climbed over the Galibier and he developed stomach cramps and diarrhoea. Unable to eat, he kept racing and kept pushing himself, managing to cling onto seventh position overall.

He still seemed in good spirits, though. At the start of Stage Thirteen, Vin Denson remembers him 'full of beans, laughing and joking.' On the early slopes of the Ventoux there was a series of attacks aimed to unseat the race leader, Frenchman (and eventual winner) Roger Pingeon. Spanish climber Julio Jiménez and Dutchman Jan Janssen went on the attack. Jiménez came second overall and won the King of the Mountains classification, while Janssen won the stage. It was clearly a make or break moment.

At some point, Simpson took amphetamines, washed down with brandy. He was experienced with performance-enhancing drugs and aimed to drive himself through his pain threshold so he could keep up as the race sorted out its top contenders. A good placing on Ventoux would have kept him in good stead for the overall finish. Denson tried to talk him out of attacking, telling him to conserve his energy, accept a place in the top twenty and focus on the World Championship later in the season. Simpson responded, 'No. I've got to move up. I'll definitely be on the rostrum.' Denson remembers the discussion well. As Simpson rode away, his teammate shouted out 'Die! Die!' in what was meant to be an encouraging call to all-out effort but ended up being awkwardly prophetic.

As the race moved above the tree line, the white rock of Ventoux reflected the heat. It was a blisteringly hot day and, fuelled by the amphetamines and a natural capacity to push his limits, Simpson simply rode until his body was so badly overheated he began to lose consciousness. He collapsed within sight of the summit, weaving so badly he lost balance and toppled over on the side of the road. Team manager Alec Taylor and long-time mechanic Harry Hall jumped out of the team car and tried to convince him to quit. He refused and, reluctantly, they helped him back on his bike.

That moment is now part of cycling folklore. As Taylor and Hall helped him remount Simpson noticed his toe straps had come undone, yelling at Hall, 'Me straps, Harry! Me straps!' The mechanic tightened them and pushed him off, with Taylor remembering his last words as a muttered, 'On, on, on.' Later, the journalist Sid Saltmarsh, writing for the canonical British magazine *Cycling*, reported the incident using the more poetic and now infamous phrase, 'Put me back on my bike!' Simpson wove along the road for a few hundred metres, then his head drooped and his legs slowed. This time, a group of spectators caught him before he toppled over. His hands were locked to the handlebars and he had stopped breathing. He was airlifted to hospital and pronounced dead that afternoon.

The reverberation of Simpson's death, and its place in cycling folklore, represents more than just the stupid excess of an over-competitive athlete or a mercenary desire to secure retirement funds. Simpson used the bike to escape the life of a factory worker. For the older club cyclists in the UK who lived a similar life, the fixation with him emerged because he chased, with great success, their collective dream of leaving the drudgery of mundane jobs and grey streets forever and taking up a life of adventure on the Continent. Understandably, when Simpson died it hit a communal nerve. As Tim Hilton remembers it:

> British cycling is familial. That is why Simpson is remembered in a personal way and why there are still disputes about, for instance, who his friends were, who loved him best, who looked after him best; and it is the family of British cyclists who take part in the communal

celebratory rides, the memorial road race held in Harworth every year and make the thousands of expeditions to the memorial on Mont Ventoux.

There's a further allure about his legend; a suggestion that he believed in what he was doing with such ardency that he was willing to kill himself for it. To believe in something that completely is rare. Few of us will feel that sort of passion as we shuffle back and forth from work each day. This is why Simpson retains his magnetism; he's emblematic of something much larger than a sporting fatality.

SOMETHING TO AIM AT

In 1982 the brilliant Scottish climber Robert Millar was asked if he saw himself in the tradition of earlier Scots cyclists like Ian Steel or Billy Bilsland. He responded, 'I'm more in the shadow of Tom Simpson.' While one was English and the other Scottish they came from the same class and faced similar prospects. Like Simpson, Millar had grown up in a drab, respectable working class part of town and found himself doing an engineering apprenticeship in a factory. One of his workmates, fellow cyclist David Whitehall, recalls Millar sneaking off to sleep, 'so he'd be well rested for training. He'd also come out with things like, 'I've perfected a new way of sleeping in the toilets', then he'd demonstrate how he could lie, with his head resting on the cistern.'

Millar was working for the glamorously named Weir's Pumps, in a factory with two thousand other employees. He hated every second of it; the crass vulgarity of his workmates, the hours of boredom, and the career path promising new frontiers of slightly better paid boredom. His biographer, Richard Moore, writes of Millar's time there:

> Working hard, going to the football and the pub, and 'pulling burds' was not only standard but required behaviour; falling asleep in the toilets while dreaming of riding the Tour de France was not.

As Whitehall recalls, Millar was the factory weirdo, with only two topics of conversation. One was 'the boredom of the factory, and how he couldn't wait to get out' and the other was cycling.

Millar tracked down Simpson's former mechanic, Harry Hall, to make him a frame, and started his career riding for Simpson's old team, Peugeot. In 1984 he bested Simpson's sixth place in the Tour by taking fourth, just under three minutes off the podium finish his predecessor had been aiming at. With a stage win and the King of the Mountains jersey, he effectively lived-out Simpson's unfinished goal.

When Bradley Wiggins, the first British cyclist to ever win the Tour, began aiming for the yellow jersey he told an interviewer, 'Tom will be watching over me on the Ventoux … What he was trying to do that day is what I'm going to be trying to do, too.' Wiggins grew up in a single parent family, living in a commission flat in the suburb of Kilburn. He may have been of a different generation but was of the same class and facing the same choices. After winning the 2012 Tour he commented, 'Kids from Kilburn aren't supposed to win the Tour de France.'

Of course, that's what's at the heart of Simpson's mythology. It's not that he was just a road cyclist per se but that he embodied an alternative that seemed impossible. To ride a bike wasn't just to race, it was to transcend. Graeme Fife opens the first chapter of his autobiography *The Beautiful Machine* reminiscing about his first ever bicycle,

I knew what that bike promised: It promised freedom. In all the years of my childhood and youth, I can't remember a time when I didn't want to escape.

Tim Hilton uses similar terms, 'The bike was my escape from the dullness and conformity', while long distance cyclist Eileen Sheridan wrote that 'It opened up for me a brand new world of opportunity and delight'. The Australian marathon cyclist Ernie Old recalls seeing a penny farthing roll into his village in rural Australia in the 1890s, writing 'I saw at once its possibilities ... Boy-like I at once began to see visions and dream dreams.'

As a thirteen year old I received a maroon red, ten-speed mountain bike with much the same sense of promise. I had just reached an age when, provided I abided by strict parameters of caution and restraint, I was allowed to leave the house without my mother's supervision. The limits of my world suddenly expanded exponentially. On the bike, I found myself cruising the immensity of unbroken suburbs. Once you left the clogged arterial roads with their snarl of lumbering motorists, the endless network of back streets formed a labyrinth of empty, secret passages taking me as far as my fat little legs could pedal.

There were limits to what you could get away with as a thirteen year old on a crappy mountain bike. I didn't know anyone else interested in cycling and had no idea people raced bikes for a living. Most of my classmates were into the normal things suburban teenagers are interested in; milling around in the McDonald's car park, binge drinking and listening to bad music. For a while I'd taken solace in those old bastions of socially inept youth; role-playing games and fantasy fiction. I read a lot of pulp fantasy novels in an attempt to insulate myself from the grim reality. Getting my first office job didn't help. Watching my young life slip away for $12.58 an hour was profoundly shocking. Worse was the inability to identify anything else to do. It was an extremely depressing time.

I snapped out of it the first time I managed to ride a really big hill. I'd purchased a hybrid road bike with clipless pedals and thin wheels. Its speed was like an epiphany; the machine made me stronger, faster, and braver. Riding that bike was like becoming a different person. I remember following the Esplanade road down along the coast further than I'd ever gone before, ending up out on the fringes of the city. A huge hill loomed in front of me, with cars groaning up the side of the bike lane. It seemed insurmountable but I started riding up it anyway, amazed at my own audacity. I was shocked when I reached the top.

After that I kept going further and further, and seeking out steeper and longer ascents. The further I went, the further I wanted to go. I lost so much weight someone asked if I had cancer but I learnt much about my body, starting with the lesson that poor hydration gave me the runs and low blood sugar produced a sensation of intense melancholy. Most of all I learnt that I was capable of a great deal more than sitting in an office all day. It was life-changing. Had there been a greater goal to commit to, perhaps I would have pursued that. But in lieu of some worthy cause, cycling became a form of freedom unto itself.

July 11th, 1975
Aurillac to Puy de Dôme

THE END OF EDDY MERCKX

The severest ordeal that nature imposes on the racer is the mountain.
The mountain: weight. Now to conquer the slopes and the weight of
things is to allow that man can possess the entire physical universe.
But the conquest is so arduous that a moral man must commit himself
to it altogether.
— Roland Barthes

There are ample stories of struggle, defeat, and death in cycling, but stories of unadulterated success are harder to come by. The exception, of course, is Eddy Merckx. While Fausto Coppi may be considered the greatest cyclist of all time, Merckx is, without dispute, the most successful. Although he lacked Coppi's romantic aura, he smashed his way through the cycling world like the Goths through Rome.

Oddly, his phenomenal career was almost sidelined before it began. In 1964, just months before he turned professional, a doctor found his heart beating at an uneven rhythm and he was subsequently dropped from the Belgian national team for the amateur World Championship. 'It was like a hammer blow to the head. I thought my life was going to change just like that', Merckx recalled. Fortunately, his mother smelled a rat, took him to their family doctor who said he was fine, and then berated the selectors of the Belgian national team until they changed their minds. Merckx raced, won, and then continued to win almost non-stop for the following decade.

In 1968, aged twenty-three, he won his first Grand Tour, the Giro d'Italia, taking the leader's, points, and mountain jerseys. He repeated the same feat in the 1969 Tour de France, beating Roger Pingeon by almost twenty minutes; one of the biggest time gaps since Coppi's 1952 victory. It remains the only time a single rider won all the prize jerseys.

From 1968 through to 1974 he won pretty much every race on the calendar; three World Championships, five Tours, five Giros, a Vuelta, Milan-San Remo (which he won a total of seven times), Paris-Roubaix (three times), Liège-Bastonge-Liège (five times), along with a host of one day classics and smaller tours. Such was Merckx's dominance that an entire generation of professional cyclists spent their careers in his shadow. This included people who, in a different era, would have been great champions. For example, Felice Gimondi was touted as the next Bartali after he won the Tour in 1965, his very first year as a professional. But like so many others, Merckx simply took all his potential victories from him. Gimondi recalls the Belgian's appearance in the professional *peloton*:

> Suddenly I had to be happy winning far less. I can't say
> I hated him. It was tough. I had trouble adapting to the
> problem he set me because all he wanted to do was win.

That was all. I had to change my mindset. There were a couple of years when it was very hard to get used to. I had to begin again from nothing.

Merckx was unusual among cyclists in that he had no specialist field. Most professional cyclists will have one area of excellence in which they focus their energies — climbing, time trials, one day races, or Grand Tours. Merckx had the unique and uncanny capacity to dominate the sport in its entirety, winning everything equally.

The only other rider to achieve such prolific dominance had been Fausto Coppi, yet his wins were interrupted by years of misfortune. Paradoxically, the ease and consistency of Merckx's victories had the effect of improving Coppi's legacy. Benjo Maso sums it up nicely:

> Gian Paolo Ormezzano writes in his *Storia del Ciclismo* [*History of Cycling*] that Merckx was 'the strongest' but Coppi 'the greatest'. This is no simple expression of Italian chauvinism. Jacques Goddet actually went a bit further and said that Merckx was the best but Coppi was still better.

Maso raises a point at odds with the popular notion of sport. Merckx won more races but when Coppi won it meant more. The Belgian won with such consistency it became routine and commonplace. When Coppi won, it was spectacular.

As Maso points out, this had a lot to do with the lens through which the Tour was seen. In Coppi's era the Tour had enjoyed not only an extremely high quality of competitors but a corresponding pinnacle in media coverage. It was the last golden age of the newspaper, before television took over. In such an environment, a journalist could write the race so it seemed like *The Odyssey*, even if, in reality, the *peloton* was acting decidedly mundane and mortal.

By contrast, when Merckx was racing in the late Sixties and Seventies, the increasing quality of television footage meant audiences could see for themselves just how far ahead of everyone else he was. Merckx would race, Merckx would win, everyone else would shuffle in behind him. It was hard to make that seem dramatic when he made it seem so easy.

The French, so fond of loss and failure, hated it. Merckx had turned their epic odyssey into just another sport and one with a very clear winner. When Merckx turned up to the 1975 Tour, he'd already won five times. By that point, the begrudging respect of French cycling fans had turned to a sense of moral outrage as their great race devolved into three weeks of watching the Belgian flatten the field, day after day. Merckx had been aware of his detractors for some time. In 1973 he abstained from racing the Tour to focus on the Vuelta. Partly this was because the Spanish cycling authorities had offered him a huge appearance fee. However, he'd also hoped it would placate the increasingly hostile French crowds lining the roads each July. Riding through their abuse had proved unnerving.

He returned in 1974 to beat an aging Raymond Poulidor by eight minutes overall. Poulidor was widely loved by the French. It was his last chance at a Grand Tour victory and it would have meant a great deal to see him in the yellow jersey. Instead, the crowds in Paris got to see yet another Merckx victory. It was a bitter pill. In 1975 the Belgian was lining up for his sixth victory, challenging Jacques Anquetil's title as the most successful Tour de France champion. Meanwhile, the French were rallying behind their new rising star, Bernard Thévenet.

Thévenet was much more in line with French tastes. He had grown up in a country town and paid his dues, gaining selection in his first Tour in 1970 only after two of his teammates came down ill just before the start. That year he went on to win a stage in the mountains and then returned in 1971 to take fourth overall. In 1972 he came ninth and won two more stages despite crashing so badly he temporarily lost his memory. In 1973 he was French national champion. With Merckx absent from that year's Tour, Thévenet came second to the brilliant and temperamental Ocaña. As he stood on the podium in the tricolour jersey, the French couldn't have been prouder.

Ill and unable to race in 1974, Thévenet returned with a great deal of French anticipation for the 1975 Tour. A new generation of rising stars were also on display, such as the Dutchman Joop Zoetemelk, who'd come second in 1970 and 1971, and Lucien van Impe who, while Belgian, had the benefit in French eyes of not being Eddy Merckx. There was real hope the Tour would be a more open affair, if only Merckx didn't simply flatten all comers and subject everyone to another grim three week parade around France.

Then the race began. On the very first road stage, Merckx attacked with such force he smashed the *peloton* into pieces. On Stage Six he battered home a decisive time trial victory and took the yellow jersey. On Stage Nine he did it again, easily winning the second time trial to assert his superiority. Two days later, the race entered the mountains. Merckx was already in the lead, two and a half minutes ahead of Thévenet. As always, he seemed unbreakable.

On Stage Eleven something finally happened to give the French fans hope. Zoetemelk and Thévenet teamed up to attack and actually managed to drop Merckx, as well as wiping out the rest of their competition. The race held together over the next few days before heading to a summit finish on the Puy de Dôme. Merckx still held a ninety-two second lead over Thévenet but the race was more open than it had been in years.

The Puy de Dôme is an extinct volcano, sticking up 1415 metres with an average gradient of 7.5% over a fourteen kilometre climb. This is deceptive, as the first eight kilometres are relatively mild before going into four kilometres at 10% to 12%. The gradient makes it particularly decisive for overall victory. It's the same road on which Anquetil and Poulidor raced side by side in 1964. It tends to favour the pure climber, being neither steady enough to develop a regular tempo nor short enough to be taken in one Herculean effort. For a rider who can alter rhythm it's possible to burn off those riders, such as Merckx, who relied on strength alone.

For Thévenet, a gifted and astute climber, the Puy de Dôme was his big chance. As the *peloton* moved onto the lower slopes, Lucien Van Impe attacked. At that point, Van Impe was arguably the best climber in the world and, as he pulled away, Thévenet looked at Merckx to see if he'd follow. To his delight, the Belgian was clearly struggling. Thévenet knew his moment had come and threw himself onto the offensive.

When the French fans lining the road on the Puy de Dôme saw Thévenet appear alone they went in to rapture. When Merckx appeared just a few seconds later, the disappointment was palpable. For one French fan, Nello Breton, it was too much. As Merckx loomed towards him, driving forward at growing speed, he swung out, punching the Belgian in the kidney. Watching the video of it, you see Merckx's cadence shift as he's hit. He clutches his side and slumps forward. Already at his limit, the blow gutted him.

Although Merckx kept the yellow jersey, Thévenet had gained time and momentum. Two days later, on Bastille Day, the Frenchman attacked again. As he did so, one of the French fans waved a sign at him; *Merckx is beaten. The Bastille has fallen.* Thévenet took the yellow jersey at the end of the stage and held it all the way into Paris, beating Merckx by a margin of two minutes forty-seven seconds. In 1977, when Merckx returned from illness to race his last ever Tour, he could only manage sixth place, twelve minutes thirty-eight seconds behind Thévenet, who took his second Tour victory.

To their credit the French fans were appalled by Nello Breton's lack of sportsmanship. As soon as he threw the punch, they set upon him, holding him in place until the police returned to arrest him. That said, they still celebrated Thévenet's win. It meant more to them than a record sixth victory for Merckx. The Belgian's physical superiority had gifted him dominance. Thévenet, on the other hand, had struggled for years to earn his yellow jersey. Whatever the impact of the punch, there was a sense the 1975 Tour had gone to the rider who deserved it most.

ASCENT

I have always enjoyed the etiquette exchanged when one cyclist overtakes another. Depending on their varying speeds, this may be a nod of recognition, passing comment on the weather, or brief discussion on component or wheel choice. There is, however, a particular class of rider to whom being passed is perceived as a grave conflict. As a general rule, this type is more likely to be wearing matching trade team lycra, using high-end equipment, and sporting Lance Armstrong paraphernalia. Notably, they also tend to be men.

On a couple of occasions I've made the mistake of attempting to exchange pleasantries with them only to find myself rebuffed with a cold silence and a glare that lets me know they don't fraternise with amateurs on mid-range

Orbeas. They evidently operate in a sphere whereby even the laziest Sunday afternoon spin takes on an aura of competition and the whole world is their unsuspecting opposition.

Some time back I was making a leisurely trip up Norton Summit, a reasonably relaxed climb with a series of short ramps interspersed by false flats and spectacular views. On one of the lower ramps, I was overtaken by one of those guys who can be described as a 'pseudo pro'. He'd been struggling away behind me for some time, mashing a big gear with the disjointed rhythm of a high school band. It was horrible. When we got onto a false flat, I slowed down to admire the view, whereupon he finally caught up with me and made a big show of overtaking, sprinting past as close as he could, splendid with his matching kit and high end Italian bike. I turned to say hello but he was busy pretending he hadn't noticed me. Unfortunately for him, the false flat ended, the road started to slope back up and he slowed down so badly he started to wobble. Inevitably I overtook him. He looked devastated.

This is the problem with treating everything like a competition. Inevitably you will be beaten. This basic truth is such an innate part of everyday life that those who ignore it must endure the almost continual indignity of being defeated. Unfortunately, there are a great many men in particular who can't reconcile themselves to this fact, and spend their lives trying to prove themselves winners. This leaves them in a continual state of discontent, chasing each elusive win until their nerves are frayed and their personalities soured. Inevitably, they grow increasingly disgruntled and unpleasant which, ironically, often exacerbates their desire to win, leading them to slake their angst through conquest over the most innocuous situations.

For those who see the world as a constant competition,

cycling is a terrible sport to engage in, and ascending is the very worst platform imaginable. Certainly, mashing away at big gears in the hills can make the muscles in your legs ripple and bulge. Unfortunately it makes them ripple and bulge with lactic acid. You can't beat a mountain. The mountain doesn't care. It is neither victorious nor interested in your defeat but, if you approach riding it as a competition, you will inevitably reach a point where you're too worn out or the road is simply too steep and you lose all love for the bike.

There's a common mantra that 'Pain is just weakness leaving the body.' This a sort of colloquial rendition of René Descarte's famous maxim of 'Cogito ergo sum', or 'I think therefore I am.' Descartes was a French philosopher and mathematician, whose work in the mid-seventeenth century had an immense influence on Western thought. It's doubtful he thought his ideas would provide an inspirational motivator for would-be athletes in the twenty-first century. Regardless, there are those who believe the brain can force the body into compliance. In this light, cycling becomes a process of willing your body to do what your brain wants, as if the two are separate entities. Nothing could be further from the truth. This is a lesson I learnt the hard way when I first began cycling in earnest. When I try to bring my body to the heel of my will, I either vomit, lose control of my bowels, or both. If you go into an ascent with the belief it'll end when you've 'conquered the mountain' you're in for a terrible awakening.

A good ascent is, almost by definition, painful and if a hill becomes too easy one will usually seek a new challenge. Cycling is a physically demanding passion and it does force a familiar relationship with pain. The problem comes when you mistake each climb as an obstacle to be defeated, rather than valuing it for the act of ascending itself. When we look at the likes of Pantani, Gaul, or Ocaña, the myth that surrounds their climbing was the role it played in unifying the various warring elements of their malfunctioning personalities. This may sound lofty but then a large part of cycling's appeal is its hypnotic, all encompassing rhythm. Moore writes of the first time he saw Robert Millar climbing:

> As he climbed the mountain his head bobbed gently and easily to the rhythm of the pedals. His style was unusual but fluid and efficient. His left knee flicked in and then out at the top of the pedal stroke, following a consistent, smooth pattern. His eyes were focused a few yards in front, yet they also appeared vacant, expressionless.

It reads like a description of an out-of-body experience, yet the sensation is one attained almost routinely on a decent climb. Pain is an inherent part of this; it absorbs all other emotions and draws one's focus onto the moment of the ascent. The aim isn't to overcome it but to lose oneself to the rhythm of the heart and lungs, the endorphin release attained through athletic endurance, and the buzz of extended oxygen debt. The combination of these elements lends ascending its meditative, quasi-religious undertone.

When it comes to cycling as a professional sport, this religious element is deeply embedded within the high mountains. Cycling has its patroness saint, the Madonna del Ghisallo, appointed by Pope Piux XII in 1949, and its own chapel on the ascent of the Il Ghisallo in Italy, where cyclists can come in pilgrimage to see relics like the bikes and jerseys of Coppi, Bartali, and their ilk.

The same Catholic lexicon is evident in the coverage of the great climbers, with legendary ascents described like religious trials, the riders like martyrs, and the outcome like an epiphany. When Gaul made the ascent of the Monte Bondone on his way to winning the 1956 Giro, *L'Equipe*'s

Christophe Penot described:

> His face deformed by cold-induced swelling, his lips thick
> and blue, as if ready to burst, and his eyes silent stammering
> cries of torment and fear. For, as sensational as he was on
> apocalyptic days, the Luxembourger thought for a while
> that he might not reach the summit, pedalling on autopilot
> without being able to fathom the stakes ... but who could
> understand?

Similarly, when Pantani was asked about his attitude to
climbing he gave the famously cryptic response, 'I love the
mountains but in the moment of exertion I am filled with
deep hatred. So I try to shorten the suffering.' Notably,
these descriptions aren't about winning but about something
more personal, hinting at the unspeakably profound. In their
compendium of Europe's great climbs, Daniel Friebe and Pete
Goding write that the most famous ascents transcend their
status as sporting stadiums to take on the aura of pilgrimage
and sacred site:

> Although most of us will never play football at Wembley
> or cricket at Lords, we can ride the Galibier or the Ventoux
> tomorrow – but we must know that it will hurt. To deprive
> oneself of that challenge, though, would be to bridle at the
> drawbridge to a private wonderland where the wheels of
> a bicycle point the high and winding way to pure elation.

They're right. Climbing does produce a sense of elation. It's
painful but beyond that is a sublime sensation that's hard to
describe to the non-cyclist.

On one of my favourite climbs I am occasionally overtaken
by a thin, elderly man, riding an immaculately maintained
steel frame. He always cheerfully wishes me a good day and I
always feel strangely comforted to see him glide past. Watching

him disappear up the road, I compare the experience to that of being overtaken by the aggressive pseudo pro and his compatriots with their Livestrong wristbands. The old man is a brilliant climber and I've never felt a sense of shame at being overtaken, even though he is twice my age. On the contrary, he has come to embody a sense of the sublime; a cadence so perfect he can enter into a state of euphoria seemingly at will. As he passes me his eyes glitter through his glasses, he beams benevolently at me in a state of rapture. Each time I watch him disappear into the low hanging clouds with a sense of awe.

It's for this reason that cycling makes icons out of diminutive climbers like Marco Pantani and Charly Gaul. They embody not so much strength but the potential for transcendence. As they hurled themselves into the most brutal of climbs the physical pain of the ascent produced a meditative moment that reconciled the extremities of their personalities. That this was a transitory harmony, afforded only by ascending the sport's holiest mountains, only added to their legend.

This is the same reason people hated Merckx. His pure physical supremacy removed the sense of the cyclist finding within the ascent a rare, transcendent and sublime contact with something sacred. Ultimately, when we watch cycling we hope to see a validation of the same sentiments that draw so many of us to riding a bike in the first place. We hope to see instances through which, win or lose, people encounter some hidden rhythm within their core and brush against their own otherwise obscured internal truth.

Of course, very few people go to the same lengths as Nello Breton in actually punching a sporting icon but then there have been very few cyclists who exercised the same dominance as Merckx. The only comparable Tour winner was Armstrong, who was also widely hated by the French.

Beyond the blatancy of his doping, his fault was the same; his wins seemed clinical and formulaic, not born out of some greater mythic truth. He found a way to make the rapturous act of riding a bike look cheap, as if he'd turned the works of Goethe, Shakespeare, Proust, or Tolstoy into a *Die Hard* sequel.

July 27th, 1998
Grenoble –Les Deux Alpes

PANTANI, ULLRICH, AND THE DESCENT OF THE GALIBIER

All action must, to a certain extent, be planned in a mere twilight, which in addition not unfrequently – like the effect of a fog or moonshine – gives to things exaggerated dimensions and an unnatural appearance.
— *Carl von Clausewitz*

There's a scene in the documentary *Hell on Wheels* in which veteran sprinter Erik Zabel questions the wisdom of descending at eighty kilometres an hour on a bicycle with narrow wheels and wire-pull breaks. The footage that accompanies it is the descent of the Galibier, eighteen kilometres of weaving, narrow road precariously placed along the side of the mountain.

While the Galibier, at 2645m, is occasionally used for stage summits, it's usually used as a hurdle before the final climb of Alpe d'Huez or the run-in to classic Tour towns like Morzine. Its length and height break the *peloton* up and produce decisive gaps between the race leaders. The road looks like someone has stuck a single lane on the side of a cliff face; the surface above the tree line is rock and patchy grass. Depending on how low the cloud cover is, the camera footage will either show the surrounding alpine passes — the Col de Joux Plane, the Tèlégraph, and the Col du Lautaret — or just a thick wall of fog and drizzle. The riders go down it in long, drawn out lines.

Usually a descent brings groups of riders back together, as the time gaps formed on the ascent are swallowed back up. The sheer length of the Galibier allows the opposite to happen, albeit on rare occasions. It was on the descent here in 1998 that 'Ice-cream' Jan Ullrich, lost the Tour to Marco Pantani, who took nine minutes out of the German, including four on the descent. On rain soaked roads, it wasn't just that Pantani forced a gap over Ullrich but that he threw his rival into a state of total confusion. Ullrich lumbered down the mountain, only resuming the subsequent climbs with the support of his lieutenants. He never got his rhythm back, lost nine minutes on the stage, and never won a Tour again.

Stage Fifteen of the 1998 Tour was blessed with appalling weather. Watching the stage, the camera footage breaks up while Phil Liggett and Paul Sherwin's crisp British accents deliver their usual array of exuberant catchphrases and clichés. The mist and grey rock combine with the sheen of water on the road to fog up the motorcycle cameras. Occasionally Ullrich hauls himself into the frame, the yellow jersey glowing on his back. The temperature was down to four degrees Celsius, alternating between rain and low cloud.

From the moment of his attack on the lower slopes of the Galibier, Pantani eclipsed everyone else. Catching the last of the day's breakaway, his cadence remained fluid, while they struggled to keep on his back wheel. By the time he hit the summit he was already two minutes seven seconds ahead of Ullrich, less than a minute off the time required to put him in the race lead. At the top of the ascent, the road was covered in cloud, with a layer of water on the ground. He sat up as he hit the peak and someone ran out and handed him a rain jacket. For a couple of hundred metres, as he began to pick up speed on the first part of the descent, he struggled to get the jacket on, with it flapping wildly on one arm. Eventually he stopped and dragged it on properly, allowing a couple of riders to catch up, including that year's polka dot jersey winner, Christophe Ronero and Rodolfo Massi.

The three of them started the descent together. The rain was so heavy that it blurred the TV images until they looked like painted figures. Pantani gained momentum quickly, leaning through the corners and sprinting to gain speed on the flats, while Massi and Ronero chased to keep up. The motorbike with the cameraman fell further and further behind, catching the riders only briefly as they slowed through the hairpin bends.

Back in the main group, second placed Bobby Julich almost crashed on the first turn, scraping behind a parked truck after losing his line. Lumbering after him, Ullrich was bewildered. With the steady fall of rain, the race coverage quickly devolved into a series of blurry images of team cars sliding across the road. About half way down Pantani became the virtual leader of the race, having gained more than three minutes on the stumbling Ullrich.

After that, the race footage broke up entirely. At some point Pantani got away from his companions and when the television coverage returned it was unclear whether he had attacked before the road started ascending again, or simply bolted away because no one else was willing to take such extreme risks on a wet descent. Behind him, Ullirch was still lost in the fog.

'Lost in a fog' pretty much describes Ullrich for the rest of the stage. Heavier than Pantani, he should have had an advantage on the descent. Instead, by the time he hit the beginning of the next climb he had already lost so much time the Tour was gone. For the Italian, it was the finest moment of his career. On the ascent, he attained a perfect rhythm that, on the descent, translated into a perfect cognition. Every action he performed seemed preordained and perfect. The Italian sporting paper *La Gazetta dello Sport* wrote,

> Among the French Alps battered by the storm, above the clouds of imagination, rises a god of the sport: he's called Marco, the strong name of an evangelist.

Unlike Ullirch, Pantani could make sense of the twists and the turns in the road as he plummeted down them at high speed.

Even after his doping had became undeniable, Pantani's attack over the Galibier remains one of the finest moments in Tour history; one of those rare points at which someone seems to possess a perfect harmony between themselves, their world, and their actions. More than any other incident that year, it defined Pantani's first and only Tour win. Of course, neither Pantani nor Ullrich ever won another Tour again. The next year, 1999, marked the start of the Armstrong era, when brute strength, a powerful team, and a carefully orchestrated doping program came to replace such virtuoso performances.

DESCENT

At one level, the difference between Ullrich and Pantani on the ascent can be measured out, at least in part, by muscle to weight ratios. The 1998 Tour was a good year for climbers. Assuming their blood values were roughly the same (reviews found both of them positive for EPO use), Pantani would have had an advantage. He was 1.72 metres tall and weighed under 60 kilograms, compared to Ullrich's 1.83m and weight fluctuating over 70 kilograms. On the descents, though, Ullrich should have been at an advantage. His greater weight should have induced a greater forward momentum, allowing him to catch up to Pantani relatively easily. Instead he lost a further three minutes on the descent, one of the few times a rider lost a Tour after being gapped going downhill, rather than the more traditional attack by a climber heading up to a summit finish.

The reasons for this are obvious when you watch old race footage. Ullrich was a rider who found a steady rhythm and stuck to it. By sheer force, he could usually set a rhythm few others could match. However, once his rhythm was interrupted, he tended to fall apart. If you watch old footage of the Galibier descent in the 1998 Tour, when Pantani attacks you can see Ullrich maintain his rhythm, confident that the Italian's attack-and-rest style can be countered by a consistent tempo. As he gets closer to the pinnacle of the Galibier, with Bobby Julich attacking him as well, he starts to get flustered. It's as if he can only digest the world, one pedal stroke at a time. Eventually he falls apart, not so much because of a physical failure as a cognitive one. By the time he hits the descent, he's fallen apart completely. Watching him go through hairpin bends is painful. Where Pantani corners like a bird wheeling, Ullrich grinds through like a truck doing a u-turn. You can almost hear the gears mashing. Lost in the fog, it's as if he can't figure out what he's meant to do.

Of course, cognition is a big part of descending. Being a naturally confused person, I always had trouble with it. I developed a love of ascending well before I began to enjoy the descents. If anything the latter was a necessary aside to the former. After the simple joy of picking out a rhythm on a long, steep climb, I would descend in a bewilderment of caution and terror, emerging from the bottom of a hill with sore hands from constantly gripping the brakes, and shell-shocked nerves from poorly plotted corners and high speed encounters with motorcyclists.

Laboriously my descending improved. I used to wet myself and start crying as soon as my speedometer crept over 45km/h, whereas now I can maintain that speed for a good sixty seconds before I'm overwhelmed with blind panic. In my attempts to learn to descend better, there are certain pieces of advice I have taken to heart. On a practical level, I'm told it's a good idea to put your weight into your pedals, rather than onto your seat. This helps lower your centre of gravity. On an open road, you're supposed to keep the pedals horizontal to the ground. Then, when you go into a turn, lower the pedal on the outside of the corner and push your weight down into it. But more widely, the major things I've learnt about descending have all been psychological. Whereas the ascent is about the rhythm of body, going downhill places the stress on the brain.

There's two cognitive themes that I've found are essential to understanding descending. The first is the notion of 'the Line' — the imaginary strip upon which one can manoeuvre a bicycle without losing balance and crashing. The second is 'the Fear' — the nerve-racking, crippling terror that something terrible is about to happen. These themes are interconnected and contain greater metaphysical truths, which I can summarize as follows.

To begin with the Line; as I understand it the average human brain is designed principally for walking. To deal with the higher speeds involved in cycling it scans the road for the twenty metres or so in front of you, detects any obstacles, and pre-empts a path along which you and your bike can manoeuvre without losing balance. You subconsciously stick to that path while your brain processes the next section of road, constantly drawing up a new path as you move over the existing one. This ever-extending ribbon of forward trajectory is the Line.

At a low speed and on flat terrain the Line is wide and generous to the point that you don't actually notice it. In such conditions, variations in direction or sudden obstacles (like a motorist opening their door or a pot hole you didn't notice) are easily avoided because you have enough reaction time and low enough forward momentum to change direction without losing balance.

At high speeds, the Line can narrow down to a couple of centimetres. At speeds of over about 40km/h your brain is obligated to process information at a much faster rate and the higher volume of momentum makes the bicycle much more sensitive to steering adjustments. In these conditions, the process of picking a good line becomes far more obvious.

At very high speed your brain reaches a point where it is required to process so much information that it is at risk of overload. As your momentum increases, your brain must become selective. What it chooses to ignore is almost as important as what it chooses to digest because such a large portion of its power is required to successfully plot a clear forward path and enable minute, subconscious decisions to be made as to how and when you should shift your weight to steer.

To that end, the average descending cyclist isn't looking at the ground five or even ten metres in front of them, and there's not much point to doing so because it's gone by the time you shift your glance downwards. Nor do you look at the obstacles upon it. If you look at, say, a broken bottle or a pothole, you will tend to find yourself steering towards it subconsciously. Generally, the descending cyclist will rely on an otherwise unique pattern of thought, scanning the ground well ahead of them, registering and picking their line, and in doing so giving their brain those valuable milliseconds required for it to tell their body how much weight to shift in what direction.

As I see it, to become comfortable at descending you need to train your brain to be more efficient in focusing on the clearest and most suitable path ahead, without getting bogged down in unnecessary details or spending too much time digesting any single fact.

There are obvious metaphysical connotations contained within this, relating to the degree to which you should be looking into the future (neither too near nor too far ahead), the amount of attention you should devote to petty obstacles, and the volume of information your brain can successfully digest to track a forward path for you. In cycling, as in life, your patterns of comprehension are changed by practice and, in both cases, the primary impediment is 'the Fear'.

The Fear is the part of your brain that tells you that around the next corner, just out of sight but headed directly towards you, there's some jerk in a four wheel drive gulping down a burger with such devotion he hasn't noticed he's merged onto the wrong side of the road. The Fear is the thing that keeps reminding you that you're going so fast you can't stop and can't steer properly. The Fear is the thing that tells you that if the guy with the burger did appear on the wrong side of the road, your brakes would be useless to stop you and would, instead, simply make it impossible for you to steer.

Like the Line, the Fear is always present. You just don't normally notice it when you're plodding along a side street at 22km/h on your way home from the shops. At 70 km/h, however, the Fear is a lot more obvious for the simple reason that you can kill yourself at those speeds reasonably easily. I've heard it said that the Veil of Mortality is thin and, from most angles, perfectly transparent, making it appear invisible. But, viewed from a particular angle, it becomes strikingly obvious that it's not only very close but extremely flimsy. The Veil of Mortality is a bit like a really well polished plate glass window, which you don't notice until the light reflects off of it or you walk into it. Riding down hills is one of the points when it's easy to see and thus requires you to develop strategies through which to deal with the Fear.

I have a great deal of experience with the Fear. I'd say it's a fairly ingrained part of my personality but until I started cycling I didn't really have a way of explaining or grappling with it. Cycling teaches you about it because it exposes you to near death incidents reasonably frequently and never is this more obvious than when you're hurtling into an unexpected hairpin bend at 50km/h. The simple answer to combating the Fear is that you need to stop thinking about it. This isn't easily done. Learning to suppress the Fear is a habit rather than event, and a habit one becomes well versed in if one rides down mountains (or, in my case, foothills) on a regular basis.

Like the Line, combating the Fear is essentially an issue of comprehension. The Fear feeds off thinking about scenarios you cannot change. The theoretical guy in a four wheel drive with the burger is a case in point – he exists always slightly out of view, just that little bit too far ahead for you to take any action but enough for you to theorize about until you start to panic. Unless one chooses to live in a cocoon, such risks are unavoidable. The lesson we can take from this is that it is extremely unhealthy to think too far into the future because you can't do much about it anyway.

What I try to do is think about the Line, focusing on continually tracking and plotting that narrow path over the next twenty, thirty, forty, and fifty metres. I find that if you devote your attention to that short distance, then you will almost certainly possess the reactions to avoid most obstacles in your path. I've avoided some terrible crashes coming down Magill Road because my brain, devoted entirely to that narrow line in front of me, has managed to detect and process not only the various cracks in the road and parked cars but also morons doing weird reverse u-turns across three lanes of traffic from an adjoining side street on the opposite side of the road. When your brain is devoted to the short-term it can work at such an optimal level it will steer you in the right direction over the long-term, both on and off the bike.

STAGE 16

July 21st, 1934
Ax-les-Thermes to Luchon

RENÉ VIETTO RIDES BACK UP THE MOUNTAIN

The gods to each ascribe a differing lot:
Some enter at the portal. Some do not!
— *Ford Madox Ford*

Antonin Magne won both the 1931 and 1934 Tours in a particular style. The journalist Geoffrey Wheatcroft credits him as 'the first truly professional rider to win by means of dedication and training rather than courage or flair.' It sounds like a backhanded compliment but, before Magne, cycling was a sport characterised by primitive equipment, ever-shifting rules, and ad-hoc training. After him, cautious preparation and the calculated reduction of risk began to replace fortune, brute strength, and audacity. Later, this would make him one of the sport's greatest *director sportifs*, guiding Louison Bobet to his three victories in the early Fifties, but at the time he seemed so austere and serious he was nicknamed 'The Monk'.

Despite the depth of their careful preparation, his victories are still proof that one's actions are always subject to fortune. At the lead of the 1931 Tour, he had two stages left to race when he was kept up late with insomnia. In an attempt to calm his nerves, he started reading his backlog of fan mail. By chance, he opened a letter from a fan who just happened to be a neighbour of one of his rivals, Belgian Gaston Rebry. The neighbour had overheard gossip around town that Rebry and his Belgian team planned to attack on a particularly difficult stretch of road on the second-to-last day of the Tour. He wrote to warn Magne of the threat.

Sure enough, the next day Rebry attacked precisely on the spot predicted, taking his team leader, Jef Demuysere, with him. The two were a formidable combination and their attack was so carefully planned and executed it opened a seventeen-minute gap on the *peloton*. Rebry went on to win the stage and Demuysere gapped all of the other GC contenders. Fortunately Magne's chance reading of the letter had allowed him to prepare his defence. He'd rallied his teammates in preparation for the attack and they'd dragged him up to Demuysere's wheel just in time. He was the only rider who managed to stay with the Belgians. It allowed him to hold his lead and take his first Tour victory, relegating Demuysere to second place.

Magne was so exhausted that he didn't race the following year. It wasn't until 1934 he came back as the captain of one of the strongest French squads of all time, including 1933 winner George Speicher, Charles Pélisser (brother of Henri), Roger Lapébie (who won the Tour in 1937), René Le Grève (who went on to win no less than six stages of the 1936 Tour), and Maurice Archambaud (who wore the yellow jersey for nine days in 1933 and would later set a World Hour record). At the bottom of the pile was a twenty-year old former hotel bellboy called René Vietto.

The inclusion of Vietto was contentious. He was young and inexperienced but he was also something of a climbing prodigy, conscripted into the team to help Magne in the mountains. He had a rough start, with flat tires on the opening two stages costing him huge swathes of time but, as soon as the race hit the Alps, he began to shine. He won Stage Seven to Grenoble, taking a three and a half minute gap over the rest of the field. Just two days later he won again, riding first over the two major climbs to win alone after a high-speed descent. Then, on Stage Eleven, he took his third victory in Cannes, where he'd once worked in a hotel. The race was half over and he was in third place overall, behind the Italian Giuseppe Martano and his own team leader Antonin Magne. Before the Tour, there'd been debate as to whether Vietto was good enough for the French team. Now the discussion was centred on whether he should be leading it.

Hoping for disunity in the French team, Martano and his Italian squad attacked relentlessly. In the Pyrenees they grew particularly determined, throwing the experienced Ettore Meini and the in-form Adriono Vignoli on the offensive in an attempt to drive a wedge between Vietto and his leader. It almost worked. On Stage Fifteen the race went up a twenty-five kilometre climb, with Magne and Vietto trying to break away from Martano and teammates. On the descent, Magne crashed, breaking his wheel. The Italians attacked, hoping Vietto would betray his leader and chase them to keep his podium place. Instead, he dutifully stopped, gave his front wheel to his leader, and waited for the team car to appear.

This was the start of the Vietto legend. The team car was miles behind him, locked up in the race caravan. As the head of the race rode on without him, Vietto was forced to wait, clutching his broken bike, while his chance of a podium finish disintegrated. He sat on a wall at the side of the road and cried out of pure frustration. It just so happened there was a photographer and a journalist on hand to capture the moment. The resulting image was on the front pages of the French sporting dailies the next day, while *L'Auto* journalist (and future Tour director) Jacques Goddet turned the incident into a moral fable of one Frenchman's capacity for loyalty and commitment to the common good. Henri Desgrange apparently hated Goddet's story; he had only begrudgingly started relaxing rules around *domestiques* giving their team leaders mechanical support and didn't like the idea that Magne's victory would be seen as reliant on Vietto's sacrifice.

For once, however, Desgrange didn't get much say in the matter. The following day, on Stage Sixteen, Vietto cemented both his own reputation for martyrdom and Magne's overall victory with what remains one of the Tour's great stories of self-sacrifice. He had crossed the first big climb at the head of the race and protected Magne as they moved onto the second big ascent, the Portet d'Aspet. There was still one climb to go, through the Ares Pass. The Italian Adriano Vignoli was well off the front, racing for the stage victory with France's other *domestique* deluxe, Roger Lapébie in hot pursuit. This left Vietto alone with Magne, fending off Martano's attacks. It was tough going. With three days left in the mountains, the Italian knew his chances to win the Tour were limited and was throwing everything he had at it.

As they made the descent, Vietto disappeared down the road. Behind him, Magne hit a rock and crashed again, destroying his back wheel. With no other French riders around him and with the team car miles behind, Magne's luck looked set to break. He found himself stuck with a broken bike while his two biggest threats for victory, Martano and his own teammate Vietto, were battling it out for the yellow jersey. The Tour seemed lost. It was unthinkable to Magne that his young *domestique* would sacrifice another opportunity to secure a position on the podium.

As it turned out, Magne had underestimated Vietto's loyalty. The younger rider had assumed his team leader was just behind him and kept up a steady pace after the descent, expecting the group to re-form. When one of the course marshals, patrolling the race on motorbike, mentioned Magne had crashed, Vietto immediately turned around, rode back up the mountain and gave his leader his wheel.

When Magne saw his young teammate riding back up the hill to hand over his bike, he couldn't believe it. Veitto had been given the chance to race for the win, and instead he turned around, utterly ruining his own chances. Magne chased down Martano and cemented his second Tour win. Vietto, however, lost a further eight minutes waiting yet again for the team car. It was the end of his shot at a Tour victory. Despite another stage win, he lost time in the final time trial (the Tour's first ever individual time trial) to finish fifth. In Paris, he complained bitterly that Magne didn't know how to ride a bike and subjected himself to crashes through technical incompetence. Magne, however, was gushing in his praise of the younger rider, whose loyalty had sealed his second Tour victory.

Vietto wasn't placated, even after joining Magne's victory lap, being declared the 'Moral Winner' and awarded the King of the Mountains prize. He was seven minutes behind a podium place, less than the amount of time he'd spent waiting for the team car after giving Magne his wheel, and it grated. By the end of his first Grand Tour, he'd already begun to develop the reputation for bitterness that would define him for the next decade-and-a-half, telling journalists, 'My main problem was that I was so unlucky.'

BAD LUCK

Magne's ten-year career finished in 1939, by which point he was thirty-five, had won two Tours with a total of ten individual stage victories, the 1936 World Championship, and three editions of the prestigious Grand Prix des Nations. As a marker of an illustrious and full career, his final victory was on the final stage of the 1938 Tour de France, when he was awarded a joint stage victory along with André Leducq, after the two of them crossed the line together. It was the end of a golden era of French cycling, of which Magne had been at the head.

By contrast, Rene Vietto's career followed a somewhat different trajectory. In 1934, he'd been the heir apparent. While his King of the Mountains and stage victories marked him as France's greatest climber, his sacrifice on Stages Fifteen and Sixteen had made him a media darling. He'd lost the Tour through loyalty to his aging leader and it had seemed only a matter of time before his self-sacrifice would be rewarded.

Unfortunately, fate follows a different path than justice. In 1935, the esprit de corps that had held the French team together began to dissolve. The Belgian Romain Maes took the lead on day one, and became one of only a handful of riders to wear the yellow jersey for Tour's entire length. He had a bit of a head start when, after crossing a railway line just ahead of the *peloton*, a train appeared, delaying the chase and letting him take the stage win with a one minute lead, which he held onto for the rest of the race.

While Vietto won Stages Six and Nine, he only placed eighth overall, more than an hour behind the leader. At twenty-one years of age he still seemed to have ample time. Unfortunately, he was mixing his bitterness with a steady diet of champagne, ultimately drawing the ire of Henri Desgrange. The Tour's founding father was at the end of his career but age had failed to mellow him in the slightest. Subsequently, Vietto was refused entry to the 1936 Tour, adding to the growing chip on his shoulder. In 1937 he wasn't even selected and his career flat-lined.

When he finally returned in 1939, Vietto had been demoted to the second tier south-eastern regional French team, albeit as its head. Much to everyone's surprise, he took the yellow jersey on Stage Four and held on to it for eleven days, finally cracking under attack in the Alps to come in second to the Belgian Sylvère Maes. Vietto was still only twenty-five. His style was more versatile than the pure climber of his earlier youth and it seemed like he was back in form, calmer, more consistent, and once again on the cusp of delivering on his early promise. And then the Second World War broke out.

While the Nazis had attempted to keep the Tour going during the war years, the Tour's new director, Jacques Goddet, refused. Regardless, Vietto kept riding professionally despite the patchy calendar of the war years. He was French National Champion in 1941, took two stages in the 1942 Vuelta, and did well in the smaller stage races that were cobbled together in Occupied France. After the war, things were radically different. For one thing, Henri Desgrange had died in 1940. Secondly, the Tour's flagship paper, *L'Auto*, had been refused permission to continue trading, based on its perceived links to Nazi occupation. The new director, Jacques Goddet promptly founded a new publication, *L'Équipe*, with backing from media baron Émilien Amaury.

Goddet himself was under a cloud of collaboration, having supposedly given the Nazis the keys to the Vel D'Hiv velodrome in 1942, whereupon they'd used it to corral eight thousand French jews for deportation to the concentration camps. Émilien Amaury, by contrast, was an undoubted Resistance hero, having fought and been captured in the initial invasion and awarded the Croix de Guerre. Under the code name 'Jupiter', he'd helped found the resistance group Rue de Lille, siphoning off heavily rationed paper supplies for Resistance newspapers and fake identification documents. More than just a financial backer, Amaury offered a degree of nationalist credibility without which the Tour may never have returned.

Goddet and Amaury hit the ground running, with a miniature version of the Tour, the Course du Tour de France, run in 1946 with five stages between Monaco and Paris. Vietto, plagued by saddle sores, dropped out of contention but shepherded his protégé, Apo Lazaridès, to victory. Just like Magne in 1934, Lazaridès owed his win to Vietto, and once again the French press were quick to heap him with praise.

It wasn't a campaign entirely without personal glory. Vietto came in second. However, third place was taken by another rider with a good deal of pent-up bile; the cantankerous, tenacious, diminutive Jean Robic. With nicknames as flattering as 'The Hobgoblin of Brittany Moore' and 'Old Leatherhead', Robic had somehow managed to turn professional in 1943, making a name for himself by finishing Paris-Roubaix with a fractured skull. When the Tour started again in 1947, he was outraged to find himself demoted to the second division France West team and widely overlooked as a Grand Tour contender.

Vietto, however, was one of only a handful of riders who had ridden a Tour before and was finally at the helm of the French national team. From the precocious youth of the 1934 Tour, he was now something of a patriarch, nicknamed 'King René'. Not only did he have more experience than his competition but also the hunger of knowing he was at the very end of his career. Aside from his age, his health was showing the drain of more than a decade as a professional; he'd had three knee operations and had an infected toe amputated (supposedly it's still preserved in formaldehyde, displayed in a bar somewhere in France). The chance to deliver on his early promise was running out.

At first, things seemed to be working; Vietto took the yellow jersey by three and a half minutes after a breakaway on the second stage of the Tour. Luck seemed to be finally with him. Jean Robic, on the other hand, was determined to make his own luck. Still smarting from his demotion, he attacked and won Stage Seven. While he pulled back time on Vietto, his attack had the unfortunate side effect of dragging the Italian Aldo Ronconi into the race lead.

Vietto wasn't too fussed. As the race entered the Alps on Stage Nine, Robic and Vietto crossed the Col de Vars together, but the older rider broke away to win the stage and reclaim the lead. By Stage Eighteen he held a lead of a minute and a half over the Italian Pierre Brambilla. Robic was more than eight minutes down, but continued to attack ferociously, although to no apparent avail. Vietto held the yellow jersey up until Stage Nineteen, with a lead of a minute thirty over the Italian Pierre Brambilla, while Robic was more than eight minutes down.

Stage Nineteen, however, was a mammoth one hundred and forty kilometre time trial, the longest in the Tour's history, and gave ample room for upset. Ironically, it was a similar late and long trial that had cost Vietto his third place in 1934. History repeated itself and he lost almost fifteen minutes along with his chances of winning the Tour forever. Brambilla took the yellow jersey while Robic dragged himself up to within three minutes of the race lead.

With only two stages left to race, and both of them on

the flat, it looked like Brambilla was the definite winner. Robic, however, kept attacking on the final stage with such abandon he forced a gap and arrived in Paris thirteen minutes before Brambilla to take the yellow jersey only on the finish line. Robic was, until Jan Janssen in 1968, the only rider to win a Tour without ever wearing the yellow jersey. Unlike Janssen, he never really looked like a threat and few had taken him seriously. Indeed, the second placed Edouard Fachleitner actually had a better time overall but Robic won through time bonuses and his audacious, freak attack on the final stage.

That was the effective end of Vietto's career. He finished the 1947 race in exactly the same position he'd finished at his debut in 1934; fifth place. While he never did reach the promise of his youth, he left cycling with the unusual record for the most days spent in yellow by a rider who never won the Tour, with a total of twenty-six days all up. It's a record he held right up until 2012, when Fabian Cancellara overtook him, taking the opening prologues in the 2007, 2009 and 2010 Tours and holding the lead until the race entered the mountains. Yet Vietto wasn't simply a *rouleur* who dominated the opening week. He had the style, form and capacity to win. What he lacked was the opportunity.

Partly it was the Second World War that robbed Vietto of his opportunity to win a Tour. He's not unique in this respect. The Italian champions Gino Bartali and Fausto Coppi both endured the same fate. Yet they still had their chance to shine. Bartali, just a few months younger than Vietto, won both a Giro and a Tour after the war, as well as a National Championship and two editions of Milan-San Remo. He retired a national icon, content with his legacy right up until his death at the age of eighty-five. Coppi's early death was tragic but he reached a pinnacle of sporting prowess that secured his place in the history books.

Was Vietto less talented, less deserving, or just less

fortunate? Perhaps it was a mixture of the three but how differently would he be remembered if circumstances had varied just slightly? If he'd stayed with Martano and won the Tour at his first appearance, or even reached the podium, what difference would it have made? Would he have been granted leadership over the French team in 1935? It's hard to believe he was less talented or deserving than 1947 winner Jean Robic. Old Leatherhead never won another Tour and his win that year hinged on luck and tenacity.

Without the interruption of the war, it's hard to believe Vietto couldn't have won at least one Tour victory. He was fifth twice, eighth once, and second once. His initial superiority in the mountains had given way to a more rounded and consistent rider. The fact he was still in contention in the 1947 race, thirteen years after his first tour start, somewhat justifies his own belief that he missed out through misfortune, not lack of skill. Whatever the case, Vietto retired in 1949, bitter at his bad luck and never having reached what he felt was his full potential. Angry at his misfortune, he retired to become a pig farmer and died, aged 74, in 1988.

July 23rd, 2008
Embrun – Alpe d'Huez

THE MEEK INHERIT THE EARTH

Whether Jupiter has allotted to you many more winters or this final one…
be wise, strain the wine, and scale back your long hopes to a short period.
While we speak, envious time will have already fled.
Seize the day, trusting as little as possible in the next.
— *Horace*

The 2008 Tour de France was inexplicably dominated by people who'd been resigned to the position of 'also-rans' throughout the previous decade. That year's winner, Spaniard Carlos Sastre had come fourth in 2006 and fifth in 2007 but had otherwise floated around in the top twenty for the previous decade. His main opponent, the Australian Cadel Evans, had endured a similar fate. After a stunning career racing mountain bikes, he'd placed eighth in his first Tour, fourth in his second, and then lost the 2007 edition to Alberto Contador by a mere twenty-three seconds.

Sastre was moving towards the end of his decade-long career, in which he'd taken top ten positions in all three Grand Tours on no less than ten occasions. Yet for the most part, he'd been consigned to the role of *domestique deluxe* for the Italian Ivan Basso at Bjarne Riis's CSC team. Basso, heir apparent to the Armstrong legacy, was kicked out of the 2006 Tour amid doping accusations. Dropped from Riis's squad, he signed with Lance Armstrong's former team, Discovery, only to be banned by the Italian National Olympic Committee. Discovery replaced him with Alberto Contador but, even after he won the 2007 race, they still pulled their sponsorship. Contador promptly moved to Astana, who were refused entry to the 2008 Tour amid accusations of doping.

With so many of its old stars and big players gone, the 2008 Tour was inevitably going to be different. Armstrong, recently retired and watching from the sidelines, was distinctly unimpressed with the result, particularly after his former *domestique* Christian Vande Velde came in fifth:

> The Tour was a bit of a joke this year. I've got nothing against Sastre … or Christian Vande Velde. Christian's a nice guy but finishing fifth in the Tour de France? Come on!

Vande Velde had just joined Johnathon Vaughter's Slipstream team. Vaughters was another ex-US Postal rider and former *domestique* to Armstrong. The two loathed each other, spatting about US Postal's doping programs with none too subtle innuendo. When Vande Velde and Vaughters proved successful at the Tour, their former boss seemed to take it as a personal affront. Sastre had barely left the top step of the podium before Armstrong was announcing his intention to come out of retirement and race the 2009 Tour, proclaiming, 'I'm doing this for my kids.'

Personally, I loved the 2008 Tour precisely because people

like Sastre and Vande Velde did well. It was the first time I'd seen the race ridden by fallible riders and its form was utterly different. After years of being won by brash, superhuman goliaths, the key contenders were the softly spoken Sastre and the eccentric and emotional Cadel Evans. Out went the testosterone-laden bravado of big men with angry faces, bellowing out their victory cries as they stormed across the line. In came the Race of the Little Guys, who won through persistence, cunning, and strategy.

The race was shaped by factors other than the noticeable absence of Armstrong and his ilk. The Tour's organisers, Amaury Sports Organisation (still bearing the lineage of Émilien Amaury, who'd bankrolled Jacques Goddet's 1947 Tour) were at war with cycling's governing body, the UCI. The ASO had refused to invite teams embroiled in drug scandals, even if they'd been approved by the UCI. That included Astana, home to reigning champion Alberto Contador. Instead, they invited a host of wildcard teams; South Africa's Barloworld, France's Agritubel (home to my favourite rider Jimmy Casper), and Jonathon Vaughter's Slipstream-Chipotle, whose modern argyle patterned lycra was like a red flag to the bulls of the Armstrong era.

The ASO added insult to injury by handing over doping controls to the French Cycling Federation and the Italian National Olympic Committee, making an open display of their distrust for the UCI's record for catching cheats. It worked; third placed Jay-Z lookalike Bernard Kohl was stripped of his accolades just after the race. On Stage Twelve, the entire Saunier Duval team was kicked out after their star rider, Ricardo Riccò, tested positive. He'd spent the whole race taunting the doping agencies. Aside from riding around with a picture of Marco Pantani in his pocket, he'd attempted to elude a drug test on Stage Four but got caught in traffic.

After disgracing his team, he was sacked and spent the night at a police station. Two years later he attempted a comeback, which ended when he was rushed to hospital, reputedly after a failed self-administered blood transfusion.

The immaculate consistency of a well-doctored team or the tireless dominance of a handful of riders disappeared. Fatigue and strategy returned to the race, making it a war of attrition rather than one of bold and sweeping attacks.

The race began to take shape on Stage Seven with a bumpy course designed for breakaways letting Luis Leon Sanchez take the win. Behind him, Sastre's CSC team used their big *rouleur* Fabian Cancellera and Stuart O'Grady to split the *peloton*, and forced the first sorting of the favourites. The race stripped down to Sastre and his teammates Frank and Andy Schleck, the Russian Denis Menchov, Spaniard Alejandro Valverde, the Basque climber Samuel Sanchez, and Cadel Evans.

The next day they were back on the flat, where Jimmy Casper managed to crash even before the race had started after getting his handlebars caught in the wheel of the rider in front of him. Stage Nine saw the first major ascents in the Pyrenees, including the Peyresourde and the Aspin. Cadel Evans crashed heavily, injuring his collarbone but racing on regardless. The mountains shaped the race. Without the recuperative properties of EPO, the conservation of energy became paramount.

As the race moved into the Alps, the lead group was quickly whittled away to just four riders, all within less than a minute of each other. At the end of Stage Sixteen, Sastre was in fourth position, forty-nine seconds behind his own teammate Frank Schleck. The soon-to-be-disgraced Bernard Kohl was in second with a seven-second gap, and Evans was third, a further second behind him. Fifth placed Denis Menchov, who had won the previous year's Vuelta, was just over a minute off the lead.

With the time gaps so close, the final stages became a tense, psychological battle, with the riders torn between conserving precious energy and seizing the chance to make a decisive move. There was no margin for error. Someone would have to make a decision to attack and, if they failed, it was unlikely they'd have the reserves left for a repeat effort.

With five stages left to go, only two chances remained for a definitive assault on the overall classification. The first was Stage Seventeen's ascent of Alpe d'Huez and the second the fifty-three kilometre time trial on the penultimate day. Of the two riders who would take the top steps of the podium in Paris, these final stages provoked different responses. Cadel Evans had placed his bet that he could exit the mountains with some minor deficit to the superior climbing skills of Sastre and Frank Schleck, and then regain lost time in the final time trial. It was a strategy of energy conservation; more subtle than the drug-fuelled attacks of the previous years but loaded with suspense. Evans was deliberately losing time with the hope of reserving his energies for the final day.

Sastre, by contrast, knew he couldn't gain time on Evans in a time trial. He also knew that he faced competition from his own teammate, Frank Schleck, aided by his younger brother Andy. The three of them shared leadership in the elite CSC team, owned and managed by enigmatic *director sportif*, Bjarne Riis.

Sastre's relationship with Riis was somewhat tense at the best of times. In his autobiography, Riis recalls their relationship by writing, 'Our conversations were a kind of battle.' By contrast, he was close to the Schlecks. It put Sastre in a tense position. To win, he had to attack at just the right moment with just enough velocity to gain time on Evans, yet simultaneously avoid being pre-emptively attacked by either Frank or Andy Schleck. It became an exercise in who would blink first, pressurized by three weeks of hard racing.

As Stage Seventeen made its way toward the Alpe d'Huez, CSC's *rouleurs* pushed up the speed, burning off as much of their competition as possible with a blistering pace over the Galibier and the Col de la Croix de Fer. At the foot of the Alpe, their dominance as a team was paying off, with the Schlecks, Sastre and their *domestique-deluxe* Kurt-Asle Arvesen controlling the race. By contrast, Evans had just one rider, veteran Belgian Mario Aerts. Only a small and elite collection of riders remained around them; Denis Menchov, Sammy Sanchez, David Moncoutie, Alejandro Valverde, Christian Vande Velde, and, racing for the wildcard South African team Barloworld, a young Chris Froome.

On the lower slopes, the race followed the endless shadowboxing that had marked the whole Tour. As the lead group thinned, the sense of pressure grew. It was increasingly obvious that any mistake would entirely reshape the race's outcome. Traditionally, the first attack tends to fail, and few opportunities for a second are afforded. This is one of the key differences of the post-doping era; the capacity to recover from the physical drain of an offensive is much lower, and thus the investment of one's energy must be more exact.

Logically one would have expected one of the outsiders, like Samuel Sanchez, to launch first in the attempt to gain a stage victory, while the contest between the overall favourites would continue simmering until the last hairpin bends before the summit. Instead, Sastre made his first attack with just over thirteen kilometres to go. Behind him, the rest of the group seemed unwilling to waste energy so early into the climb. Eventually Evans' *domestique*, Mario Aerts, began to drag the race back together.

Ahead of him, Sastre slowed his pace to study the situation, watching as Aerts pulled the group within metres of his back wheel. Then he launched his second attack and behind him, the lead group started to crumble; Menchov disappeared and the lead riders began to fight among each other. At eleven kilometres to go Evans finally began to panic and to chase in earnest, whereupon both of the Schleck brothers alternated in their attacks, aiming to break his rhythm. Yet there seemed to be no cohesive strategy; instead the continued spats prevented any of them from making a decisive manoeuvre.

Sastre, by contrast, remained utterly fixated on the finish line. Over the remaining ten kilometres of the ascent, he forced a lead of almost a kilometre-and-a-half back to the squabbling riders behind him. As he came into the final run with the crowd screaming at him, he sat up, kissed the cross hanging around his neck, and went over the line with his head bowed. It was the absolute pinnacle of his sporting life. Frank Schleck and Evans didn't arrive for another two minutes, giving Sastre a lead of one minute, twenty-four over Frank Schleck and one minute, thirty-four over Evans. It was still a tenuous margin with the final time trial yet to come but the Spaniard had banked that his attack had gained just enough time to give him a buffer against Evans. In the end, it proved sufficient; the Australian could only trim the lead down to fifty-eight seconds, allowing Sastre to take his first and only Grand Tour victory.

CARPE DIEM: CARLOS SASTRE

I always look back at Sastre's 2008 victory as a unique alignment of the right man, in the right place, at the right time, making the right decision. Sastre held his nerve longer than his competitors, chose his moment to attack with greater clarity of thought and, in those crucial minutes on Alpe d'Huez, gave his commitment completely. It was his sense of tranquillity that marked Sastre from Evans. The Australian had gone into the race as the favourite but he seemed to attract misfortune, crashing so badly on Stage Nine he cracked his helmet, and then launching into a series of comically awkward encounters with the local press. By the time he made it into the yellow jersey on Stage Ten, he seemed on the edge of breaking, weeping openly as he hugged and kissed the Tour's soft toy lion mascot.

Certainly other factors came into play; Sastre's CSC team were much stronger than Evans' Silence-Lotto, and Bjarne Riis's watchful eye and bulbous scalp exercised a near reptilian cunning. But the race still seemed to be testing something more ingrained than the merely physical and, whatever the mitigating factors, there's no doubt that, at the crucial moment, it was Sastre who seized the day.

Of course, both riders benefited from the decline of the doping programs so characteristic of the Armstrong years. Sastre was one of the few riders of his generation to have never been implicated in a doping scandal. Had he been born a few years later and raced against a cleaner *peloton*, perhaps he would have won more often. On the other hand, if he'd been born a few years earlier perhaps he would never have had the chance to step out from behind the long shadows of Armstrong, Pantani, Ullrich, Landis, and the generation of medically-enhanced winners who had taken precedence over the past decade.

Much the same could be said of Evans. In the 2005 Tour, he'd come in eighth. Of those who beat him, all seven were later implicated in doping scandals. In 2006 his fifth place was upgraded to fourth after Floyd Landis was disqualified and the only rider above him to avoid implication in drug scandals was Sastre. In 2007 Evans came in second and Sastre was upgraded to third after the disqualification of Levi Leipheimer for doping.

It's been said that clean riders like Evans and Sastre had their best years stolen from them. This assumes success is based on merit, thwarted by the duplicitous nature of cycling's cheats. Maybe — but then so, too, is it based on luck. Consider the case of the Tour's first winner, chimney sweep Maurice Garin. Born in 1871, he was barely over five feet tall, and reputedly once traded by his parents in return for a block of cheese. Of all the malnourished chimney sweeps to ever exist, the statistical chance of Garin being born at the dawn of a sport he just happened to excel in beggars belief.

Of course, part of the majesty of the Tour is that it makes obvious the impact of chance and luck; Rene Vietto may well have won the Tour had he not lost his best years to the Second World War, and the same could be said of a host of other riders now long since forgotten. At a further extreme, an Australian like Russell Mockridge could have had far greater success had he not been born on the other side of the world in a country that didn't particularly care about professional cycling. This myriad of coincidences, good fortune, and timing is part of the wonder of the Tour. It produces a rare moment in which its contenders may prove themselves.

This is part of both the tragedy and the appeal of Cadel Evans in the 2008 Tour. Theoretically, he had greater opportunity than Sastre but, at the decisive moment, he made the wrong decisions. When Sastre first attacked on the Alpe d'Huez, Evans' *domestiques* closed down the gap. Had Evans focused on chasing Sastre, he may have lost the stage but kept a margin he could have reclaimed in the time trial. Instead, he engaged in a cat-and-mouse game with Frank Schleck. Watching the stage coverage, you can see the moment it happens, with the pace slowing and the riders re-grouping. If you watch the stage closely, you can count out maybe three or four minutes in which his indecision cost him the race.

While there's stylistic differences in their performances, from Sastre's pure climber to Evans' consistent grind, I think there's a certain emotional distance between the two as well. Perhaps this was because Evans had been kicked in the head by a horse as a child. While it initially seemed he'd suffer brain damage for life, the only long-term damage was supposedly a penchant for more overt displays of feeling. Perhaps it's this intensity of sentiment that blinded his capacity to act at the decisive moment on the Alpe d'Huez.

By contrast, Sastre always came across as decidedly calm, persistent, and driven by something beyond simply winning. In an interview with him for *Cycling News* just after he'd retired, he said:

> Nothing is easy in life. Maybe I'm wrong … I'm not a judge: I don't know whether I took the right path and someone else the wrong one. But at the time I never wasted my time thinking about whether I was doing the right thing. I did it at the start of my career and I wasted energy but I eventually learned how I could get through with my training and hard work and still get satisfaction.

Gérard Vroomen, Sastre's director at his final professional team, summarized him by saying,

> Carlos has this way of talking … He can sound like a philosopher. You think you know what he means but you're never one hundred per cent sure.

One wonders if it was this philosophical capacity that kept him slugging away at the top end of a sport despite being routinely beaten by chemically-enhanced riders. Without any clear chance of reward for his efforts, he remained entirely committed to his vocation until, almost by chance, the landscape shifted around him and he was able to win.

I consider Sastre's career to be the ideal illustration of Horace's much-quoted adage, 'Carpe diem' or 'seize the day'. This is often cited as a feel good adage on living in the moment and pursuing life to the fullest. It's a perception that says more about the enforced optimism inherent to our modern age, driven upon us by the kind of wealthy ex-hippies who now make inspirational calendars and keep a steady stock of 'dream catchers' and tie-dye t-shirts.

Horace's original implication is that the gods control one's fate, grim death and misfortune are always in the wings, long-term plans are bound to fail, so one should make use of the immediately available opportunities. If those opportunities, through some wonderful trick of fate, happen to be grand in scale, such as winning the Tour with an attack on Alpe d'Huez, then all the better.

Sastre's take on this is unique. Philosophically, he's right that nothing is easy in life, and it's hard to tell if you're on the right or wrong path. The Fates may conspire to alter the outcome of whatever path you choose, and it's presumptuous to believe success is purely a matter of making the right choices. Conversely, the failure to make choices is a choice unto itself, and a choice that will inhibit one's chance of victory far more completely than fortune ever could alone.

STAGE 18

July 21st, 1986
Briançon to Alpe d'Huez

A FRENCHMAN, AN AMERICAN AND A MILLIONAIRE ON ALPE D'HUEZ

Hunters for gold or pursuers of fame, they all had gone out on that
stream, bearing the sword, and often the torch, messengers of the might
within the land, bearers of a spark, from the sacred fire. What greatness
had not floated on the ebb of that river in the mystery of an unknown
earth! … The dreams of men.
-Joseph Conrad

The first time I ever saw Bernard Hinault in action was at the 2008 Tour de France, twenty-two years after he'd retired. The French rider Samuel Dumoulin was on the podium, accepting the award for his stage victory, when a protester jumped in front of the camera. Out of nowhere, Hinault appeared — aged and clad in smart casual but still instantly recognisable — he barged the intruder off the stage and then joined the security guards in hoisting him away.

Seconds later, he re-appeared to guide Dumoulin through the ritual of hand shaking with the waiting dignitaries.

Serious, fearless, and vicious, the five time Tour winner is still known as 'Le Blaireau' or 'The Badger' because of his tenacious, indefatigable will to fight. Along with Anquetil, Bartali, and a mere handful of champions, he controlled the *peloton* by sheer force of personality. There's an amazing image of Hinault riding Paris-Nice in the early Eighties, when the race was stopped by striking shipyard workers gathered on the road. Hinault rode into their midst and simply began throwing punches. In the background a young and confused Phil Anderson can be seen looking on while Hinault wades in to the fray, fists flying.

When Hinault won his last Tour de France in 1985, it marked the end of an era. The next year would feature the first ever Tour win by a rider from outside the heartland of Western Europe — and an American at that. With Greg LeMond's victory in 1986, the sport went global. It wasn't an easy transition. LeMond came to symbolise the New World and Hinault the Old, and the battle between them was made all the more intense because they were racing for the same team, La Vie Clare, owned by flamboyant millionaire Bernard Tapie. The supreme moment of their conflict occurred on July 21st, 1986, with Stage Eighteen's ascent of the Alpe d'Huez.

To understand the impact of that stage on the Tour's history, we need to understand its context and protagonists. Greg LeMond's difference from Hinault could not be more pronounced. He reminds me of Luke Skywalker; blond, open-faced, devoted to the cause but with a sort of 'Innocent Abroad' fragility. Hinault is the quintessential French *Asterix* caricature; the indefatigable Gaul holding out against the foreign invaders. In contrast to the Frenchman's sheer force, LeMond mixed fragility, determination, and an almost naïve belief in justice and truth. When the two ended up on the same team it was a recipe for conflict on a grand scale.

It started when LeMond was signed-up to ride as Hinault's *domestique-deluxe* in 1985. In return for LeMond's loyalty, Hinault pledged that their roles would reverse the following year. LeMond would help Hinault to a record fifth victory and, in 1986, Hinault would help him become the first American Tour winner. Inevitably, it became a clash of not only their personalities but the shift of cycling into a new age.

By 1986 LeMond had ridden the Tour twice, finishing third in 1984 as a *domestique* for Laurent Fignon, and second while working in the same role for Hinault's La Vie Claire team in 1985. There's a theory that LeMond could have won the 1985 Tour and certainly Hinault, usually impervious and dominating, had shown a degree of weakness previously unimagined. In the past, he'd been almost as all-consuming as Merckx, winning the Tour in 1978, 1979, 1981, and 1982, the Giro in 1980 and 1982, the Vuelta in 1978 and 1983, the 1980 World Championship, and most of the Classics.

By the mid-Eighties, after years of smashing away at gigantic gear ratios, Hinault had been left with a knee injury that had already forced his withdrawal from the 1980 Tour while in the yellow jersey. When he won the 1982 Tour, it was clear retirement wasn't far off. He sat out the 1983 Tour, still nursing his knee. In his absence, his team, Renault, appointed his former *domestique*, Laurent Fignon as leader. Fignon won and Hinault's relationship with *director sportif* Cyrille Guimard began to fracture. It was clear he needed a new team if he wanted a fifth Tour victory.

Later that year Hinault teamed up with Bernard Tapie to set up an entirely new squad. The title sponsor, La Vie Claire, was a chain of health food stores within Tapie's substantial business empire. Yet the 1984 Tour was a disaster; Hinault was beaten into second place by Fignon and the loss rankled. The two were very different — Hinault's Breton pragmaticism and tenacity were in stark contrast to the university educated Parisian, Fignon. Like the Anquetil/Poulidor battle some two decades earlier, it was a clash between differing French identities. Waiting in the wings, was Fignon's new, American *domestique*, Greg LeMond.

The American was vital to Fignon's win. He had the strength and pedigree of a champion. The race wasn't even over before Tapie and Hinault were trying to poach him away from Renault. On Stage Seventeen, Fignon had just taken the yellow jersey with a summit finish atop the Alp d'Huez. That night, LeMond was staying in the ski resort on the mountain and, after dinner, he stepped outside to admire the view. Out of the darkness, a motorcycle emerged, driven by a beautiful woman. She told him Bernard Tapie wanted to see him, and then sped him away on the back of her bike to a meeting in a hotel room with Tapie and Hinault.

Tapie supposedly opened the conversation with, 'How would you like to make more money than you ever dreamed of?' LeMond was offered the first million-dollar contract in cycling, as well as royalties from the sale of the new Look pedal, the first of the now ubiquitous clipless pedals. In August, less than a month after Fignon had taken his second and final Tour victory, it was announced LeMond was moving to support Hinault to win the race for a fifth time in 1985.

Their relationship was always going to problematic. Hinault's star was falling and LeMond clearly had the capacity to win in his own right. Indeed, there's some suggestion this is why Tapie brought them together; win, lose or draw, the spectacle of the rising American star and the French stalwart would attract its own attention. LeMond had served his apprenticeship and now knew he could win the Tour. Hinault knew his time was limited and he wanted to make the most of his final years. Additionally, while the two had starkly different characters, they both knew they were champions and neither particularly trusted the other to share the limelight.

The definitive text on their relationship is Richard Moore's *Slaying the Badger*. Documenting the moment at which their relationship showed its first major crack, Moore interviewed Australian rider Phil Anderson. He recalled the cracks starting to show on Stage Fourteen of the 1985 Tour, when LeMond had finished in a breakaway group into Saint-Étienne some two minutes ahead of Hinault. This itself wasn't much of a problem. Hinault was still more than three minutes ahead of him but, on the run-in to the finish line, Anderson collided with Hinault's Canadian teammate Steve Bauer and, in the resulting crash, Hinault fell heavily. As Anderson recalls it,

> Hinault knew I was a good friend of Greg and I think he thought I was trying to knock him off on purpose, or something crazy like that.

Hinault ended up with a broken nose, a gash to his head, and two black eyes. Moreover, he broke a new pair of Ray Bans. He was outraged.

Hinault's luck cracked again on Stage Seventeen, a two hundred and nine kilometre beast of a stage through the Pyrenees ascending the Aspin, Tourmalet, and Luz Ardiden. He was clearly off his game and began to slip away from the lead group on the second ascent. By contrast, LeMond was now in third place overall, riding ahead with the second-placed Stephen Roche. Leaving Hinault behind, the two of them crossed the summit of the Tourmalet with an elite group, including future Tour winner Pedro Delgado and phenomenal Columbian climbers Luis Herrera and Fabio Parra. Hinault fell three minutes eighteen seconds behind, meaning LeMond needed a mere ten second gap to become the leader of the Tour with one mountain left to go.

Delgado immediately launched an attack, racing for the stage win, with the two Columbians chasing. LeMond's brief for the stage was to shadow Stephen Roche, ensuring a win for La Vie Claire in the event Hinault cracked. It was the Tour's key moment. Had Roche and LeMond worked together, they could have smashed open the distance back to Hinault, putting the American in first place with a healthy margin, Roche in second, and leaving the veteran Frenchman in third. Instead, LeMond followed team directions and refused to help Roche. Subsequently, the two were caught and came in three minutes behind the stage winner, albeit still a minute and a half ahead of Hinault. When the race finally came into Paris, LeMond was a mere minute forty-two seconds behind Hinault. Had he attacked on Stage Seventeen, LeMond almost certainly would have won the 1985 Tour and both he and Hinault knew it.

In the last days before Hinault took his final win, the two were already in open conflict. In a peace deal brokered by Tapie himself, Hinault promised to repay LeMond's loyalty by helping him win victory in the 1986 Tour. Recounting the event to Moore twenty-five years later, Hinault recalled, 'I told him, "Next year, it's you who'll win the Tour, and I'll be there to give you a hand".' When he won in Paris, he told journalists he had no intention of going for a sixth Tour victory in 1986, declaring he'd retire after helping LeMond take his first win. 'I'll stir things up to help Greg win and I'll have fun doing it', he declared, 'That's a promise.'

Whether he kept that promise is a matter of some debate. Hinault says he did, LeMond says he didn't. Either way, their terse relationship made the 1986 Tour one of the most thrilling races in decades. Everything went relatively smoothly until the

Stage Nine individual time trial. LeMond powered through the sixty-one and a half kilometre course until a broken wheel forced a bike change, costing him somewhere between thirty and sixty seconds. He still came in as the second fastest rider, a mere forty-four seconds behind Hinault. After the stage, LeMond slowly began to suspect a change in Hinault's attitude, a suspicion that whatever he'd said publically, the French champion held his own private rule that the outcome of that time trial would decide whether he worked with LeMond, or whether he worked for a sixth victory for himself.

The following day, whether from the stress, the heat, the poor food or, as he believes, a 'bad peach', LeMond contracted severe and violent diarrhoea. Paul Kimmage famously detailed it in his autobiography:

> LeMond was in trouble today. He had a bout of diarrhoea. He rode by me with thirty kilometers to go, surrounded by his *domestiques* bringing him to the front. God, the smell was terrible. It was rolling down his legs. I know if it was me I would have stopped. I mean, it's only a bike race. But then I'm not capable of winning it. He is and I suppose that's the difference.

LeMond himself recalled the story to Richard Moore with a humour presumably improved over time:

> It didn't feel like it was going to be diarrhoea, but oh, my God, it was so severe. I just felt the shorts go wooooop! And it fills my shorts, then slowly dribbles down my legs into my shoes. I mean, literally, it was dripping into my wheels, it was flying off the spokes.

Eventually he reached the finish line, scrambling through the crowds to get to the team's camper van. He continues:

I go over to the team's motor home … I'm rushing in, I go in, and I go to open up the toilet, and they've removed it. It's full of boxes of postcards. The one sitting where the toilet was… God, the irony! Imagine a box about this high (he gestures about four feet) with all these Hinault postcards. There had to be 30, 40 thousand of these cards … I took them all out of the centre so I could sit, like it was a toilet seat… and I sat there for an hour and a half.

On Stage Twelve the race entered the Pyrenees and things went from bad to worse. Hinault and fellow French La Vie Claire rider Jean-Françoise Bernard broke away with Spaniard Pedro Delgado. Delgado was going for the stage win but, as Hinault and Bernard disappeared away from their supposed team leader Greg LeMond, things became confused.

Hinault worked with Delgado to push the time gap out, while LeMond sat back in the bunch. To chase down his own teammate would have brought mass hatred from the French fans, given Hinault's standing as a five-time Tour champion. At the same time, with the gap growing ever greater, LeMond began to suspect this wasn't some tactical manoeuvre but that Hinault was trying to gain enough time to reinstate himself as La Vie Claire's undisputed leader and seize a record-breaking sixth victory. As the stage progressed, his suspicion turned to a certainty. In a panic, LeMond attacked with Luis Herrera, clawing back a minute but still conceding time. Hinault had taken the yellow jersey with an overall gap of five and a half minutes.

LeMond was furious at the betrayal. Hinault didn't seem to care. He attacked again on Stage Thirteen over the Tourmalet, gaining three minutes by the ascent of the Aspin. This time LeMond was less trusting and chased him down on the Peyreseourde. When Hinault attacked a second time, LeMond and his new American teammate, climber Andy Hampsten made an attack of their own. Hampsten towed his team leader for as long as he could and then LeMond unleashed a week's built up angst, pulling the race apart, winning the stage and regaining more than four minutes on Hinault. The two were now separated by a mere forty seconds. On Stage Seventeen, the Tour entered the Alps, with Hinault in the yellow jersey, followed by LeMond, and, in third place, the Swiss national champion Urs Zimmerman. Hinault knew the next few days would decide the overall winner but when LeMond and Zimmerman disappeared up the road he couldn't answer. LeMond took his first yellow jersey.

This set the scene for Stage Eighteen, considered by some as the greatest stage in the Tour's history. Running from Briançon over the Galibier, Télégraphe, and Croix de Fer, the stage ended with a summit finish at Alpe d'Huez. It was Hinault's last chance and he threw everything at it. Attacking a mere forty kilometres into the one hundred and sixty-three kilometre stage, he split the *peloton* and dragged away a small group. Try as he might, though, he couldn't escape LeMond.

Hinault attacked ferociously again on the ascent of the Télégraphe, blasting off everyone but Bauer, LeMond, and a Basque rider, Pello Ruiz-Cabestany. By the time they hit the top of the Croix de Fer, they'd already forced a three-minute gap but Hinault wasn't content, and attacked a third time on the descent. Plummeting downhill at 90km/h he didn't even slow when he opted to take a high-speed piss. LeMond was the only rider who could stay with him.

At the foot of the descent, preparing for the summit finish on Alpe d'Huez, LeMond emerged as the stronger of the two. Hinault was beginning to tire and the American was waiting to attack when their team owner Bernard Tapie drove up to them. He told LeMond, 'You've won the Tour, Greg. But this is really important: Let Hinault lead – it's his last Tour – and let him win the stage.'

LeMond agreed but, as they started climbing, he became nervous. He neither trusted Hinault nor the swarms of French fans on the side of the road, who had believed they might see a record sixth win for their hero, and were none too pleased to see an American victory instead.

Hinault claims he told LeMond, 'You stay calm, don't panic, and we go to the finish together.' For once, he kept his promise, towing LeMond through the crowd. LeMond was ecstatic and conciliatory, patting Hinault's back and telling him, 'Thank you. This has been a great stage for you and me, and I hope we're both winners.' Hinault crossed the line first and it looked like a passing of the torch; the older rider guiding his young disciple to his first victory, taking one last stage victory for old time's sake.

The goodwill lasted about twenty minutes, until the press conference in which Hinault declared, 'The race isn't over.' In practice, of course, it was. LeMond had enough of a time gap to cement his place as the race's winner and the spectacle of the two men crossing the line together had been the pinnacle of the race; the image that would be remembered for years after. Yet Hinault dragged it out, opting for a psychological if not an actual victory. Instead of riding towards Paris like a conquering victor, LeMond spent the rest of the race thinking he was going to be physically attacked or have his bike sabotaged, telling journalists:

> If I don't win because of an accident, and Bernard wins because I've been knocked out by some rider in the *peloton*, I just say it will be his worst victory ever, and that's a bad way to go down in history.

It didn't help calm his nerves when the Tour's director, Jacques Goddet, turned up at his hotel room, telling him, 'You must be very careful, Greg. There are a lot of people who want to see Hinault win.'

It wasn't idle chatter. Just before the final time trial, with three days left to race, he was testing his bike when one of the pedals fell off. After the Alpe, it was virtually certain LeMond would win but Hinault kept him fighting for it right up until the final stage. In an article for *Rolling Stone*, Trip Gabriel recounted the impact the Tour had on its first American winner:

> The Tour de France has taken the youthfulness out of LeMond's face, glazing his small, blue eyes and stretching his skin tightly over the contours of his skull. At twenty-five, he was like the survivor of a death camp, hanging on to first place overall in what the French papers called a 'march through hell'.

The physical drain was evident, but the Alpe d'Huez had left a deeper mark on LeMond. In Paris, he reflected on what he'd learned, telling journalists, 'You can never trust anybody. Life is that way.'

ON SUBLIME AMBIGUITY: 'THE TOUR IS WON ON THE ALPE'

Jean-Paul Vespini wrote an entire book on the Alpe d'Huez, describing it as 'a climb that delivers a verdict – absolute, impartial and final.' Contemplating the popular adage, 'the Tour is won on the Alpe', he continues:

> To truly gauge the significance of this climb in determining overall victory, we must focus our attention on the yellow jersey. By doing so, we see that in seventeen of twenty-five ascents, the winner of the Tour was in yellow following Alpe d'Huez. In general, Tour winners must make a supreme effort to either save the jersey or consolidate their lead... even in the years when the Tour is not decided on the Alpe, the race can certainly be lost there.

He's right in one respect; ever since Coppi won the Tour with an attack on the first ever ascent in 1952, the rider with the yellow jersey at the top of the Alpe d'Huez almost always goes on to win the Tour.

On the other hand, the verdict isn't always absolute or final. Armstrong took the win on both the Alpe and the Tour in 2001 and 2004 only to lose them both to doping charges in 2013. Landis cemented his lead on the Alpe in the 2006 Tour and lost it for the same reason. The three fastest times for the ascent all belong to Marco Pantani, all of which were almost certainly influenced by doping. The top ten fastest times were all set by riders later implicated in doping scandals, including not only Armstrong, Landis, and Pantani but Ullrich, Riis, and Virenque. While Vespini is correct in saying the Alpe d'Huez passes a verdict, the meaning of that verdict is subject to debate.

The LeMond–Hinault battle leaves an equally ambiguous legacy. At the end of the 1985 Tour, Hinault had told reporters, 'I'll stir things up to help Greg win, and I'll have fun doing it. That's a promise.' Richard Moore, writing about their rivalry after interviewing both of them a quarter of a century later, revisits this comment:

> Let's look at this pledge afresh. Whether Hinault intended

it or not, there is a sublime ambiguity at play. Was he saying he would put himself at the service of LeMond or that, by 'stirring things up', the likely – or possible – outcome would be a LeMond win? Was his priority victory for LeMond or fun for Hinault? What, in fact, was he saying?

LeMond took it as a promise and a promise unfulfilled. By contrast, when Moore asked if he'd betrayed his younger teammate, Hinault had a different recollection:

> He thought so. I didn't. Never. I'd given my word and I wasn't going back on it. I didn't pay attention to what was being said. I gave my word from the first day. I don't have to justify everything I do. He had nothing to worry about.

Even after twenty-five years, the verdict remains undecided. When we watch footage of the two of them crossing the line on the Alpe d'Huez, the meaning is still unknown. Hinault boasted in his autobiography, 'I could have had his scalp on Alpe d'Huez' yet continues to claim he helped LeMond, and LeMond says the exact opposite. Then there's their boss, Bernard Tapie. When he cruised up to LeMond in the team car and told him to let Hinault win, it should have marked the end, but Hinault never conceded defeat and, as far as we know, Tapie never told him to.

Tapie isn't visible in the footage of LeMond and Hinault crossing the line on the Alpe d'Huez but his role adds an additional element beyond the simplistic clarity of sporting victory and loss. He was one of those 'entrepreneurs' who appeared in the Eighties, floundering in the cash bubble that blew up with globalisation. A bit like Australian Alan Bond's sponsorship of America's Cup winning yacht Australia II, Tapie's investment in sport was drawn partly from love, partly as a promotional tool for his business, and partly out of a desire for glory. He'd started La Vie Claire as a chain of health food stores and set up the cycling team ostensibly to publicise it, hiring Hinault as much for his status as a French icon as his capabilities as an athlete.

La Vie Claire went on to be one of the most dominant teams of the 1980s. When Tapie grew bored of cycling he moved on to football, buying the Olympique de Marseille football team, which he steered to five French championships and victory in the Champions League in 1993. The following year, the team was embroiled in a match fixing controversy, with Tapie at its core. He'd also entered into a political career, as Minister of City Affairs under Pierre Bérégovy's left-leaning French government. Bérégovy later shot himself after losing an election and becoming embroiled in corruption charges and losing. Tapie, also implicated in corruption, ended up in prison.

For a while, bankrupt and unable to return to politics or business, he became a filmmaker, clawing things back together until he was caught up in a tax scandal. The documentary *Who Is Bernard Tapie?*, describes him simply by saying, 'If he were American, he'd be president by now. Or he'd be in the electric chair.' His team was unique. With their jerseys inspired by the Modernist artist Mondrian, they ushered in a new era of cycling. Partly that was due to Tapie's bankroll. When he gave Greg LeMond a million dollar contract, it utterly revolutionised the pay and contract system for top riders, bringing it closer to other blockbuster sports, like football and basketball.

Beyond that, the team introduced a degree of modern technology in their training and equipment, adopting carbon frames, clipless pedals, heart rate monitors, and the now standard computerized speedometers. Moreover, directorship was handed to the eccentric genius Paul Köchi, who had pioneered training based on hard data. Köchi had seen LeMond win the 1983 World Championship, remarking,

> He had a different way. Nothing to do with the traditional mentality in Europe, which I wanted to cut. I wanted nothing to do with that and I had different ideas about how my teams should work.

Indeed, Paul Köchi is an apt personification of the La Vie Claire team. He didn't conform to the rules of the Old World; gone was the semi-feudal era when team *soignoirs* relied more on superstition and amphetamines than physiology and science. Gone was the age when the sport was almost exclusively an affair for Catholic Western Europe, ruled by France, Belgium, Italy, and Spain. La Vie Claire was the first big team of the globalised era and it brought with it a degree of ambiguity inherent to that age. If the rules of the Old World were fading, what exactly were the new rules?

Köchi told Richard Moore, 'Cycling is a play sport: it's a game. I tell my riders in the morning, "OK, today we play cycling! Let's play cycling!"' The team's three great protagonists, however, all played by different sets of rules. For LeMond, fresh from the US and entering cycling afresh, cycling was a sport, dictated by the rules and conventions of fair play. For Hinault, as Köchi observed, it was a game; 'Hinault liked the game', and it was a game that continued both on and off the bike. For Tapie, it was another part of his empire; a means of promoting his companies but also of promoting himself, his legacy, and reputation. Accordingly, all three raced for different ends. LeMond's goal was a sporting one; the yellow jersey and the overall victory, for Hinault it was, as he said, 'fun'. He was driven by the game itself.

Yet the key to understanding the legacy of their contest on the Alpe d'Huez is Tapie's approach. For him, the race wasn't about the winner or the way they won but the story it told and the glory it generated. He was writing another chapter of his own legacy and the role of his characters was to generate intrigue just as much as to win bike races. The LeMond-Hinault clash was far greater in scope than any win by an undisputed champion backed by a unified team could ever be.

There's a greater parable within their clash; as the rules of the game change, so too does its meaning and the way we play it. Do we watch the Tour, like LeMond, because we want to see a clean sporting victory, or because we want to see a drama or a fable? Do we dress up in outrageous lycra attire and haul ourselves, out through the buzzing traffic and up through the local hills, purely out of a desire for fitness, or is there some element of a game we're playing? If it's just a game, why not stay at home and play something quiet and dignified like chess?

Cycling's an odd sport. Ultimately, whatever it looks like from the outside, it's always been professional and, up to a point, Hinault and LeMond were just doing a job — a job in which winning isn't necessarily the desired outcome. Tapie was the only one doing it entirely of his own volition. But then one of the great things about the LeMond victory was that he seemed to drag the game back into alignment with the things we love about it; he was neither a pragmatist like Hinault, nor a storyteller weaving a piece of myth like Tapie. When he won the 1986 Tour the implication was that if you wished and worked for something hard enough, you could overcome grotty commerce and pessimism. The game and its petty rules could be transcended and the dream could become reality.

STAGE 19

July 26th, 2006
Pornic - Nantes

LANCE ARMSTRONG WINS AGAIN

*To think of these stars that you see overhead at night, these vast worlds
which we can never reach. I would annex the planets if I could; I often
think of that.*
— *Cecil Rhodes*

Lance Armstrong won the final time trial in every Tour
of his reign, with one exception. In 2003 it was taken
by Scottish rider David Millar. This was the only one of
Armstrong's seven Tour victories in which he'd looked at risk
and his failure to dominate in this final test was emblematic
of his struggle to control the race. In previous years it had
been more or less a personal victory parade before he arrived
in Paris with margins of six or seven minutes, having never
really looked in serious trouble.

In 2003 Armstrong faced a particularly determined set of
attacks. In the mountains he'd been under pressure from an
elite group of Spanish climbers, including the Euskadi duo

Heimar Zubeldia and Iban Mayo, and ONCE's team captain, Joseba Beloki. But the bigger threat was Jan Ullrich, who'd won the race in 1997 and come second on no less than four occasions. After several years of varying form and wildly fluctuating weight, the German seemed to have sorted out his various demons. In the opening prologue, race commentator Paul Sherwin offered the backhanded compliment, 'No one could call this man Porky.'

A year earlier Ullrich had been dropped by his team, T-Mobile, after a drink driving charge. He'd also been given a six-month ban for taking ecstasy and amphetamines while out partying. With a new team, Bianchi, it looked like he'd finally fulfil his promise of a second Tour victory. Plus, after four years of total dominance, people were bored of watching the American US Postal team cruise to clinical victories. Growing rumours of Armstrong's drug use were matched by growing discontent amongst the French fans.

By Stage Eight Armstrong had taken the yellow jersey, with Ullrich two minutes behind him. The gap stayed the same as the race moved through the Alps. But then came the first individual time trial and Ullrich took back more than a minute and a half on Armstrong over a mere forty-seven kilometres. It left him just thirty-six seconds down, the perfect position as the race entered the Pyrenees. Given that Ullrich had already taken five seconds from Armstrong in the six-kilometre opening prologue it was entirely reasonable that he could limit his losses, perform well in the final time trial on Stage Nineteen, and fulfil the promise of his 1997 victory.

This potential to upset Armstrong's bid for a fifth consecutive win made the 2003 Tour the first since 1999 that actually seemed like a competition. Until the doping allegations came out, many would have said it was one of the best Tours since the Fignon, Hinault, and LeMond clashes of the mid-Eighties. Certainly, it had a tension that had been lacking in the previous four editions, where Armstrong's formula had been simple — dominance in the time trials, consistency in the mountains combined with one or two deliberate, powerful attacks, and, underlining it all, a powerful, devoted team exercising total control over the race.

Armstrong's US Postal team was especially strong, including his fellow Americans Floyd Landis and George Hincapie, along with the first Columbian to wear the yellow jersey Victor Hugo Pena, multiple Vuelta winner Roberto Heras, and Russian veteran Viatcheslav Ekimov. In time, virtually all of them would be implicated in doping scandals linking back to the team itself. In the Stage Four team time trial, they'd used their collective force to win the stage and produce a buffer of forty seconds over Ullrich's third placed Bianchi squad. If not for that, Ullrich would have been in yellow after his performance on the Stage Twelve individual time trial.

On Stage Thirteen the German attacked as the race entered the Pyrenees, cutting the gap between the two down to fifteen seconds. On Stage Fifteen, he attacked again. When the group came back together on the final climb, Armstrong crashed after colliding with a spectator, and then almost crashed a second time after his foot slipped off the pedal. It was poor timing, as Iban Mayo had just launched his own offensive, dragging Ullrich after him. Depending on who you believe, when he heard Armstrong had crashed Ullrich either waited or didn't. Either way, the Texan produced one of the great rides of his career, catching and dropping the lead group, to win by forty seconds on the uphill finish into Luz Ardiden. It gave him the one minute and seven second lead he took into the final time trial on Stage Nineteen.

With his earlier victories, Ullrich had already shown he could reclaim the time he needed to win. There was a real hope that he would win and take the closest Tour victory in more than a decade. As it turned out the final time trial, between Pornic and Nantes, was the first in that year's Tour to be visited by bad weather. With Armstrong and Ullrich the last to ride, spectators and journalists had ample time to work themselves into a fever pitch. In steady rain, Ullrich surged off the start platform with a massive 137.5 inch gear, needing to gain one and a half seconds per kilometre over Armstrong to win. He was fastest through both the first and second time checks, although not by a wide enough margin. But the course was producing its time splits towards the end, when it shifted from hard slog to a far more technical final section, complicated immensely now by the rain slicked roads.

Armstrong had already ridden the course in training, paying his usual attention to detail. His teammates, including expert time trialists like Landis, Hincapie, and Ekimov, had all raced the course earlier and reported back that the final section was dangerous. Ullrich, by contrast, had watched a video of it the night before in his hotel room. The difference in preparation showed — barraging into the final, technical finish, Ullrich took a roundabout too fast and the bike slipped out from under him, hitting the ground with such force sparks flew off the rear derailleur, while he slid across the road into hay bails on the outside of the turn. He finished in fourth place, eleven seconds behind Armstrong's third position. It was the fifth time Ullrich was to come second in the Tour, and Armstong's fifth win.

THE REDEMPTION OF DAVID MILLAR

The winner of the Stage Nineteen time trial was the young Scottish prodigy David Millar. He won, despite crashing, with an average speed of 54.36km/h, just below Greg LeMond's time trial record speed of 54.54km/h. He'd spent most of the year training for the Tour's time trials, under pressure from his Cofidis team to bring in a win big enough to justify his contract. They had high expectations; he had won the prologue in 2000 and held the yellow jersey for three days, and then won a stage in 2002.

Yet 2003 started badly when a motorbike hit him while he was training. Cofidis pushed him to keep racing while he was still injured and his form suffered. Under substantial pressure, Millar's Stage Nineteen time trial victory was capped by a subsequent win at the World Championship in Canada to salvage an otherwise lacklustre year.

Interestingly, in his autobiography Millar devotes little attention to his victory on Stage Nineteen and focuses, instead, on the prologue he lost at the start of that year's race. Soaring towards the finish, his chain had fallen off, costing him vital seconds and gifting the win to the Australian Bradley McGee. Millar's mechanics in the French Cofidis team had undertaken what they claimed was a 'weight saving' measure, removing the front derailleur from the bike. Unfortunately, somewhere between this piece of mechanical innovation and the use of an untried sponsor's chain ring, nearly all the chains of Cofidis riders simply fell off once they started riding. Millar's came off as he was powering down the finishing straight looking almost certain to win. Yet, writing about it almost a decade later in his memoir, *Racing Through the Dark* it's not so much the mechanical fault he focuses on but the win it effectively gifted to McGee:

I crossed the line two-hundredths of a second behind Australian Brad McGee. It was divine justice. Brad, one of my closest friends, had managed to stay clean, despite everything. I couldn't help thinking that that was the way it was supposed to be.

Millar had been using EPO since 2001. He continues:

Brad knew that I had been prepared and we both knew that what had happened in the Tour prologue was right – that it was karma – and that he was supposed to win. I had told him this the next day. Brad understood that I had made my decisions and yet he did his best not to judge.

The loss evidently meant more to him than his capture of the World Time Trial championship a few months later. It was one his greatest wins, yet his memory of it is decidedly sour:

I had a crushing victory. I was so much quicker that I realised I would win at the halfway point. In fact I spent the last ten kilometres trying to save energy, so that I'd be good for the road race three days later. After I'd won I stood on the podium, listening to 'God Save the Queen.' I was World Time Trial champion, yet I felt almost nothing. I should have been choked, moved, just as other athletes were at that moment. I wanted to experience that feeling. Instead, I just thought: 'Job done'.

It's a damning confession that strikes at the heart of the doping dilemma. Beyond the argument as to fairness or sportsmanship, or the desire for an authentic victory is the grim suspicion that a life's dream can be reduced to nothing more than a job. It's the same sensation you get as a kid when you finally realise that Father Christmas was just a farce put together by your parents. No one dreams of doing a mundane day job and, to find out the champions of your sport are doing just that, devalues the whole thing so badly it's like you've been watching the postman do his rounds.

Herein lies the rub at the heart of the Armstrong Era. When Lance Armstrong was finally convicted of doping it wasn't just that an individual athlete had been caught, nor was the problem to do with endemic corruption within the sport's upper echelons. Armstrong himself embodied a dream; a dream of a man who could overcome cancer just as he overcame the world's hardest sporting contest. He wasn't just an athlete and he most certainly wasn't just an entertainer doing a job. He was proof that success and, indeed, survival were a matter of will power. This dream allowed cycling to transcend the confines of Western Europe and burn through the Anglo world like wildfire. It brought millions of viewers and billions of dollars to the sport.

The Armstrong Era had begun when he joined the Motorola team in Europe in 1992 and ended one year after his second retirement, with the US Anti-Doping Authority's 'Reasoned Decision' stripping him of his seven Tour wins. During that time, cycling had grown from an almost exclusively European sport to one of global proportions. That growth occurred in unison with, and largely because of, Armstrong. He was to the cycling industry what Cecil Rhodes was to the British Empire: its agent of expansion, the emblem of its conquest, and ultimately the proof its corruption.

Of course, Rhodes made his fortune through the conquest of land and minerals rather than riding a bike but, like Armstrong, it was an economic conquest made possible through an ardent belief in a higher cause. Of his vicious and mercenary forays into Empire building, he commented,

I contend that we are the finest race in the world and that the more of the world we inhabit the better it is for the human race.

For all his brutality, violence and exploitation of the African people and their land, Rhodes was driven by a belief the ends justified the means. The same thing could be said of Armstrong. When he stood on the top step of the podium in 2005, having won his seventh and final Tour, and told the crowd 'I'm sorry you don't believe in miracles', he wasn't reflecting on a career spent simply selling a product but one of chasing dreams.

Unlike Rhodes, Armstrong never actually killed anyone but then his conquest didn't require land or minerals. Yet cycling is still an industry, albeit the raw material it mines and sells is more esoteric in nature. David Millar tries to explain it in his autobiography, rapturously describing cycling's 'epic human accomplishment on a grand scale, performances as seemingly close to super-human as I'd seen in sport.' Roland Barthes puts it only slightly differently when he asks:

What is sport? What is it then that men put into sport? Themselves, their human universe. Sport is made in order to speak the human contract.

Prior to watching the Tour, I'd never really 'got' sport. I'd played field hockey in primary school but found football terrifying, cricket bewildering, and team sports characterised by a degree of competitive angst way out of proportion to the schoolyard forums in which I'd competed. Getting screamed at by my classmates while playing tunnel ball didn't fill me with the competitive urge or an overwhelming camaraderie so much as a belief that I was surrounded by pre-adolescent lunatics.

By high school I'd given up on sport entirely, retreating into literature and music. The years of my youth I might have invested in cycling, I spent playing in bands that never really went anywhere and writing fanzines. Oddly, when I did finally fall for cycling, its allure was much the same as my love of music and writing. They allowed me to reach my limits and unleashed a rush of otherwise rare emotion.

Pierre Bourdieu once noted that 'Music is the 'pure' art par excellence. It says nothing and has nothing to say.' The same could be said of cycling. Given the all-consuming physical effort it extracts from its participants, and the transcendental, screaming passion of the fans on the side of the road, it obviously says something, yet it does so without recourse to words. Like great literature and art, sport produces meaning, but it has no author. The Tour de France does this on the scale of a symphony or an opera; it's Wagnerian, like watching *The Ring Cycle* in full but with more lycra and lower body fat ratios.

The first time I saw Armstrong race in the flesh was at the start of his 'comeback' in 2011. Thanks to some dubiously accounted-for state funds, he made his return in my hometown of Adelaide at the Tour Down Under. It was the start of the season and the race was used as a sort of glorified team holiday/training trip. With a stage start around the corner from my house I headed over to wander among the team cars and enjoy the post-race ambience. When a rather weighty older man shuffled up to me and asked, 'Where's Lance?' I pointed to the thronging crowd a little further up the road and he shuffled off to pay homage.

A couple of days later, Armstrong announced a morning ride on Twitter, resulting in a seething mass of old guys on Treks filling the Esplanade road along the coast. At the time, the questions about his doping had gone from a well-founded suspicion to almost undeniable. Regardless, the local council gave him the keys to the city and his appearance fee was rumoured to be in the millions. To the best of my knowledge, this is the only time the City of Adelaide has given its city keys to someone under investigation by the US Federal Government for perjury and fraud.

I'd never really understood Armstrong's allure but, on the side of the road, waiting for the Tour Down Under to start, his presence was immense. While it's a pretty small event on a world-scale, there were other big name riders there; local hero Stuart O'Grady, Queensland's former green jersey winner Robbie McEwen, former Tour winner Oscar Pereiro, and Cadel Evans. The year before, Miguel Indurain had been the guest of honour but no one really seemed that interested. Armstrong had a magnetism all of his own, which dragged the sport along behind it.

As he later acknowledged, much of that magnetism was because he told the story of a dream realised; the legend of a guy who had survived cancer and gone on to win the Tour de France seven times in a row. As Armstrong himself told *Cycling News* after his confession, it was a story he worked to construct but also one people wanted to believe:

> I controlled the narrative but I think the wave of momentum helped to control it. I was at the front of it but whether it's the sport, the industry, the cancer community, there was this wave of momentum that was the narrative. And along the way there were people that had different opinions and that momentum rolled over them.

Both on and off the bike he foisted the idea that it wasn't chance or luck that made one a winner, either at the Tour de France or over cancer; it was force of will. This is a deeply appealing story to tell; the idea that you can become anything you desire through sheer belief, insulated from misfortune or poor circumstances.

When he finally admitted to doping, one of his justifications was that, as his competitors also doped, it was merely a breach of the rules, rather than a breach of sportsmanship itself. Unlike Hinault, Armstrong wasn't there to play a game, but nor was he just there to make money. He was always chasing a dream; the same dream Greg LeMond had chased a decade earlier. But there was a fundamental difference between the two of them; Armstrong thought you could alter the rules of the game if the dream proved otherwise unachievable.

Unfortunately, if you're allowed to move the goalposts, that does tend to undermine the meaning of the game. Summarizing his former boss, Tyler Hamilton writes in his autobiography, *The Secret Race*, that it's this element of chance that makes sport itself so enthralling and it was this element that the Armstrong narrative devalued:

> The reason we love them (sports) – the reason I got involved in the first place – is that they're unpredictable, surprising, human. To me, that turned out to be Lance's problem: he couldn't let go of this idea that he was destined to be a champion, and he couldn't let go of the power that allowed him to control his performance so precisely. It's the oldest paradox: Lance could withstand just about anything, but he couldn't withstand the possibility of losing. And that, in my opinion, is not normal.

I think he's right. After all, Armstrong didn't win just through force of will — he won through meticulous doping, training, cover-ups, and intimidation — and he was eventually caught out.

Of course, it wasn't just Armstrong who wanted to believe it was a triumph of will that made him a success. From the insipid journalists like John Wilcockson, who made their living out of documenting the Armstrong myth, through to the old guy asking me 'Where's Lance?' at the Tour Down Under, or the Adelaide City Council giving him the key to the city while he was under federal investigation; people wanted to believe and they kept believing in the Armstrong lie, even as it fell apart around them. They did so because it's comforting to believe you can control the world through force of will, you can overcome cancer by believing in yourself, and you can ascend to the pinnacles of your chosen vocation with sheer self-determination. It's a beautiful idea because it means you and you alone control your fate but it's also a lie. This was the problem with Armstrong's doping; in the end, it wasn't just the nature of his blood values but that millions of people had come to the sport believing in what turned out to be a fiction.

STAGE 20

Grenoble – Grenoble
July 23rd, 2011

CADEL EVANS FINALLY WINS THE TOUR

But by the grace of God I am what I am: and his grace which was
bestowed upon me was not in vain; but I laboured more abundantly
than they all.
— *1 Corithians 15:10*

When Cadel Evans finally won the Tour de France in 2011 it was like entering an alternate universe where all logic ran in reverse; as if North had become South, hot had become cold, up was down, and losers were winners. Even as he powered to victory in the final time trial, I kept waiting for the planet to realign itself. Surely, I thought, the laws of physics would recognise there had been a fundamental miscalculation, gravity would suddenly reassert itself, and Evans would come plummeting back to ground in another of those innocuous crashes that had ruined his chances in the past. When he crossed the line in the yellow jersey, the mode of his victory was so different from those of the Armstrong years it felt like a seismic shift had occurred in the fabric of the universe.

I sat up late, waiting for him to launch out of the starting ramp. After a spirited defence on Alpe d'Huez, he was a mere fifty-seven seconds behind race leader Andy Schleck, and just three seconds behind Frank Schleck. The two brothers had, with their all-imposing CSC team, pushed for a repeat of Sastre's 2008 win, albeit minus the Spaniard. In the three years since Evans had last appeared on the Tour's podium it had become accepted logic he would never win the Tour de France; not so much that he couldn't, but that he wouldn't. It seemed inevitable that he'd panic, falter at the final step, or simply be struck down by some inane piece of bad luck.

I'd been having conversations about why Cadel Evans wouldn't win the Tour on a seasonal basis ever since his near-miss with victory in 2007. That year he had ceased to be one of the also-rans; eighth in 2005, fourth in 2006 (later upgraded after Landis was disqualified). That year he came so close. Alberto Contador beat him by a mere twenty-three seconds in one of the closest Tours ever. The Spaniard was a star on the rise; the only rider who could follow the Danish savant Michael Rasmussen on his terrifying ascents. When the Dane was disqualified, he held on to the advantage he'd gained in the mountains but things could have been so very different.

I still think Evans could have won in 2007. Right up until the final time trial, I thought it was possible. On the Stage Thirteen time trial he'd been more than a minute ahead of Contador. He went into that penultimate stage with a one minute, fifty second gap. All he needed was one of those awe inspiring, domineering victories we'd got used to seeing when Armstrong won the Tour; a final, brutal display of strength and control. Of course, it never happened.

On the upside, Evans would be retrospectively awarded the wins for both the individual time trials after the riders who'd beaten him, Alexander Vinokourov and Levi Leipheimer, were disqualified for doping. Unfortunately, the time bonuses usually awarded to stage victors didn't apply in the time trials that year. If they had, Evans would have retrospectively won the Tour by a slender seventeen seconds.

Contador was absent from the 2008 race. His new team, Astana, had been ostracised thanks to the sins of their former star Vinokourov. In his wake, the Australian was the favourite. When he pulled on the yellow jersey on Stage Ten, his difference from Armstrong couldn't have been more obvious. Armstrong would never have cried on the podium, let alone kissed the little toy lion mascot. Evans was such an innate eccentric; wrapped in a towel at a stage finish he berated a journalist, 'Don't stand on my dog or I cut your head off!' Initially I thought he'd cracked but then it turned out his dog, Molly, was actually at the finish line, just outside the camera's field of vision.

This, of course, raised the question as to why you'd bring your dog to a stage finish at the Tour de France. The thing went viral. A particularly unflattering image emerged of Evans, holding said dog, in which they both appeared to be pulling the same goofy grin. Then there was the sudden aggression at a journalist who touched his shoulder, the head butting of a cameraman at a stage finish, and the way he always sounded right on the cusp of tears, always pouting, griping about some injury or perceived injustice. When he lost to Sastre in 2008, it wasn't a huge surprise.

In 2009, the conversation started again — could Evans do it? No, Contador was back and too good, Andy Schleck had grown too strong, he'd crack under the pressure again, he'd crash, he was too old. There was still a desire to see him win after coming so close over the past two years but he seemed such an unlikely contender. Evans was fickle, frail and fallible, and so very unpolished — the exact opposite of Armstrong's steely determination.

In Australia, cycling was exploding on the back of the Armstrong legacy and strong performances by our macho sprinters Robbie McEwan and Stuart O'Grady, veteran Michael Rodgers, and Mark Renshaw, lead-out man to the phenomenal Mark Cavendish. Amid that, no one really knew what to make of Evans. He was like the anti-hero of Australian sport; embarrassingly emotional, more akin to the kid everyone picked on at school than the one who'd always been winning the annual Sports Day ribbons.

In 2009 he was thirtieth, way off the mark. His team fell apart on the Stage Four team time trial and he lacked form in the mountains, coming in behind his own *domestique*, Jurgen van den Broeck. Shortly afterwards, his biography came out. Titled *Close to Flying*, it was informally re-titled *Close to Crying*. The usual conversations emerged when I ran into cycling friends. 'So Cuddles had a bad Tour,' one of us would say. 'Think he'll ever win a Tour?', the other would reply. 'No. 2008 was meant to be his year but he lost it on the Alpe. Too many tears. Couldn't see Sastre attack.'

Then he surprised us all by winning the 2009 World Championship. It was strangely euphoric; he actually attacked, riding away to win alone on the final slopes of a hilly course. Our hopes revived. In the lead up to the 2010 Tour, his form seemed good. He had a new team, he seemed happier. He took the yellow jersey for a single day but then crashed, broke his elbow and was dropped on the first serious climbs. It was horrible to behold; as the lead group whirred away in the first real cull of the GC contenders, Evans simply fell out the back of the *peloton*. Passed by lesser riders, he seemed an object of pity even to them, with consoling hands placed on his shoulders as he struggled to the finish line in tears.

And then came the 2011 Tour. Each night I'd sit up watching the race and every time I heard Evans' name I'd be expecting news of a crash, a mechanical fault at a crucial moment, or a break he'd failed to follow. Yet, inexplicably, he held on, matching Contador's attacks, dragging up to the Schlecks as they burst away on another violent ascent. Come Stage Seventeen, he was second behind Thomas Voeckler. For anyone else, you would have said it was the perfect position to be in. Voeckler was of no concern; he would crack in the mountains. Evans held a lead of four seconds over Frank Schleck and a minute and a half over Andy. The Schlecks could attack in the mountains but then there was the final, forty-two kilometre time trial on the penultimate day. He was by far the better rider against the clock. All Evans had to do was limit his losses.

Had he been any other rider, he would have been considered a good bet. But with two summit finishes, on the Galibier for Stage Eighteen and the Alpe d'Huez on Stage Nineteen, it felt inevitable he'd do something wrong; crash, cry, fail at the crucial moment. Somehow Cadel Evans would let himself get pummelled into submission by the trio of Contador and the Schleck brothers. Contador, back from a ban for suspect doping, seemed intent on proving himself, and Andy Schleck, riding for a new team, had already come second twice, and had grown in strength and skill with each loss. Evans, by contrast, seemed past his prime.

When Andy attacked with sixty kilometres to go on Stage Eighteen it looked like an even more grandiose replay of the Sastre victory. Evans was left behind with Frank Schleck, Contador, Ivan Basso, and a lead group who automatically began shadowing each other. The gap grew up to more than four minutes with only fifteen kilometres left to race. Then, inexplicably, Evans moved to the front. His special skill isn't so much the fiery attack as the gruelling defence. When he finally started to chase he wasn't able to drop his competition but he certainly thinned their ranks. With everyone else trailing in his wake he cut the four and a half minute gap down by two minutes in less than ten kilometres. It left him a minute and a quarter behind Andy Schleck, a distance that was, theoretically at least, surmountable in the final time trial.

Of course, there was still one mountain stage left to go, on which both Contador and the Schlecks would seek to widen their gap, and in which Evans could re-assert his capacity to fail at climatic moments. Sure enough, he had a mechanical just before the descent of the Galibier, as the race produced the decisive group for its final clash on the Alpe. I must admit, I thought that was the end of it and fully expected him to lose time. Yet somehow he not only caught up on the descent but easily stayed with the main group, chasing Contador and stage winner Pierre Roland to cross the line with the Schlecks.

This left the Stage Twenty time trial as the deciding moment of the 2011 Tour. In first place was Andy Schleck. His brother, Frank, was second by fifty-three seconds. A mere three seconds further down was Cadel Evans, in third place. It was a veritable replay of the 2008 race. Technically, Evans was a sure bet. Based on their previous results, the Australian would outpace both of the Schleck brothers by at least a couple of minutes.

Yet, I still didn't believe he could do it. There'd be the inevitable stupid crash or a bungled wheel change and he'd end up in tears in the arms of his wife on the finish line. Evans' wife, Chiara, had become a celebrity in her own right for her awkwardly earnest Twitter comments on how cute Cadel was, what their dog Molly was doing, and pictures of their son. Her tone had the aura of protective determination you'd expect from someone's over-supportive mum at a school sport's day. Again, it only served as a reminder of how different things were to the Armstrong days, when his rock star fiancé Sheryl Crowe could be seen milling around at stage finishes. Out on the course, Evans looked much the same; his face puffy and red, oddly lumpy in BMC's red and black Lycra, clamping his lips together. With the time trial running in reverse order, he left the start gate third to last.

Six minutes later, Andy Schleck started. At the first time check, he was already twenty-seven seconds down on Evans. By the second it was approaching two minutes. At the finish line, the Australian had beaten him by two minutes and thirty-eight seconds, taking second place on the stage behind time trial specialist Tony Martin, and beating Contador by more than a minute. If only he'd produced such a stellar performance in either 2007 or 2008 he might have won another Tour.

As Evans stood on the podium in Paris, the Australian sports commentator Mike Tomalaris openly admitted, 'I didn't think I'd see this day.' Australian singer Tina Arena was led on to the Champs Élysées to sing the national anthem. Arena is, in Australia, the kind of singer your aging aunt might like and the perfect accompaniment to Evans, who stood swathed in the Australian flag and unfashionably teary-eyed. He thanked everyone in his high pitched voice and concluded, 'I couldn't be happier than to be standing up, right here, in the middle here.'

The two Australian commentators, Tomalaris and Phil Anderson (the first Australian to ever wear the yellow jersey) sounded equally overwhelmed. At home, on my own, I was surprisingly elated. After years of Armstrong victories, there was something so distinctly unlikely about Cadel Evans standing on the top of the podium; he was too short, too stocky, too goofy, and too emotional. Yet he'd still done it.

There was something so decidedly mortal about his victory that it felt redemptive, after years of the sport being dominated by the kind of aggressive, macho jerks you'd expect in elite level sports. I felt guilty for doubting him for all those years, indeed doubting him even as he rode to victory, but then he was so unlike the champions we'd grown to accept through the Armstrong years that the thought of him winning just didn't make sense.

ON THE MERITS OF PERSISTENCE

At the 2009 Vuelta a España, Cadel Evans lost the race after one of the most comically inept wheel changes ever seen. Perfectly positioned to win, he was heading over one of the final major ascents when he flatted just before the summit. With the team car nowhere in sight, he was stuck on the side of the road until, eventually, a neutral service vehicle turned up. Based on the subsequent fumbling they had, presumably, never even seen a bike before, let alone changed a tyre.

After an interminable delay, his team car turned up with a replacement bike but by then it was too late. After starting the day in second place, just eight seconds off the lead, the bungled wheel change cost him one minute twenty-three seconds. To add insult to injury, his mechanic forgot to give him a drink bottle with the new bike, leading to a ten second penalty after he finally got a replacement too close to the finish line. When the race ended in Madrid, he was third, one minute thirty-two seconds behind Alejandro Valverde.

When he finished that particularly infamous stage, Evans sobbed, 'I don't deserve this. I do everything right in this fucking sport and I don't deserve this shit.' With his poor showing in that year's Tour de France, his Silence-Lotto team had announced he'd be sharing leadership with their new star recruit, Jurgen Van den Broeck. Evans grumbled about politics and stress. Perhaps he didn't 'deserve' to lose the Vuelta due to a wheel change but then this begs the question as to whether winning, or success in general, is ever a matter of rewards being deserved.

Coincidentally, a decade earlier the Vuelta had been the race at which Lance Armstrong simultaneously returned from cancer and announced his presence as a potential Tour contender. Up until that point, he'd been more focused on one-day races and stage victories. He was too heavy, muscular, and aggressive to race over endless mountains with the consistency required for a Grand Tour win. In his four previous Tour de France appearances he'd withdrawn three times and come thirty-sixth once. Reminiscing about it in his autobiography, *It's Not About the Bike*, he declared

> On October 1, 1998, nearly two years to the day after I was diagnosed, I completed the Vuelta. I finished fourth, and it was as important an achievement as any race I'd ever won …What's more, I nearly won the toughest mountain stage of the race, in gale-force winds and freezing temperatures. The race was so tough that almost half the field retired before the finish. But I didn't quit.

The next year he took his first ever Tour de France victory, beginning the great cancer comeback story that made him famous. A decade later, when Floyd Landis's accusations rumbled through the media, Armstrong told journalists, 'It's our word against his word … I like our word. We like our credibility.' When that failed to placate journalists, he went further, 'We like our story'. And there was, indeed, a lot to like about it. It was the story of a man defined purely by his own actions. As Armstrong himself had written:

> I believed in belief, for its own shining sake. To believe, in the face of utter hopelessness, every article of evidence to the contrary, to ignore apparent catastrophe - what other choice was there? We are so much stronger than we imagine, and belief is one of the most valiant and long-lived human characteristics. To believe, when all along we humans know that nothing can cure the briefness of this life, that there is no remedy for our basic mortality, that is a form of bravery. To continue believing in yourself ... believing in whatever I chose to believe in, that was the most important thing.

It's a delightful truism; just believe in yourself and everything will be all right. This sort of adage was, in varying forms, applied to Evans on message boards across the internet — he had lost because of a lack of mental fortitude, because he was a whinger and a wimp, always seeking to blame his team, his bike, or some other misfortune. To admit that he might be perennially unlucky was to pose the possibility that effort did not necessarily reap reward. If we admitted it in Evans' case, we had to admit it in our own. No matter how hard we trained or studied or persevered or worked, our dreams might not come true. Moreover, we would also have to admit that luck played some part in our good fortunes — that perhaps our promotions, new cars, good houses, and educations owed more to the fluke of being born white and middle class than any real merit on our part.

Evans' failure in the 2009 Vuelta suggested that the best laid plans often go awry, whereas Armstrong's fourth place in 1998, not to mention his Tour victories, suggested success was the inevitable reward for those who believed, worked hard, and never quit. This homage to self-determination was central to Armstrong's appeal and when it turned out to be false the disappointment was palpable. At the start of his own successful Tour campaign in 2013, Bradley Wiggins summed up the Armstrong legacy with his usual concise wit, 'As you get older you start to realise Father Christmas doesn't exist, and that was always the case with Lance.'

This is true for his victories both on and off the bike. Armstrong didn't overcome cancer through willpower. Cancer doesn't care about willpower. Whatever his strength of will, Armstrong also benefited from the freak physiology of a top athlete and the statistical rarity of being a wealthy American with access to the very best medical care available. Had he been born poor, born outside the West, or subject to any of a number of entirely arbitrary factors, he would have died like so many others. It's hard to imagine all those people who have died of cancer simply lacked the will to live.

This goes some way towards explaining why Cadel Evans' victory in 2011 came as such a shock. He had come to personify the frustrated rage and misery of a man whose dreams are constantly thwarted. There was something of the myth of Sisyphus about him; eternally pushing his boulder up the hill, only to have a minor mechanical or a seemingly insignificant crash leave him on the side of the road while his hopes and dreams rolled away from him. At the same time, his moping proclamations that 'I don't deserve this' spoke of some deep-seated but entirely misplaced sense of privilege. Did he really believe the world had a moral obligation to reward him?

Of course, we're all subject to a continual reinforcement of themes such as 'Follow your dreams' and 'Be true to yourself!' Someone stuck a motivational calendar up in my old office containing these very phrases. I suppose it was meant to be comforting. Certainly, the idea of futility is far less appealing. We want to believe dreams are rewarded on merit, which is why we liked Armstrong. He told us all we needed was self-belief. Conversely, Evans worked so hard to win so little. His endless struggle and perseverance contained within it the horrible suggestion that, no matter your merit, no matter how deserving you were, you could labour in vain.

To admit his fortunes were detached from personal effort would have been to accept the notion that our own labours might be for nothing. So, a less confronting rationale was sought for Evans' losses — to explain his failure as the result of some internal fault on his part. That he lost because he didn't have 'the mindset of a champion', that he was too cautious, too whiney, and too eccentric.

When Evans did eventually attain his great victories, it was astounding. Just after that fateful Vuelta, he took the 2009 World Championship. As he launched that final attack into Mendrisio I found myself on my feet, jumping up and down with glee. When he finally won the Tour de France in 2011, I buzzed with simple joy for days. But why? Was I pleased he'd got the win he deserved? This would imply I thought others were less deserving — and I didn't. If anything, Andy Schleck had the stronger moral claim. He'd already been second twice, runner-up in 2010 by a mere thirty-nine seconds. It was the exact amount of time he'd lost after an inopportune mechanical fault on Stage Fifteen. His conqueror, Alberto Contador, was subsequently embroiled in a doping scandal and would be stripped of his win two years later. Schleck had laboured hard, attacking time and time again, but he would never get to wear the yellow jersey in Paris.

So what did Evans' win in 2011 mean? Within it there was something more complex than morality; something about perseverance in the face of chance. He'd simply been slugging away for so long, training so hard, submitting himself to such stress, that his stars had finally aligned. It was almost statistical. Perhaps that sounds cold but look at it in a different light. If one's chances are a hundred-to-one, the margin for success is slim. Yet if one fails to compete at all, no matter how noble one's dreams or deserving one's merits, the chance is nil. This says little about positive victory but it does say something about human agency. The will to compete may not ensure victory but, without it, defeat is certain.

STAGE 21

July 23rd, 1989
Versailles – Paris

LAURENT FIGNON'S FAULT

Will a Self, and Thou Shalt Become A Self
— *Nietzsche*

Laurent Fignon began the final time trial of the 1989 Tour de France with the yellow jersey and a fifty-second lead over Greg LeMond. Twenty-seven minutes and fifty-five seconds later he had lost the Tour by a mere eight seconds. He had raced the fastest time trial of his career, taking third place on the stage with an average speed of 53.59 km/h. LeMond, however, had set a new record of 54.55km/h, covering the course in a phenomenal twenty-six minutes and fifty-seven seconds. With the controversial use of aero bars, the American won the stage and seized the yellow jersey at the last possible moment. After three thousand, two hundred and eighty-five kilometres, Fignon had been tried and found lacking in the final eighty metres. Despite having won the Tour twice, in 1983 and 1984, it was this final loss that would be his legacy.

The time trial was the conclusion to a long, tightly contested Tour in which Fignon and LeMond had traded the race lead back and forth in fierce competition. After a battle royale on the Alpe d'Huez, Fignon had delivered what looked like the knockout blow, dropping LeMond just four kilometres from the summit to claim more than a minute. The next day, Stage Eighteen, he took an emphatic stage victory in Villard-de-Lans and secured the fifty-second buffer he would hold right up until the final metres of the race.

The final time trial was only twenty-four kilometres long and seemed like a formality. LeMond was a great time trialist but few thought he was that great. When he beat Fignon in the Stage Five time trial, it took him seventy-three kilometres to secure fifty-six seconds. It was thought he could take back maybe thirty seconds over twenty-four kilometres but not enough to win. Fignon's victory looked so certain the French papers had already plastered his face across their front pages.

After years of injury and bad luck, the French champion had returned to the kind of form that saw him pummel both Hinault and LeMond into submission to take the 1983 and 1984 Tours. Back then, he'd looked like the next Eddy Merckx, until he'd somehow knocked his achilles tendon against his pedal and it inexplicably turned into tendonitis. By 1985 the problem was so bad he needed major surgery, stifling his chance of a third successive Tour win and a shot at the Giro, in which he'd come second the year before. Years later, he wrote, 'Fate plays curious tricks on sportsmen. You can fall victim to the smallest thing.'

It took Fignon years to fully recover. After winning the 1988 Milan-San Remo, the French fans thought he was back on top but his Tour performance was pitiful and he was dropped on Stage Three. As it turned out, this too was bad luck. Unable to comprehend his poor form, he was lamenting his failure in the hotel bathroom when he shat out a tapeworm measuring almost two metres. After a few brief moments in which he was 'terrified. I thought I was expelling my intestines', there came the relief of at least knowing what the problem was, even if it did meaning dropping out of the race.

Parasite free, he arrived at the 1989 Tour driven by a will to win far beyond his original, youthful exuberance. Fignon knew that, at age twenty-nine, his chances for a third win were running out. Around him, the race was also changing as the sport spread beyond its European heartland. LeMond had become the first American winner in 1986 and Stephen Roche the first Irish champion a year later. French dominance was no longer assured.

The Tour's long-standing director, Jacques Goddet, finally retired in 1986 and the new management had launched a dubious campaign to attract greater commercial interest. Fignon was appalled, writing in his autobiography that they'd devolved the great race into 'a kind of travelling circus,' with cars and helicopters full of corporate guests interrupting the racing:

> The lack of respect for the tradition of the Giants of the Road and the myth of the Tour and its history horrified me. It felt like the end of an era.

He was right. Fignon's career was the last vestige of a different world. The year he retired, 1993, was the same year Lance Armstrong won the World Championship. With the exception of Laurent Jalabert's 1995 Vuelta win, the French would go decades without a Grand Tour victory.

It was also the dawn of the EPO era. Fignon had few problems discussing his occasional amphetamine abuse but he was horrified as blood doping warped the sport. When his former *domestique* Bjarne Riis won the 1996 Tour, Fignon recognised the onset of a sport that had forsaken its authenticity for spectacle. Looking at the Tour's grand history, he reflected:

> From Coppi to Hinault, passing through the eras of Anquetil and Merckx, there was no magic that could dose up lesser riders to compete on equal terms with the greats. Exceptional human beings, like their extraordinary exploits, were authentic.

What does an authentic victory mean when the same ends can be achieved with a good doping program? For Fignon, it was a question that struck at the heart of his life on the bike:

> I was myself and nothing else. I was just a man who did what he could to beat a path towards dignity and emancipation. I did my best to be a human being.

The inherent risk of such an approach is that doing one's best doesn't necessarily produce either dignity or emancipation. Waiting in the start ramp for the final time trial of the 1989 Tour, Fignon had yet to confront this truth. He had less than half an hour of racing left. The champagne was already chilled and he felt certain of his third Tour victory. It would also give him the elusive Giro-Tour double, achieved only by the truly great; Coppi, Anquetil, and Merckx. He could finish his career by entering the Pantheon of the sporting gods.

LeMond had started two minutes before him, racing with the controversial aid of an aerodynamic helmet and aerobars. Today these are considered standard in cycling but, at the time, they were entirely new and extremely contentious. Most cyclists rode the time trials with bullhorn bars and, perhaps, disc wheels. LeMond incorporated grips traditionally used in triathalons, allowing him to crouch in a more aerodynamic position. Unique for the time, he also adopted an aero helmet, decreasing his drag even further. Debate raged as to whether this was legal but the UCI's referees allowed it.

Fignon, by contrast, raced with no helmet and his ponytail flapping in the wind. He did have disc wheels, and a smaller front wheel to afford some aerodynamics, but he'd chosen to race the old fashioned way; reliant on his physical strength and skill. The difference between the two men couldn't have been more marked. LeMond looked like something out of science fiction. Fignon, with his glasses and thinning hair, looked almost antiquated. As an added indignity he'd developed saddle sores in the final days of the race and sitting on the bike was particularly painful. Leaving the start line, he committed himself to this one last effort.

In front of him, LeMond had opted to race without being told his time splits. Turning a 55x12 gear, he barrelled through the time checks well ahead of everyone else. After eleven kilometres he already had a twenty-one second interval back to Fignon. By the fifteen-kilometre mark, the gap was out to twenty-four seconds. Then, over the final ten kilometres, Fignon began to struggle while LeMond's speed increased. On the final straight of the Champs-Elysées, the race could still have gone either way. In the last two hundred yards, LeMond caught the man in front of him, 1988 winner Pedro Delgado, to cross the line with the best time. He had always been a superb time trialist, but the aero bars and helmet had elevated him to new heights.

Fignon, coming on to the same stretch a few minutes later, was struggling with his bike, gasping for air and starting to panic. Right down until the final hundred metres it still looked like he could win. All he needed was a handful of seconds. The crowd watched the clock. Mere metres from the finish it ticked over the fifty-second mark. LeMond raised his arms in victory. Eight seconds later, Fignon crossed the line. He had lost the Tour by the smallest margin in history.

Still in his yellow jersey, Fignon collapsed. He'd come third in the stage and ridden the best time trial of his career, yet still lost the Tour. On the podium, an elated Greg LeMond tried to console his decidedly glum opponent, telling him, 'Cheer up, you still won the Giro.' Fignon took little solace in this. Over the next few days, he found himself constantly counting to eight over and over again. Years later, he could still recall the sensation, writing, 'the more I counted, the more aware I became of what a derisory amount of time it was. You can't do anything in eight seconds!'

For three days after he lost, Fignon was in a state of devastation. He knew he'd never win another Tour and, indeed, he never even made it to the podium again. In his autobiography, he remembered the days immediately following his defeat:

> How could I have lost? How could I have allowed it to happen? For hours and hours I felt sorry for myself. It was the only thing in my head. There was no flavour in anything I ate. Just moving felt like an effort. It was like being in a coma. 'Watch out for sorrow, it's a bad habit,' wrote Flaubert.

After three days, he crawled out of the shower, looked at his face in the mirror and had a revelation: 'There was no room for rational thought. It wasn't my way to feel I had been victimised. It was entirely my fault. The good parts and the bad.'

Was it his fault? Certainly, he could have adopted the same time trial bars and aero helmet as LeMond. A specialist in aerodynamics later estimated that if he'd simply cut off his ponytail the reduced drag would have been enough to save him those eight seconds. But Fignon chose how he raced. He hated LeMond's scientific and mathematical approach to cycling. He wanted to win through audacity, courage, and skill. There's something to be said for this. When he was offered EPO later in his career, he rejected it, choosing to face defeat rather than risk an inauthentic victory.

In his autobiography, he asked, 'Can a man's character be represented in the way he rides a bike? If so, has cycling said all it can say about me?' His loss in 1989 said a good deal about him — about his persistence, his devotion to his sport, and his willingness to give his all. But it also spoke of things beyond his control. The world around him was changing, and those changes shaped his fortune. He saw that final time trial as the emblem of that shift:

> Many people feel that this is the day that divides two radically different kinds of cycling. Is that surprising? The craftsmen were defeated by mass-production. Handmade goods were overwhelmed by factory-made stuff. Individuals were submerged in the anonymous mass. The people's heroes were strangled and the glory of the Giants of the Road trickled away.

It's hard to read this and believe he was just writing about cycling. Perhaps it sounds grandiose, but as Armstrong rose to fame over the following decades the world changed. Fignon made his choices. In 1993 he retired and left the sport to its future.

In 2010 Fignon died of cancer, aged just fifty. In the months before his death, he told an interviewer, 'I don't want to die… but if there is no cure, what can I do? I'm not afraid of dying. I just don't want it to happen.' Perhaps it comes across as fatalistic, but he'd had ample time to reflect on the gap between what we want and what we get. His greatest rival, LeMond, was the first to admit Fignon never had the chance to reveal his true depth:

> I see him as one of the great riders who was hampered by injuries. He had a very, very big talent, much more than anyone recognised. For me he was one of the greater champions that was not recognised.

Oddly, given their somewhat fractious relationship, the American also remembered him very fondly off the bike, recalling, 'He was a great person, one of the few that I find was really true to himself.'

Had it not been for tendonitis, tapeworm, and Greg LeMond's aero bars, it's highly likely he would have triumphed at least once more. When he won in 1984 the time gaps had been huge; he finished more than ten minutes ahead of second placed Bernard Hinault and almost twelve over LeMond. He won a total of five stages to achieve a mammoth victory. Yet he was always remembered for that final defeat. It seemed so fickle. All it would have taken is a slight tail wind on an earlier time trial, a better-timed attack on Alpe d'Huez, or a minor mechanical and the whole thing could have ended differently.

THE FINAL STAGE

Laurent Fignon retired the same year Lance Armstrong won the World Championship. Two decades later, he would die of cancer. Armstrong, diagnosed with the same disease in 1996, not only 'defeated' it but went on to 'win' the Tour seven times. In his first autobiography, written in 2000, Armstrong wrote, 'I am very firm in my belief that cancer is not a form of death. I choose to redefine it: it is part of life.' It's in stark contrast to Fignon's own reflection, 'I don't want to die at fifty but, if there is no cure, what can I do?' One is the statement of a man who believed his will was limitless, the other of a man who accepted that some things were insurmountable.

When Armstrong stood on the podium at the end of the 2005 Tour de France and proclaimed, 'I'm sorry you don't believe in miracles', most would have agreed he was a far superior cyclist to Fignon. His seven Tour victories eclipsed Fignon's two. Armstrong's career was almost destroyed by his cancer, yet he came back even stronger, while Fignon's best years were wiped out by nothing more dramatic than tendonitis and tapeworm. But when the doping allegations finally overwhelmed him and Armstrong made his requisite confession on Oprah, a different tale emerged. As his former *domestique* Tyler Hamilton said of him, Armstrong 'couldn't let go of the power that allowed him to control his performance.'

By contrast, Fignon defined himself by pitting his will against the uncontrollable. He needed variables beyond his control through which to find himself. To that end, he virtually threw away his victory in 1989. Nothing prevented him from adopting the same tools as LeMond; the aerobars and helmet. If the expert was correct, just cutting off his ponytail would have saved him eight seconds in wind resistance. He chose not to. This was an ideological choice rather than a simple case of obstinate naivety. Fignon spent the rest of his life critiquing LeMond as forerunner of an era in which cycling devolved from a beautiful art to a grim science; the age when mass production supplanted craftsmanship and heroes became anonymous. He wouldn't be complicit in its decline.

After all, what was the point? To win a place in the Pantheon through trickery didn't make you a god. Fignon saw cycling as a trial and he wanted to be judged by the way he rode his bike, not the seconds of drag he saved through his choice of handlebars. He didn't race just to win. He raced to prove himself. Through the Tour de France, he could find the proof he wanted, but for it to mean anything it had to contain the potential for defeat.

When we consider where the sport went after 1993, his point becomes clear. For Armstrong, the limits were optional; mere technicalities to be thought through and surmounted. If the gods hadn't granted him the necessary haematocrit, VO2 max, or testosterone to achieve his dreams, then he would will them upon himself. He knew he was destined to be one of those Giants of the Road and, if transcendence required falsely inflated blood values, then so be it.

Armstrong wasn't the first to make this choice. Bjarne Riis' 1996 Tour de France victory was the first undoubtedly owed to EPO. Riis had never had the makings of a Grand Tour winner before then. As a young man, he loved cycling and committed himself to it completely, training for hours, studying the bike, and pursuing any opportunity for improvement. As a teenager, he dreamed of competing for Denmark in the 1984 Olympic Games. After finishing a race in Germany, he was excited when the national coach, Otto Olsen, beckoned to him at the finish line. As he wheeled his bike over, Riis could almost feel his dreams brushing up against his fingertips. Then Olsen told him, 'I think you should go home, hang your bike on a hook and give up riding.'

Riis refused to give up. He turned professional two years later. It was a grim journey, riding for minor teams with no security and little real support. Eventually he had a lucky break. He was asked to ride for Fignon's Super U team, where he became an extremely devoted *domestique*, committing himself tirelessly and selflessly to his captain. Fignon was impressed and the two liked each other. After working to support the French champion's successful Giro campaign, Riis was selected to ride the 1989 Tour. He was there when LeMond won on the final day, standing with the team entourage at the finish line, watching in horrified silence as the clock ticked over. It was a landmark moment for him just as much as Fignon.

Remembering his time with Super U years later, Riis recalled one particular piece of advice Fignon gave him, 'You can never win on your own.' Fignon recognised a victory required one's team, without which the numerous variables thrown up in a Grand Tour were insurmountable. Perhaps Riis misunderstood or perhaps the sentiment got lost along the way. The Dane knew he couldn't perform at Fignon's level on his own and began visiting Professor Francesco Conconi. When he came third in the 1995 Tour his haematocrit level was 56.3%, fifteen percent higher than his normal level. The next year, when he won, he was given the nickname of 'Mr Sixty Percent' for his consistently unusual blood values. He knew he couldn't win alone so he altered who he was. The era of blood doping had arrived.

In 2007 Riis admitted to doping throughout his career. No one was particularly astonished. In his autobiography, he was surprisingly blunt about why he did it:

The decision to continue to use EPO and cortisone through my career was mine alone, and was a choice I'd made having thoroughly thought it through. No one was forcing me to swallow the pills, or holding me down while they injected me with EPO. I was choosing to inject myself, and it was a consequence of me deciding that I needed to dope in order to race at the level I wanted to compete at. It was my responsibility and no one else's.

It's a comment uncannily reminiscent of Fignon's belief that both the good parts of his career and the bad were 'entirely my fault.' The difference is that Fignon took responsibility for those limits beyond his control; for the tapeworm, tendonitis, and LeMond's aerodynamic handlebars. His limits showed how far he could go, who he was and proved his true worth. Riis, like Armstrong, made decisions to overthrow his limitations and make himself anew.

The difference is profound. At one level, it is purely about desire. There's no question that Riis studied, trained, and pursued his sport with the diligence of a champion. What he lacked was the natural physical talent but, instead of seeing this fault as his cross to bear, he made decisions to expand his physical boundaries. This is entirely understandable. We've all wanted to be better than we are, convinced that if only we were smarter or stronger, fortune would smile on us. If we can supplement our faults to achieve our desires, it's tempting to do so.

However, there's something else at play, beyond desire; an idea of how the world should work, in which effort and reward are linked. Geoff Drake's history of 7-Eleven, the first American team in the European *peloton* and their struggle to find success on the Continent, hints at this:

> Even the most gifted athletes cannot will themselves to victory. While isolation and independence drove the athletes, there wasn't a single one who thought, at some point, that his efforts shouldn't be worth more, that sacrifice and physical prowess should amount to something in this world. Hard work was always a tool they had their disposal, but it was not sufficient.

It's a truism to believe hard work yields rewards. Undoubtedly, the truly determined can drive themselves to a level of effort that demands respect. For a young athlete, it might be common to have begun serious training in their mid-teens. By the age of twenty-one they might, like Armstrong, find themselves in Europe, riding and training relentlessly, having forsaken family, education, employment, and security. This can all be achieved by will power but, at some point, as Drake points out, other variables come into play and these are largely subject to blind luck.

But what if you could will yourself to greatness? The idea has a powerful allure. This is the sentiment behind the fable of Icarus, the legend of Faust and, ultimately, the conundrum at the heart of Armstrong, Riis, and their ilk. It raises fascinating questions; if greatness is defined by the capacity to confront one's limits, what would it mean to overcome them at will? How would you know your own worth? And where would you draw the line?

Sporadically people make the argument that doping should simply be considered as part of the legitimate preparations for a race. The winner, after all, is simply the best performing athlete, and how they get there is a secondary issue. When the first scandals broke out about the use of EPO, Armstrong's doctor Michele Ferrari famously countered, 'EPO is not dangerous, it's the abuse that is. It's also dangerous to drink ten litres of orange juice.' Perhaps blood doping could have been put in the same category as injecting vitamins or taking protein supplements.

Arguments against this attitude based in morality and health are plentiful; poorly administered doping kills athletes, the line needs to be drawn somewhere, and there's always the usual innocuous commentary about fair play. These are all sporting arguments but they fall short of explaining why doping is so reviled. Jeremy Whittle, former editor of the *British ProCycling* magazine, encapsulates it best,

The essence of doping is cheating and the essence of cheating is defeatism. Doping says, 'This can't be done any other way; this can't be achieved through hard work or talent, through intelligence, determination, and honesty.'

This attitude didn't necessarily help Whittle's career. As a journalist he was, along with Paul Kimmage and David Walsh, on Armstrong's media blacklist. Armstrong once described him as a 'snake with arms'. Regardless, his book, *Bad Blood*, is one of my favourite cycling memoirs. Whittle interviewed one of Armstrong's former *domestiques*, Frankie Andreu, who was one of the first to admit to doping. Describing the choice, he explained,

> I knew what I was doing was wrong, but I had been getting my butt kicked for ten years… I was fine with that – even though I knew I'd get on the start line and wasn't going to win. But then I cracked and got tired of putting up with that. So I did it. But I didn't feel totally guilty about it, because everybody else I was competing against seemed to be doing it.

We've all been in a similar situation at some point. We've all worked hard just to have our efforts undermined by some petty upset or injustice beyond our control. For most of us doping doesn't present itself as a solution. Maybe this is why it has drawn such condemnation. Our own lives are marked by the confusing and ambiguous hand of fortune and we expect to see our sporting heroes subject to the same forces. Indeed, the contest against uncontrollable fate is what defines the Tour's great champions. Coppi's immaculate, perfect victories are enhanced by his poor fortune off the bike. It's as if the gods had turned a blind eye to his wilful supremacy on Alpe d'Huez, knowing they'd extract their dues through his incongruous death from malaria. We can see the same logic at play in the lives of the sport's other great martyrs — Pantani's miserable decline and drug addled death, Ocaña's shot gun suicide, and Charly Gaul's descent into isolation.

Even among those of a less dramatic bent there's the same sense that fate hasn't been cheated but fought, bargained-with, or eluded until such time the debt becomes insurmountable. The first man to win the Tour three times, Lousion Bobet, died of cancer before he reached old age, as did the first five-time winner, Jacques Anquetil. Russell Mockridge returned to Australia from the pinnacle of the sport only to be struck down by a bus. It was as if they'd given their all to achieve the sublime, knowing full well they'd pay for it later.

This also explains why cycling is a sport that champions its losers. René Vietto wasn't an icon because he won but because of the honour with which he lost. The same could be said of Poulidor or Evans. They played the game with total commitment, knowing full well there was no guarantee they'd ever be rewarded. Of course the Tour de France isn't about the pursuit of justice — nor is it about winning. There's always the promise of a glittering, perfect victory but it's not the main thing. The race is shaped more by its losses; the unrewarded persistence of a breakaway caught metres from the line, a contender brought down by a crash, a lead lost through a moment of weakness or drained away in the final metres of a time trial. But nor is the Tour only about loss. No one watches, let alone rides, a Grand Tour, through their love of futility.

What defines the Tour is the spectacle of its competitors facing their limits; the play of fortune, physicality, sheer effort, and determination. Each stage is a trial and we wait to see who will find their threshold and who will exceed it. But it's the trial we're watching. This is the problem with doping; if human limits can be surmounted at will, then the trial loses all meaning and, if trying doesn't mean anything, what's the point? Winning and losing are both pointless without a context. What binds them, as Roland Barthes points out, is an idea that people are defined by their actions. Naturally, those actions are subject to chance, blind luck and circumstances beyond our control. This can make them seem futile; what does it matter if you work, strive, and persist only to be beaten at the line? Yet this doesn't imply that things are meaningless. On the contrary, the Tour de France draws its meaning from the constant battle between human will and the hand of fortune.

SOME SUGGESTED FURTHER READING

Cycling has always been a literary sport, and cycling fans are fortunate to have such a wide array of high quality writing available to them. For those interested in pursing further reading, I offer some notes on the sources and texts I've cited herein.

For general reference, I relied heavily on Bill and Carol McGann's multivolume *The Story of the Tour de France* (Dog Ear Publishing). The McGann's also publish *Bike Race Info* (http://bikeraceinfo.com/index.html), which is the best online resource of Tour facts. I also used Geoffrey Wheatcroft's *Le Tour* (Pocket Books 2003) and Chris Sidwell's *A Race for Madmen* (Collins 2010). The Wikipedia entries on the Tour get some of the details wrong, but on the whole are a tribute to the collective energy of cycling fans. Owen Mulholland's writing, combined with Brett and Shelly Horton's photographic archive, makes *Cycling's Golden Age* (Velo Press, 2006) a good, quick reference point for the sport's best years. For work specific to the mountains I like Daniel Friebe and Pete Goding's *Mountain High* (Quercus 2012), Jean-Paul Vespini's *The Tour is Won on the Alpe* (Velo 2008) and Richard Yates *Ascent* (Van der Plas 2006).

For contemplation of the bicycle itself, *Zinn and the Art of Road Bike Maintenance* by Lennard Zinn (Velo 2005) is invaluable, as are Delong's *Guide to Bicycles and Bicycling: The Art and Science* (Chilton 1976) by Fred Delong, and Sam Tracy's *How To Rock and Roll: A City Riders Repair Manual*. David Herlihy's *Bicycle* (Yale University Press 2004) was my main reference for the history of the bicycle as a machine. If you can track it down, James Wagenvoord's *Bikes and Riders* (VNR 1972) is a delight, and it's also good to have a copy of Richard Ballantine's *Richard's Bicycle Book* (Pan 1972). Lastly, Sheldon Brown's website (http://sheldonbrown.com/) is brilliant. Sadly, Mr Brown died in 2008.

Cycling has a wealth of great biographies, some of which I've cited at length. Matt Rendell's *The Death of Marco Pantani* (Orion Books 2006) is superb, as is *Kings of the Mountains*, his tribute to Columbian cycling (Aurum Press 2002). Also on Marco Pantani, Manuela Ronchi's *Man on the Run* (Robson Books 2004) offers an insider's account of his decline. For information on Jacques Anquetil, I turned to Paul Howard's *Sex, Lies and Handlebar Tape* (Mainstream 2008), for Merckx I recommend Daniel Friebe's *Eddy Merckx* (Ebury Press 2012) and William Fortheringham's *Half Man Half Bike* (Chicago Review Press 2012). Fotheringham's *Fallen Angel* and *Put Me Back on My Bike* (Yellow Jersey Press 2003) cover Fausto Coppi and Tom Simpson respectively (Yellow Jersey Press 2009). Alistair Fotheringham's *The Eagle of Toledo* (Aurum 2012) is the best book I've found on Federico Bahamontes. Aili and Andrews McConnon's *Road to Valor* is a wonderful account of Gino Bartali's life (Crown 2012). Richard Moore's *In Search of Robert Millar* (Harper Sport 2007) is a personal favourite, as is his *Heroes, Villains and Velodromes* (Harper Sport 2008), but his best work is *Slaying the Badger*, on the Lemond/ Hinault conflict (Velo 2012). While he never rode the Tour, it's still worth reading *Reg Harris* by Robert Dineen (Ebury Press 2012). For a biography of a team, Geoff Drake and Jim Ochowicz's *Team 7-Eleven* (Velo 2011) is a decent overview of the rise of US cyclists in Europe. The UK equivalent is Jeff Connor's *Wide-Eyed and Legless* (Mainstream Publishing 2011), which follows the far less successful ANC-Halford's team, but is a far better written.

For Australian fans, Martin Curtis's *Russell Mockridge: The Man in Front* (Melbourne Books 2008) is a rare history of one of the nation's greatest athletes. I haven't been able to track down a copy of Mockridge's own autobiography, *My World On Wheels* and have cited from Curtis's excerpts. I've also used *Cadel Evans: Close to Flying* by Rob Arnold (Hardie Grant 2010). More generally, there's Rupert Guiness's *What A Ride* (A&U 2009). Australian readers should also be familiar with the irreplaceable *Ride* magazine, published by Rob Arnold and out quarterly. Ernie Old's *By Bread Alone* (Georgian House 1950) is virtually impossible to track down but a great book. I'm happy to say I have a signed copy, dated to 1957, when Mr Old was eighty-three.

There's a subgenre of cycling autobiographies written before the sport commercialized in the English-speaking world, usually written directly by the athletes themselves. In the UK, Mousehold Press has re-published some of these, including Vin Denson's *The Full Cycle* (2008) and Allan Peiper's touching *A Peiper's Tale* (2005). Mousehold also published Jean Bobet's *Tomorrow We Ride…* (2008), which is a gem. Jean Bobet is as good a writer as his brother was a cyclist. Similar to Bobet's work, Laurent Fignon's autobiography, *We Were Young and Carefree* (Yellow Jersey Press 2010) is charismatic and wise.

Particularly under Pat McQuaid's time at the UCI, women's cycling has been badly under supported. The volume of published writing by or about female cyclists is much lower than it should be. I've cited from a couple of autobiographies that deserve a far larger readership including Beryl Burton's *Personal Best* (Springfield Books 1986) and Eileen Sheridan's *Wonder Wheels* (Mercian 2009). Sheridan's autobiography, originally published in 1956, is one of my favourite books.

I'm thankful to *Rouleur* magazine, which published a rare interview with her among their other excellent articles.

In making sense of doping, the obvious starting points are Paul Kimmage's *Rough Ride* (Yellow Jersey Press 2007), Willy Voet's *Breaking the Chain* (Yellow Jersey Press 2002), David Walsh's *From Lance to Landis* (Ballantine Books 2007) and *Seven Deadly Sins* (Simon and Schuster 2012), along with Jeremy Whittle's *Bad Blood* (Yellow Jersey Press 2008). Written by the riders themselves, there's David Millar's *Racing Through the Dark* (Orion 2011), Tyler Hamilton's *The Secret Race* (Bantam 2012) and, less openly, Bjarne Riis's *Stages of Light and Dark* (VSP 2012).

For those of a philosophical bent, I opened the book with Roland Barthes' *Mythologies* (Vintage 2000), and relied on his *What Is Sport* (Yale University Press 2007) and *The Eiffel Tower and Other Mythologies* (Noonday Press 1979), which includes the essay 'The Tour de France as Epic'. I've also cited from Pierre Bourdieu's *Distinction* (Harvard University Press 1984) and Jean Baudrillard's *The System of Objects* (Verso 1996) and a few other sources I vaguely remember from my under graduate studies, such as Nietzsche, Robert Browning, Shakespeare, Goethe, and Motörhead.

Finally, there are the books I like the best. Paul Fournel's *Need for the Bike* (University of Nebraska Press 2003) was a revelation when I first read; one of the first intelligent texts on sport I'd encountered, beautifully written with a superb translation by Allan Stoekl. Benjo Maso's *The Sweat of the Gods* (Mousehold Press 2005) is a unique critical history of the sport, drawing out its interweave of commerce, modernity, and human toil. My final suggestion is Tim Hilton's *One More*

Kilometre and *We're in the Showers: Memoirs of a Cyclist* (Harper Perennial, 2005). This book is a masterpiece. It was one of the first books on cycling I read and profoundly changed the way I thought about the bike and the sport. I cannot recommend it strongly enough.

ACKNOWLEDGEMENTS

Thank you to my mother Dimity, Diana Smith, Lisa Dempster, John Hunter, Stan Mahoney, and the Format Collective.

Additional thanks to the numerous people who contacted me with encouragement after the publication of the original version of this book.